Paris, a New Rome

Paris, a New Rome

—

Edited by
Michèle Lowrie and Barbara Vinken

DE GRUYTER

ISBN 978-3-11-133473-8
e-ISBN (PDF) 978-3-11-133477-6
e-ISBN (EPUB) 978-3-11-133480-6

Library of Congress Control Number: 2024931725

Bibliographic information published by the Deutsche Nationalbibliothek
The Deutsche Nationalbibliothek lists this publication in the Deutsche Nationalbibliografie;
detailed bibliographic data are available on the internet at http://dnb.dnb.de.

© 2024 Walter de Gruyter GmbH, Berlin/Boston
Cover image: Cy Twombly, Roman Notes, 1970, A Set of six offset colour lithographs Sheet:
34.2 x 27.6 in. © Cy Twombly Foundation, Courtesy Galerie Bastian, Berlin.
Typesetting: Integra Software Services Pvt. Ltd.
Printing and binding: CPI books GmbH, Leck

www.degruyter.com

Acknowledgments

Joint research for over a decade prepared the ground for this volume. In 2012, we taught two seminars, one at the Center for Disciplinary Innovation, housed in the Franke Institute at the University of Chicago, the other at the Ludwig-Maximilians-Universität under the auspices of the then Centre Flaubert. Our topic was the long afterlife of Roman figurations of civil war in French literature. We decided at the end of the second seminar that we needed to write it up. The result is our book, *Civil War and the Collapse of the Social Bond: The Roman Tradition at the Heart of the Modern*, which came out with Cambridge University Press in 2022. As we wrote, more and more material emerged that surpassed the scope of the book. We knew already, but also discovered in more detail, how widespread and multifaceted the Roman model was and remains for Europe and America. The figuration of France as a new Rome, from both French and other perspectives, was an especially prominent motif. To explore this dimension would require the participation of a larger group, working from a broader angle – chronologically and nationally in substance and from diverse methodological and disciplinary perspectives. Hence, we organized a conference, from which this volume arises.

We heartily thank the University of Chicago Center in Paris for funding to bring us together and the Deutsches Forum für Kunstgeschichte for offering an additional stylish venue in Paris. Thomas Kirchner, Director of the DFK, was an intellectual partner in organizing the conference. We thank him, as well as his staff, for material support. We also thank the staff of the Center in Paris, under the guidance of Sébastien Greppo, for making our meeting seamless. This was a special feat as the world opened again after the pandemic. Originally scheduled for 2020, the conference finally took place in June, 2022. We are tremendously grateful to Hanna Sohns for her assistance in pulling the volume together.

ML and BV

https://doi.org/10.1515/9783111334776-202

Contents

Acknowledgments —— V

Michèle Lowrie, Barbara Vinken
Introduction: With and Against Rome —— 1

I Before Paris

Susanna Elm
"*Le Jour de Gloire*" – Augustine of Hippo on Glory, Renewal, and the Law of War in the *City of God* (Book 1) —— 11

Anselm Haverkamp
Second Romes, and no Sense of an Ending —— 31

II Early Classicisms

Tristan Alonge
Néron et Louis XIV au miroir racinien : *monstre* ou *grand prince naissant* ? —— 51

Larry F. Norman
Versailles, A New Rome? Perrault and the Quarrel of the Ancients and Moderns —— 67

III Classicism Enlightened and Revolutionized

Philip Hardie
Translatio laudum*. Rubens' Maria de' Medici cycle, and Voltaire's *Henriade —— 89

Christine Tauber
Jacques-Louis David's Roman Revolutions in Paris —— 113

IV Romanticism and Realism

Barbara Vinken
Heinrich von Kleist's Napoleanic Romans in the Teutonic Woods —— 143

Stephan Leopold
Empire – Typologie – Apocalypse —— 161

V Palimpsests beyond Origins

Andrea Frisch
Calendars, Commemoration, Containment: The Saint Bartholomew's Day Massacre(s) and Roman Practices of Commemorating Defeat —— 183

Michael P. Steinberg
The Cry of Laocoön. Myths and Countermyths of the Founding of Cities —— 201

Michèle Lowrie
Epilogue: Before Rome —— 223

List of Contributors —— 227

Figure Credits —— 229

Michèle Lowrie, Barbara Vinken
Introduction: With and Against Rome

Siding with or against Rome has been a central act of self-definition for European letters, arts, and politics from Late Antiquity to Late Modernity, up to and including the present. The paradigm of ancients versus moderns remains a consistent baseline in the telling and making sense of history. Europe is Roman, since, like the Romans who translated Greek culture, Europe keeps retranslating Latin letters, arts, and politics. However shared the Roman inheritance may be, it hardly unifies. Which Rome is the model, the Republic or the Empire? The Rome of imperial conquest or of civil war? The glorious conqueror who extended universal peace, the rule of law, and infrastructure – roads and aqueducts – or the detested tyrant who imposed domination? Or worse, the corruptor of republican liberty and source of putrefying decadence? To borrow Livy's words, the question was whether Rome offered an *exemplum* to "take for ourselves or our commonwealth" or one we should "avoid, foul in inception, foul in outcome" (*Preface* 10). Rome always returns, but which one? To complicate things further, various capitals – actual or notional – competed to establish themselves as Rome's rightful heir and to redefine, reform, or erase Rome to legitimate their claim to inherit its preeminence. *Translatio Romae* is a unitary discourse to the extent that Rome – to translate *translatio* into Greek – remains the central, structuring metaphor, but the discourse itself is the site of endless contestation, for power and over values. Our introduction situates the papers in this volume within a larger narrative.

France presents itself as a privileged locus for Rome's return since the beginnings of its history and *L'âge classique* was particularly obsessed with defining France as a new Rome. But the prehistory to French classicism has become obscure. We begin therefore with papers on Late Antiquity and Medieval Rome to show that continuation and rupture are not incompatible and furthermore may be inflected together in various ways. One tendency attempts to erase and supplant Rome with a newly defined *civitas*. Another resists Rome while using its model to legitimate its present reinstantiation. These periods establish the Christian gesture of overcoming through appropriation.

In Rome's translation from Trojan origins, an alternative to the mainstream of imperial power politics has always been available, though this alternative has remained endangered and obscure in the blinding hindsight of history as written by the victors. Vergil's *Aeneid* attests to the possibility of a different foundation, one based on love and openness to refugees and suppliants, whose promise is cruelly belied by Rome's history of civil war, internal division, and imperial con-

https://doi.org/10.1515/9783111334776-001

quest.[1] The question of Roman identity ripples across the poem: Is Rome Italian or oriental? What are the moral and aesthetic stakes of each position? This question is never definitively answered. In the dominant reception however, the celebration of empire and all it stands for prevails.

For Eusebius, the Roman Empire provides the vehicle for the Roman Catholic Church. Augustine says no and rejects Rome and its politics out of hand.[2] His *City of God* opens a space apart from the earthly politics tainted by Rome's example. As embodiment of worldly error, the *civitas terrena* in its paradigmatic form, Rome was crippled by an internal split whose primal scene was foundational fratricide, Romulus' murder of Remus, the political analogue to the Old Testament story of Cain and Abel, which universalizes the foundation of human history as bloody conflict. In its war of all against all, Rome turns out to be no shining republic on a hill. Susanna Elm shows how Augustine renarrates the sack of Rome to devalue Roman militarist values and deny Rome her glory. Rome is instead a daughter of Babylon. In Augustine's interpretation, Rome's value was a negative anti-type of the *civitas Dei* to come. Within the *civitas terrena,* Rome was the first degraded republic, which served God's plan only as the dark shadow of the true *res publica,* whose heavenly ideal was prefigured by Jerusalem. Rome reveals all that has failed between God and men, men and women, between fellow men. Augustine's degradation of Rome, however, cannot eliminate its status as preeminent model. It remains the standard-setter of all that needs overcoming. Therefore, *The City of God* establishes a new foundation – based on *gloria Dei*, not *gloria belli* – that overwrites and rejuvenates classical Rome. This gesture of overwriting and rebirth becomes paradigmatic.

While we concentrate mostly on ideological redefinitions, it is important to acknowledge that Roman influence was also material. In Anselm Haverkamp's reading, a no less radical, but conflicting self-re-conception of the Roman legacy arose in the series of Romes after Constantine's division of the Empire. Following Augusta Treverorum (Trier) and its competitor Colonia Agrippina (Cologne), Aix la Chapelle (Aachen), Charlemagne's capital, emerged as yet another "second Rome." Each inflects the Roman inheritance differently. The legacy of imperial administration remained strong in Trier. In the case of Cologne, explicit citation of Rome's republican heritage opposed the bad emperors who ruled under Jupiter's sign. The Holy Roman Empire innovated ideologically by putting *translatio imperii* on a new basis. Counter to the ancient city's model of domination, a very different Roman figure becomes exemplary for Charlemagne's new Rome: the of-

---

1 Lowrie and Vinken 2022, Ch. 3.
2 Lowrie and Vinken 2022, Ch. 4.

ficer Martin, later bishop of Tours, who shared his coat, *capa,* with a beggar in the image of Christ. His *capa,* preserved in the *capella* of the royal court chapel, legitimated Carolingian administration by a metaphorical transfiguration. The *caritas* instantiated in St. Martin's gesture refigures the new *imperium,* translated from Rome, according to Christian values, but the reinvestment of the Roman republican model in cities like Cologne established a counter-model that informed Early Modern civil society in opposition to the dominant imperialism. The extent to which Aix was able to synthesize these strands remains an open question.

The hope not just to follow but surpass or overcome the example of ancient Rome in all its complexity becomes a strikingly central motif in French history and literature. The gesture, predicated on the structure of Christian overcoming, can be redirected to redefine aesthetic worth as well as the ideals governing the exercise of power. The nature of the Rome to be surpassed, however, remains disputed. In the Renaissance, Rome appears as a glorious model for both politics and letters in Ronsard, but a decadent failure in Du Bellay.[3] Ronsard's *Franciade,* which styles its author a new Virgil, has the legendary Trojan child Astyanax survive, so he may found the royal house of Valois. Racine follows Ronsard and names the son of Andromache and Hector the founder of the French dynasty. This gesture corrects the classical tradition, in which Astyanax's death during the Trojan War effectively ends Priam's lineage. The translation makes France a second heir to Troy after Rome according to an alternative dynasty. Paris, a new Troy, supplants glorious Rome in a story that succeeds and notionally surpasses Virgil's *Aeneid.* Against Ronsard's model of succession, which leaves Rome and its glories intact as models for imitation, Du Bellay forwards a disquieting *translatio*: his Rome has always been in ruins. Classical Rome and the Rome of the Catholic Church alike have become emblems of *vanitas,* models we cannot help but imitate, even if they should be avoided.

Before the *siècle des lumières,* the heroes of classical Rome may have absorbed Christian norms but evoking them nevertheless asserts a modern will to power. As Foucault has highlighted in his last lectures, the "Jupiterian" urge is strong, especially in France.[4] The sheer preponderance of the Roman discourse reaches a new apogee and is especially prominent in Corneille, where it sustains the model of the absolute ruler. There are wrinkles, however. In Philip Hardie's reading of Rubens' cycle depicting Marie de Medicis at the Louvre, encomium and praise transfer Roman panegyric discourse, with its mix of myth with history, to a female regent without fundamentally questioning her authority. Rather, ico-

---

3 Vinken 2001.
4 Foucault 2011.

nography produces a synthetic personification of Roma, Juno/Maria/Marie, and France to sustain the greatness of the *grand siècle*. Despite feminine inflection, Roman parallels may be assumed to be laudatory – until, that is, they have to do with a bad emperor. Tristan Alonge challenges a scholarly taboo by reopening the question of Racine's uncanny fashioning of Louis XIV as Nero and probes the limits of the interpretation *à clef*. Does the crazed tyrant *par excellence* rub off on the sovereign? Or does the mirror of the prince, shining Louis' glorious visage back onto himself, spur him to remake and reform any traces of Nero in the salutary image of his securely Christian reflection? A further question is whether pleasurable identifications can escape the burden of moral judgment.

Rome's formative reach turns not just on political legitimation, but on the structure of discursive and visual idioms. In Larry Norman's analysis of contemporary jockeying over the evaluation of Versailles, a late seventeenth century guidebook, astonished that France's new seat of government fuses the old and new Rome together, simplifies the contestation over aesthetic values under Rome's banner in Perrault and Boileau. The Roman paradigm is again polyvalent. The contrast between *anciens* and *modernes* blurs through intermediary references to Renaissance and contemporary Romes. Furthermore, even the Rome of Augustus was understood to be already modern, and therefore paradoxically a model for and argument in favor of future modernities – the case in point being Louis XIV and the aesthetic of his court in the arts, sciences, and letters.

Voltaire's enlightened panegyric of Henri IV, the *Henriade*, as Hardie shows, makes obsessive parallels between Henri and Aeneas, but lets them go when they would violate contemporary norms of decorum. The Roman inheritance is not just allusive, but thematic and discursive – with a good dose of the self-consciousness about fiction and hyperbole typical of Roman literature. The epic shares representational strategies and tropes with Rubens' Marie de Medicis cycle, which in turn derive from Roman imperial panegyric. All deploy a moralized and divinized spatial hierarchy that leads to apotheosis and makes the ruler analogous to the gods – already in Claudian a hybrid of pagan and Christian. Similarly, the language of discord, which tells the plot of historical civil wars in consistent imagery, inflects an abstract opposition between order and disorder in cosmic terms that legitimate monarchy.

Christine Tauber demonstrates how Jacques-Louis David's neo-classical iconography articulates an ideological commentary on rapid political change through formal means. Leading up to the French Revolution, the Roman figures in the *Serment des Horaces* and *Les licteurs rapportant à Brutus les corps de ses fils* stress republican ideals: unity and personal sacrifice for the common good. Similarly, the hero of *Socrate buvant la ciguë* instantiates autonomy at the same time, paradoxically, as the value of subordinating oneself to Athens' democratic regime. But with the Restoration of monarchy, now at least constitutional, David's *Léonidas* embodies a starker contradiction: heroic solitude, yet another tragic sacrifice for the good of the whole, comes in the homoerotic and pastel register of Rococo boudoir painting. Tauber stresses David's emptying of the republican register as he became disillusioned with the Republic's failure and, a loyal citizen, was enlisted to glorify Bonaparte. Roman glory, in Elm's reading of the *Marseillaise*, had already been tarnished.

In the wake of the Enlightenment, the challenges of European imperialism shift the paradigm again. Rome loses authority but retains potency. Rome no longer represents an ideal to be surpassed. Instead, it becomes a curse haunting European history, one that could neither be abandoned nor overcome. This curse acted out blindly, in perpetuity, without progress. Marx's formulation of history as eternal return, at the opening of the *Eighteenth Brumaire of Louis Bonaparte*, which returns once as tragedy, and once as farce – always in Roman costume – was perhaps the most despairing formulation of this curse's inevitability.[5] The Roman republican values of the French Revolution yield to imperial domination under Napoleon and are further degraded by the cruel complacency of Napoleon le Petit's reign.

Heinrich von Kleist's *Herrmannsschlacht* (1808) degrades the Romans as a proxy for Napoleonic overreach.[6] But in Barbara Vinken's hands, Kleist's play refuses to tell the birth of the German nation as a story of Arminius' wholesome, just war against Roman expansionism. Napoleon's mapping of colonial imperialism onto Roman imperialism created the expectation that overthrowing the Romans would figure German liberation from the French, and so the play was falsely understood. Against nationalist ideology, Kleist stages a re-run of the Roman civil wars, in which the difference between friend and enemy dissolves. No national identity exists to be rescued from imperial domination, whether Roman or French, no German authenticity is at stake. All are as terrible as the Romans and we become Roman by opposing them. We are against them *and* with them at the same time. For Kleist, Europe's politics of translation brings no redemption.

Rome came back to haunt Paris, turned from republican liberty or imperial glory, in what became tellingly named an "Oriental Renaissance."[7] In this figuration, Rome may have dominated the world, but Rome herself was already undermined from within, captivated by the spell of Babylonian idols. Vergil's nightmare of Carthage as Rome's alter ego, Lucan's of Egypt as the locale where Caesar goes native, Augustine's charge that Rome was merely a second Babylon – the orientalism that threatened Rome's self-understanding in antiquity came home with a ven-

---

5 Lowrie and Vinken 2022, Introduction & Ch. 1.

6 Vinken 2011.

7 Vinken 2020; Vinken 2015; Vinken 2015a.

geance. Myth criticism after Friedrich Creuzer, the most influential orientalist of the earlier nineteenth century, reached the terrible realization that the Roman Church, whose legitimacy rested in part on its claim to have reformed pagan Rome, was nothing but a "pseudomorphosis" of idolatrous cults – Baal, Cybele, the Cults of the Great Mother. The question of what returned together with Rome in Paris was thus not only a political inquiry, not only a question of imperial tyranny versus a new republic. Imperialism began to reveal "orientalism" as its fatal *arcanum*, with the ideology of the new, post-Revolution republic as its latest, corrupt guise. The question also became a matter of epistemology: Did the cruelty of myth and pagan religions persist under the veil of Christianity in the late Roman empire, to return in blindness to darken the ambitious goals of the Enlightenment?

The most successful writer of the day, Émile Zola, saw the Second Empire as the mythic return of devastating Babylon, coming alive in its metaphorical counterpart: the tyranny of Napoleon III. The most thorough, historically grounded analysis of Rome in the light of the nineteenth century was written by Gustave Flaubert.[8] In bitter satirical fashion, his novels' plots in *L'éducation sentimentale* and *Mme Bovary* expose Paris as a fake Roman republic, that is not undone, but fulfilled in the French Empire. Rome had returned as a Babylonian tyranny under the guise of the post-revolutionary republic. Victor Hugo, another self-styled Vergil in *Quatrevingt-treize*, also presents the Terror as falsely republican, but nevertheless truly Roman in its decadence.[9] Maupassant showed Paris firmly in the grip of Babylonian idolatry at the heart of the Church, as a dance around the golden calf of power and sex.[10] Stephan Leopold traces the inflections of Rome's return according to a double temporality that is fundamentally typological. Such a layering of past and present was already operative in Vergil's *Aeneid*: his Trojans prefigure the Romans in the way French literature's Romans prefigure the French. Even when the Romans are reviled – and sometimes their decadence is embraced – the teleological drive reassures, if only in its epistemological certainty. The novels of Zola, Stendhal, Flaubert, Balzac, and Proust, however, subvert such clarity. They pervasively and consistently convert, each in their own way, the typological return of the past into a new and apocalyptic temporality where the future becomes open to the terrifying end of time itself.

Andrea Frisch finds a palimpsestic overlay in the French adoption of the Roman practice of commemorating black days by inscribing them into the calendar. The *dies Alliensis* of Rome's defeat by the Gauls even makes its way into a Cath-

---

8 Vinken 2015a.
9 Lowrie and Vinken 2022, Ch. 5.
10 Vinken 2020.

olic humanist calendar, alongside the Biblical Exodus, the capture of Jerusalem during the Crusades, and the recent death of Erasmus. The massacre of Protestants on the feast day of St. Bartholemew offers a case study for the manipulation of "ideologemes" that are open to (re)interpretation and can serve changing political agendas. Minimal inscription fragments at the same time as the annual cycle of calendrical time preserves. Rome becomes one signifier among others. Emptied of meaning, it nevertheless continues to circulate. It wields transactional power without specific content by the sheer force of tradition.

Leading with Hector Berlioz' *Les Troyens*, the first opera performed at the Opéra Populaire de la Bastille, built to commemorate the storming of the prison in 1789, Michael Steinberg contrasts transcendent, divinely sanctioned myths of origin with human, secular myths of beginning in his review of a panoply of refoundational moments. In each, silence, transferred voice, the human – as opposed to divine – gesture, or a tone of melancholy blocks any potentially triumphalist nationalism. Berlioz' counter-teleological pulse downstages the Romans' march into Rome – an ironic quotation of an earlier triumphal theme – as backdrop to a chorus of Carthaginians, which curses Aeneas' descendants while their city goes up in flames. Any identification of the Romans with the French, either at the opera's composition in 1856–1858, a decade after the '48 Revolution, or at the bicentenary celebration of the French Revolution in 1989 diffuses. Similarly, Daniel Chester French's Lincoln Memorial, parallel to Michelangelo's Moses, is contemplative, not triumphalist. The Roman fasces on Lincoln's massive chair, which notionally symbolize republican unity, in alignment with Lincoln's primary political aim of holding the United States together, cannot maintain their other symbolic function – to represent the state's right to punish citizens – before Marian Anderson's voice, inaugurating the memorial in 1939, and Martin Luther King's citation of her in 1963. Against Mussolini's adoption of the fasces to bolster his oppressive regime, Lincoln's contemplative gaze recognizes the ever-unfinished business of refoundation, even as his statue was reappropriated as a symbol of civil rights. Emancipation, trumping unity, leaves the fasces-bearing, slave-holding Romans behind.

To the extent that the perennial recourse to ancient Rome – as model or anti-model – binds together a cohesive tradition, the logic of this gesture asserts a unity beyond modern identity politics, which depend on defining them against us, to resist nativist assumptions about national character, French, German, Italian, American, etc. All share pluralistically in the same polysemous inheritance, for good or ill. All are Roman and all resist Rome without needing to agree on what exactly is shared. The unity underlying the discourse, however, no longer depends on defining Rome as origin. The substantive connection becomes thin. Instead, Rome's figuration persists discursively, as a translation to be further translated.

This volume tells a story about Rome's figural potency, all the more because what it figures has been ambivalent from the beginning. This cultural discourse remained prevalent until the Second World War. After that, it became sporadic. It is not clear whether *any* of the various Romes need come back at all or what the rejection of Rome altogether may stand for. Hence, Rome's strong return, when least expected, dressed in a panoply of conventional tropes, surprisingly reinvigorates a metaphor most had left for dead. In Michel Houellebecq's *Soumission* (2015), Augustus returns in an all too well-known story.[11] His alter ego, Mohammad Ben Abbes, provides an allegedly moderate solution to internal discord. The Muslim Brotherhood candidate offers an electoral compromise that destroys a republic, rent by civil war, under the banner of restoration and establishes an oriental tyranny in its stead. Globalized imperialism, modeled on Roman forms, unmasks yet again the inner Orient,[12] wearing the latest Roman fashion. Houellebecq's caricature of political Islam satirizes not the orientalized other but the French self. The toga, however outmoded, remains ever available for reappropriation.

As an epilogue, Michèle Lowrie explores French popular culture as yet one more site of ambivalence for thinking about ancient Rome, specifically, the *Astérix* comics and imagery used by the Gilets Jaunes. Once again, rejection of the topoi of the Roman discourse cannot help but use the language of tradition in its rejection. The ambiguity of the Roman *exemplum* persists despite – or because of – the energy devoted to its erasure.

Bibliography

Foucault, Michel. *The Courage of Truth: Lectures at the Collège de France, 1983–1984*. New York: Palgrave Macmillan, 2011.

Lowrie, Michèle, und Vinken, Barbara. *Civil War and the Collapse of the Social Bond. The Roman Tradition at the Heart of the Modern*. Cambridge: Cambridge University Press, 2022.

Vinken, Barbara. *Flaubert Postsecular. Modernity Crossed Out*. Stanford: Stanford University Press, 2015a (originally published in German: *Flaubert. Durchkreuzte Moderne*. Frankfurt am Main: Fischer 2009).

Vinken, Barbara. Ed. *Translatio Babylonis. Unsere orientalische Moderne*. Paderborn: Fink, 2015b.

Vinken, Barbara. *Bestien. Kleist und die Deutschen*. Berlin: Merve, 2011.

Vinken, Barbara. *Du Bellay und Petrarca. Das Rom der Renaissance*. Tübingen: Niemeyer, 2001.

---

11 Lowrie and Vinken 2022, Ch. 6.
12 Vinken 2015b.

I Before Paris

Susanna Elm

"Le Jour de Gloire" – Augustine of Hippo on Glory, Renewal, and the Law of War in the *City of God* (Book 1)

Allons enfants de la patrie,
Le jour de gloire est arrivé!
Contre nous de la tyrannie
L'étendard sanglant est levé!
Entendez-vous dans les campagnes,
Mugir ces féroces soldats?
Ils viennent jusque dans nos bras
Égorger nos fils, nos compagnes!

Unlike most national anthems, France's *La Marseillaise* has been a world-wide hit thanks to its association with the French Revolution ever since the French National Convention adopted it as the revolutionary anthem in 1795. Its original title, *Battle-Hymn of the Rhine Army*, is less well known.[1] Composed in Strasbourg in 1792 when France had declared war against Austria, the *Battle-Hymn*'s fiery language immediately resonates, especially for those who are familiar with the language of the Roman Republic and of the later Roman Empire. Children of the fatherland (*patria*) are rising up against the bloody standards tyrants wield against them by means of ferocious soldiers ready to cut the throats of women and children; foreign cohorts and phalanxes of mercenaries seek to enslave the defenders of liberty, whose valiant furor nevertheless spares the vanquished . . . The late Roman Gallic authors who had composed panegyrics in praise of late Roman emperors would have been proud to see their calls for the defeat of tyrants who had enslaved Rome so faithfully reiterated.[2]

The deep and complex interplay between Roman republican ideals and the French revolution has received a great deal of scholarly attention. Not by accident, long before she published *On Revolution* in 1963, Hannah Arendt had thought about Lucan's evocation of Cato the Younger's suicide at Utica after his loss against Caesar in a civil war.[3] Lucan's understanding of Cato's defeat because his actions

---

[1] Written by Claude-Joseph Rouget de Lisle: Robert 1989.
[2] Nixon and Rodgers 1994.
[3] Luc. *Phars.* 1.128: *victrix causa deis placuit, sed victa Catoni* (the victorious cause pleased the gods, but the defeated one pleased Cato); Arendt 2000 [1963] 11, 14, 17, 28–32, 124–129, 142; Tassin 2007, 1109–1126.

https://doi.org/10.1515/9783111334776-002

did not yield the desired outcome crystalized Arendt's distinction between liberation and freedom.[4] In what follows, I will not engage Hannah Arendt's conception
of the French Revolution. However, I would like to point out that one of her central
concerns in the *essai sur la revolution* address "the perplexities of beginnings."[5]
Can those who engage in revolution create a new order? If they institute a new
order, to what extent does that order limit the freedom of future citizens to devise
their own? Are revolutionary founders liberating anyone but themselves? For
Arendt, the French Revolution really initiated something novel. Rather than relying
on earlier models of circularity and restoration (revolution, *revolvere*), for her the
French revolution introduced linear time as a vector of modernity, "the notion that
the course of history suddenly begins anew."[6]

Such questions – the relationship between war, civil war, violence, restoration or foundation, that is, the relationship between a new order and notions of
time – immediately bring to mind not so much Lucan or Livy as another author,
whom scholars of Arendt's *On Revolution* discuss far less frequently. Surprisingly
so, because this author had influenced Arendt since her 1929 dissertation on *Der
Liebesbegriff bei Augustinus*.[7] Admittedly, Augustine's writings, including his *City
of God*, which will be at the center of what follows, are rarely associated with revolution.[8] Nor for that matter are they quoted in the context of war with the exception of his 'just war theory.'[9] Rather, as Arendt's dissertation indicates, Augustine
is understood as a theoretician of love and peace. Moreover, many of the themes
he developed for example in the *City of God* became fundamental theological max-
ims and are central to the history of ideas, such as the earthly and heavenly city
and how they intermingle, the nature of desire, sin and redemption, or the nature
of time. Consequently, these themes dominate scholarship. However, the author of
the *City of God* was also a master theoretician of war, including civil war.[10]

---

4 Controversially received when it was first published, partially because of Arendt's idiosyncratic
approach to the Roman republic, *On Revolution* has recently found new appreciation: see the con-
tributions in the special issue of the *European Journal of Political and Cultural Sociology* 1, 2014;
Roza 2016, 85–96; König 2017, 185–209; Wedin and Wilén 2020, 19–45; in general, see Jonas (1969).
5 Arendt [1963] 2000 208; Gordon 2017, 107–128.
6 Arendt [1963] 2000, 21, 27–28, 34–36; Pocock 1975, 3–30 is fundamental; cf. also Gordon 2017,
110–111; Järvinen and Örestig 2019.
7 Arendt 2003.
8 August. *De Civ. D.* (= *CCSL* 46–47). Trans.: Dyson 1998. Trans. and commentary: Walsh 2021
[2005] (books 1–3). Commentary: Clark 2021 (books 1–5).
9 Mostly on the basis of a slender paragraph in Book 19 of the *City of God*. Markus 1983, 1–13 is
foundational; see also Markus 1970, 33–44, 52–57. Wynn 2013, 9–32, argues that Augustinian influence on 'just-war theories' is essentially a twentieth century phenomenon.
10 Wynn 2013, 213–217; Tornau 2021, 53–80; but see now Lowrie and Vinken 2022, 144–192.

Augustine began the *City of God* in response to Rome's sack by Gothic federations under the leadership of Alaric in the summer of 410. The sack prompted Augustine to preach several sermons in Carthage in the immediate aftermath in the presence of refugees who had fled the city's destruction.[11] Rome's destruction had sent shockwaves through the empire and many wondered why such a disaster occurred in Christian times. Many considered it the traditional Roman gods' revenge for the empire's recent turn to Christianity, and the eternal city's destruction called in question the eternity of the empire as a whole.[12] Augustine's sermons in 411 and the *City of God*, which he began in 412, offer his explanations and responses. God, in his wisdom had not in fact permitted Rome to be destroyed. Rather, Christian barbarians had captured the city to correct its inhabitants such that they, at last, could begin to understand the true meaning of Christian Roman virtue.

1 The Law of War *(ius belli)* and the *City of God*, Book 1

War was at the root of Augustine's *magnum opus*.[13] Rome's sack offered him the opportunity to reconceptualize, recast, or, better, to create in new ways the foundation of Rome, of the *res publica* and the *imperium Romanum*. That was a significant driving force of the *City of God*. In Hanna Arendt's sense, then, Augustine used Rome's recent calamity to start the *imperium* and its history anew. To achieve this, he re-formed and overwrote in the *City of God* the foundational works of the *imperium Romanum*, prominently among them those of Cicero, Livy, Vergil, Sallust, Lucan, and Varro.[14] War had been at the center of Rome's *imperium* and thus of its foundational narratives: foreign war or the crushing of external foes so that they could be integrated into the ever-growing *corpus imperii* (3.1), and near constant civil war as heralded by Rome's fratricidal foundation (3.17).[15] Consequently, war was as central to Augustine's *City of God* as it had been for the authors who narrated Rome's rise and its divine eternity, *imperium sine fine dedi*, as he made clear

---

11 Elm 2017, 51–75.

12 Recent research has rightly moderated the long-term impact of the sack, but that does not diminish its immediate effect on many of the empire's inhabitants: van Nuffelen 2015, 322–329.

13 Scholarly discussions of Augustine's views on concrete warfare have been reticent: Weissenberg 2005; Wynn 2013, 265–295; Zwitter and Hoelzl 2014, 317–324.

14 Conybeare 1999, 59–74; Clark 2007, 117–138, 2021, 9–11; Elm 2020, 85–90.

15 Conybeare 2010, 139–155; Clark 2018, 54–62; Tornau 2021, 53–80.

when citing Vergil's rendering of Anchises's prediction for Aeneas's dependents in his preface.[16]

Indeed, as I have argued elsewhere, Augustine structured the opening of the *City of God* in Book 1 according to the "law of war," *ius belli*.[17] Other terms Augustine used in Book 1 are *mos* (tradition) *belli* or *bellorum* and *consuetudo* (custom) *belli*.[18] The essential elements of the *ius belli* or law of war Augustine has in mind are captivity, "devastation, slaughter, looting, burning and affliction" (1.7).[19] For those who knew their Livy, Vergil, and other Latin authors, that sequence vividly evoked descriptions of the *urbs capta*, the captured city.[20] In other words, when speaking of *ius belli* in Book 1, Augustine had in mind neither proper ways of declaring war nor *ius belli* as parameter permitting a more "humane" conduct of war as discussed by Cicero, Livy, or Ambrose (often referred to as *ius in bello*). Rather, he spoke about the historic experiences how captured cities suffered, time and again, as narrated in foundational works and felt in life.[21]

Because Augustine illustrated his *iura belli* through the evocation of the *urbs capta* and through exemplars such as Marcus Regulus and Job, (Arendt's) Cato the Younger and Judas, as well as Lucretia, he also spoke about *ius belli* in the sense of justice in war. Augustine's exemplars Christianized the law of war by refashioning Roman virtues as Christian through the example of Rome's sack and its endurance as means of correction.[22] Augustine's principal point in the first five books of the *City of God* was to demonstrate that the traditional notion according to which the gods guaranteed Rome's eternal *imperium* because of its *pietas* was false since the only guarantor of true eternity was the Christian god. He demanded a different kind of *pietas*.[23] Therefore, by divine design, as Augustine had

---

16 Verg. *Aen.* 1.278–279; MacCormack 1998, 175–224.

17 For the *ius belli* see Cic. *Off.* 1.34–40; Ambr. *Off.* 1.29, 139; August. *Ep.* 189.6 to Boniface (*CSEL* 57, 135); Meconi 2021, 19–38 emphasizes different aspects when highlighting four structuring elements of Book 1; Elm, forthcoming.

18 *Mos* or *mores*, "the way things are done," covers both "custom" and "morality;" *ius* usually covers both positive law and a sense of justice, but in Book 1 Augustine uses *ius* more in the sense of *mos* and *consuetudo*, which also means custom; Dodaro 2004, 11.

19 Augustine's use of *ius belli* is also different from later discussions, beginning with Gentili and Grotius: Vergerio 2017.

20 Paul 1982; Kraus 2020; Lavan 2020.

21 Cic. *Off.* 3.107: *Est autem ius etiam bellicum fidesque iuris iurandi saepe cum hoste servanda*; cf. Ambr. *Off.* 1.29, 139: *quae* [sc. *iustitia*] *etiam hostibus reservatur*; and 1.29, 140: *Liquet igitur etiam in bello fidem et iustitiam servari oportere*. Wynn 2013, 136 and 143 uses *ius belli* and *ius in bello* interchangeably. For Christian conceptions of a more 'humane' war prior to Augustine see e.g. Swift 1970. For the correct ways to declare war with particular attention to Livy see e.g. Santangelo 2008.

22 Elm 2017; for Roman exemplarity as key to law see Lowrie 2016a, 2022.

23 Wu 2007, 27–31.

already emphasized in the sermons of 411, Rome was sacked but not destroyed. Rather, God in his mercy had flogged eternal Rome like a master an unruly slave or a good father a disobedient child, so that it could correct itself and learn true *pietas*. This required a painstaking adjustment of all the civic virtues that had made the Romans Roman.[24] In short, Rome's "Christian" citizens had to be corrected so that they would re-form *gloria belli* to *gloria Dei*.

In Book 1 Augustine again emphasized that Rome's sack by ferocious and bloodthirsty but Christian barbarians was a mere corrective flogging by contrasting it to "the usual custom (*morem hostium*) of an enemy when sacking a city" (1.4): Rome's sack had been "mild" – *mite* (*immanitas barbarum tam mite apparuit*, 1.7). Recent scholarship has corroborated this assessment by highlighting that this sack, though of great symbolic value, did not lead to Rome's fall.[25] However, by calling the sack mild Augustine might not have had the actual experience in mind. After all, he was making a number of (polemical) points. One of these points was to stress the contrast between foreign and civil war. Throughout Book 1 Augustine emphasized that this time Rome had been sacked by "foreign nations (*nationes*)," that is, by barbarians and hence in accordance with the laws of external war (though this time foreigners crushed Romans rather than, as was customary, vice-versa). Significantly, then, this sack was not the result of civil war, the worst of all wars about which Augustine has also much to say in the *City of God* (for example in Books 3 and 19): "What rage displayed by foreign nations, what ferocity of the barbarians, can match the horror of this victory of citizens over citizens?"[26] Indeed, in the decades preceding the *City of God* civil wars rather than foreign ones had been the most frequent and savage threats to Rome – if not to the city itself than to the empire it embodied. Civil war, *bellum civile*, utterly shattered the social bonds, the *vinculum societatis* or *sociale* in the terms of Cicero and Augustine, tearing apart everything from the family to the cosmos in ways that made reconciliation an extra-human endeavor; hence the significance of *religio* as binding.[27] That Rome had been sacked by foreign barbarians instead of other Romans thus demonstrated that the Christian god had wished to spare the city in this instance from the fate it had so frequently endured since its fratricidal foundation: this sack had been mild – by comparison.

---

24 Swift 1987; Harding 2008, 39–55.

25 Piccaluga 1995; Mathisen 2013; Salzman 2015.

26 August. *De Civ. D.* 3.29 on the civil war between Sulla and Marius; at *De Civ. D.* 3.13 and the abduction of the Sabine women, which Augustine, quoting Lucan's *Pharsalia* on the civil war between Caesar and Pompey, considered "wars . . . worse than civil" (*bella . . . plus quam civilia*; Tuttle 2021.

27 Cic. *Rep.* 1.49; August. *De Civ. D.* 15.16; Lowrie 2016b; Lowrie and Vinken 2022, 11–13.

2 The Laws of Capturing a City

Though less brutal than it might have been during a civil war, Rome's sack, as Augustine freely acknowledged, had been savage. After all, the *ius belli* or law of war that structures Book 1 involved captivity, "devastation, slaughter, looting, burning and affliction" (1.7). Book 1 addresses them in sequence, which also distinguishes it from the remaining 22 books of the *City of God* that no longer refer to this disaster directly. At the same time, Book 1 opens the entire work and contains many of the themes more fully developed later.[28] Beginning with his famous repudiation of Vergil's claim – "you, Roman, remember you own arts: to rule the world with law, impose your ways on peace, grant the conquered clemency, and crush the proud in war" (Verg. *Aen.* 6.851–853)[29] – Augustine stressed how much the fate of Rome's defeated inhabitants differed from that customarily suffered as a result of the laws of war: "Acts that the law of war would have permitted elsewhere were forbidden" (*ubi fuerat interdictum quod alibi belli iure dicuisset*; August. *De Civ. D.* 1.1); "contrary to the usages of war (*morem bellorum*) the cruel (*truculenti*) barbarians spared them" (1.1). True, "whatever devastation, slaughter, looting, burning and affliction was committed during that most recent calamity at Rome, all this was at any rate according to the custom of wars (*consuetudo bellorum*)" (1.7). But this time "a new and unprecedented standard in such affairs" had come to the fore and in what follows Augustine explicates this new standard (*novo more/ novus mos*) and what it proves.

Augustine began with the first law of war, captivity. That law meant that the conquering barbarians savagely killed and sought to capture as many Romans as they could, driven by bloodthirst and greed. Whose life the victors spared, were saved, *servus*. Hence, such a *servus* or *serva* became their property or slave; in short, the fate normally suffered by those Romans had conquered they now endured themselves.[30] However, these ferocious yet Christian barbarians, Alaric's Goths, spared those who had sought refuge in Christian basilicas and the shrines of martyrs, "large areas selected to contain a great throng."[31] Granting sanctuary or asylum in a place of worship was unprecedented. "Many histories have been composed of the wars waged before Rome was founded and after her rise and accession to imperial power. Let our adversaries read these histories and cite any instance of a city captured by foreigners in which the conquerors spared those they found seeking refuge in the temples, or of any barbarian commander who

28 Clark 2021, 5–36; O'Daly 1999, 74–75.
29 Trans.: Bartsch 2021, 148.
30 Lavan 2013, 73–123.
31 See also August. *De Civ. D.* 5.23 for a comparison to non-Christian Goths.

gave direction when a town was entered, to spare those who they found taking refuge in this or that temple" (1.2).

All one needed to recall was Vergil's description of Troy. Its capture was the most famous exemplar of the laws of war in action, the *urbs capta* par excellence.[32] By comparing Rome's capture to that of Troy, Augustine both emphasized that traditional connection between these two cities, one of which had preceded the other, and at the same time highlighted why Rome merely suffered correction.

> In the former liberty was lost, in the latter preserved; in the former captivity was enforced, in the latter proscribed; in the former the defeated were forced into slavery as property of the enemies who had conquered them, in the latter they were conducted to freedom by the merciful . . . Perhaps Vergil, poet that he was, made it all up? No. On the contrary, he has depicted the usual custom (morem hostium) of an (foreign) enemy when sacking a city [. . .] (1.4).

Next Augustine addressed looting and its inevitable consequence, famine, and intense mortality. "They lost all they had." But what does such a loss mean? Did they lose "their faith? Their godliness? The goods of an inward man who is rich before God?" Certainly, to lose all earthly possessions was harsh. But it allowed "those who lost their earthly riches in the sack . . . to say with one [exemplar] sorely tempted but never conquered," none other than Job, "'naked came I out of my mother's womb, naked shall I return into the earth. The Lord gave and the Lord has taken away" (1.10; Job 1.21). Of course, many, including Christians, rejoiced that "they had laid up their earthly riches in a place where, as it happened, the enemy did not break through," falsely assuming that this was a stroke of luck when instead they should have considered this an opportunity to rid themselves of sinful attachment to their worldly possessions; had they given away their possessions freely they would now not been saddened by their loss (1.10; cf. 1.9) – a divine teaching moment. The "many persons, including Christians, [who] were laid low by the protracted famine" as inevitable consequence of looting, should draw similar conclusions. "Those whom the famine slew it rescued from the ills of this life, as does bodily sickness and those it did not slay it taught to live more moderately; it taught them to fast more diligently" (1.10) – harsh correction, to be sure, but correction – as most of Augustine's contemporaries knew very well – could not be achieved without harshness.

"Many Christians were slaughtered and many were consumed by a variety of dreadful deaths. If it is hard to bear, however, it is at any rate common to all who have been born into this life. I know this: no one has ever died who had not been going to die eventually" (1.11). What matters is not when and how one died, but what happens after death, "into which place [one] will be brought by dying."

---

32 Kenty 2017; Kraus 2020, 17–20.

Christians know that they will be brought to a better place, so even a terrible death can do little harm. But "so great was the massacre that not all the bodies of the dead could be buried" (1.12). Certainly, a terrible state of affairs but not one that should make survivors feel guilty; While not calling for an end of the care for the dead, Augustine reiterated that the absence of proper burials though painful for the survivors did not affect the fate of the deceased.

After a second return to the consequences of captivity in Book 1.14–29, to which I will return, Augustine focused on the corrosive effects of plundered wealth and the luxury it afforded the victors. True, Rome had been captured by foreign enemies, but what would a world without external foes mean? Everyone who had read Sallust – and that means most of his audience – knew the answer.[33] When Rome's chief rival Carthage had finally been destroyed, the ensuing "peace" and the immense material abundance it generated had caused insane desires and innumerable vices (1.30). Civil war inevitably followed, conducted with such cruelty that Romans suffered more from fellow citizens than they had from external foes. Finally, Rome's overwhelming lust for domination (*libido dominandi*) became concentrated in a few men who enslaved all others so that they could indulge their perverted luxuries, including theatrical shows (1.31–32). Even in this current calamity, Rome's citizens still go to the theater (1.33)! No wonder that harsh correction was called for. But God's corrective capture had been mild, as exemplified by the new form of asylum introduced by the invading Christian barbarians, which had endowed Romulus's asylum with its true, Christian meaning.[34] In short, the *urbs capta* as outlined by Vergil for Troy and Livy for Veii structures Augustine's Book 1.[35] Like his precursors, Augustine used the laws of war and the trope of the captured city, familiar narrative pattern, to provide his audience at the moment of writing and those reading him in the future, with new Christian ways to come to terms with yet another experience of age-old horrors.

3 Laws of War II: Captivity, Torture, and Sexual Violence against Men and Women

In Book 1.14–129, Augustine returned once more to the laws of captivity. "But many Christians, they say, were also led into captivity" (1.14). That is a great misery, of course, but even in captivity, "God the Comforter did not desert them" (*nec Deum*

---

33 Aug. *De Civ. D.* 1.30; Sall. *Cat.* 10–12 and *Hist.*; Clark 2021, 75–77.
34 On Augustine's recasting of Romulus's asylum: Benjamins 2022, 162–176.
35 Livy 9.4.12–14; Aug. *De Exc. Urb.* 6; Elm 2017, 53–56; Kraus 2020, 27–29.

defuit consolator), but helped them endure. Scripture offers other examples of followers of the true God made captive, but "they" (traditional Romans) too have "among their most shining men" exemplars who endured captivity even voluntarily for the sake of religion. Their most famous exemplar was the commander (*imperator*) Marcus Regulus (1.15).[36] If Regulus's captivity with its extreme tortures did not cast aspersion on *his* religion, Augustine points out, then his co-religionists and his (imagined) opponents, should likewise refrain from casting aspersion on the Christian god because his followers too had been captured. At least the Christian God never deserted his own in their suffering. With that Augustine momentarily set aside the true quality of Regulus's virtue until Book 1.24.

Instead, Augustine next addressed an aspect of captivity which "as Sallust, a historian famous for truth, writes, Cato himself did not omit to mention . . . in the speech which he delivered to the Senate . . . 'Maidens and boys are violated; children plucked from the embrace of their parents; the mothers of families endure (*pati*) whatever might be the pleasure of the victors . . . In short, all is filled with arms, corpses, slaughter, and lamentation'" (1.5).[37] One essential component of captivity resulting from foreign and civil war was sexual violence (here *raptus*) of maidens, boys, and mothers of families. This was so because those taken captives were now enslaved and as such sexually available to their masters.[38] One frequent consequence of this particular law of war was that "many have killed themselves (*se interemerunt*) for fear of falling into the hands of the enemy" (1.22).[39] Moreover, as Augustine's adversarial interlocutors are quick to point out, during Rome's recent sack "violations (*stupra*) were committed not only on married women and young women intending to marry (*virgines*), but also on consecrated virgins (*sanctimoniales*)" (1.16). Nevertheless, Augustine was adamant that Roman Christians should not kill themselves (1.16). By doing so, he argued, they would murder an innocent person, themselves, out of mistaken notions of honor and shame or modesty (*pudor* covers both) that equated sexual violence with loss of *pudicitia*, modesty or purity.

---

36 Marcus Atilius Regulus had defeated Carthage during the first Punic war, but his terms of surrender were so draconian that the Carthaginians resumed fighting and captured Regulus. They then sent him to Rome to negotiate peace and a prisoner exchange, but Regulus urged his fellow Romans to reject all terms. Because he had been bound by oath he returned to Carthage and captivity and was tortured to death; Clark 2021, 60.
37 Sall. *Cat.* 51.9; Clark 2021, 46–47.
38 Harper 2011, 442.
39 The term suicide is a twelfth century neologism that became widely used in the sixteenth and seventeenth century. It incorporates Augustine's rejection of self-killing he had first outlined in what follows: van Hooff, 1990, 243–250; Shaw 2011, 735–770, n. 46; Webb 2015, 212–213.

Augustine knew that "the infliction of pain (*dolor*) [and] and the gratification of lust (*libido*) is possible on the body of another" (1.16). However, he argued, that did not affect the purity (*pudicitia*) of the sufferer who did not consent to such violence. "*Pudicitia* is a virtue (*virtus*) of the soul, and has as its companion (manly) courage (*fortitudo*) which resolves to tolerate any evil whatsoever rather than consent to evil. But no one (*nullus*), no matter how great-souled and modest (*magnanimus et pudicus*), has it in his power to control what is done to the flesh, but only what the mind (*mens*) will consent to or refuse" (1.18).[40] *Pudicitia*, Augustine continued, "must be numbered among the good things of the body such as strength (*vires*), beauty (*pulchritudo*), good health (*sana valetudo*) and so forth" (1.18). These too can be diminished (for example through age), but their loss does not determine whether or not a life was well lived and hence virtuous (1.18). "Though our discussion is forced into the narrow space between shame (*pudor*) and rational explanation (*ratio*), we say that neither faith (*fides*), nor piety (*pietas*), nor that virtue which is called chastity (*castitas*) is really at stake" (1.16). No one, therefore, who has suffered sexual violence or is terrified by its imminence should resort to self-killing.

Augustine's position, formulated not so much "to return an answer to outsiders as to bring comfort (*consolatio*) to our own," was unusual (1.16). Others such as Ambrose considered self-killing in expectation of sexual violence at the hand of a captor a matter of choice between two kinds of force, *vis*, making it acceptable even if it violated the Scriptural precept "you shall not kill" from which only soldiers in wartime were exempt (1.20–21, 26).[41] To illustrate his position, Ambrose evoked Pelagia who had 'martyred' herself (*exemplum martyrii*) by drowning rather than endure sexual violence, but he also adduced the most famous example, that of Lucretia, whom Augustine's interlocutors may well have called upon as well. Augustine too turned to Lucretia. However, rather than praising her self-killing as honorable and courageous, he made her into an *exemplum* why killing oneself in response to sexual violence was fundamentally mistaken. Livy had made Lucretia's sexual violation by Tarquinius, his threat to expose her to shame, and her subsequent suicide which led to the expulsion of Rome's kings,

---

40 Will and consent are therefore central to Augustine's argumentative moves, which then leads to questions as to how lacking consent can be made visible and hence proven; consent and it implications have thus been at the core of much scholarship on the passages discussing Lucretia: Webb 2013; Bahlberg and Muehlberger 2018; Barry 2020; Smith 2020, 237–257; see also Azam (2015).

41 Ambr. *Virg.* 3.7.32–3; Tert. *De exhortatione castitatis* (*SL* 2) 1.1; 13.24, he also adduces Dido; Quint. *Inst.* 5.11.10.: *admirabilior in femina quam in viro virtus. Quare si . . . accendatur aliquis . . . ad moriendum non tam Cato et Scipio quam Lucretia.*

into a foundation narrative of Rome's republic. Augustine instead recast her as an example of misunderstood *pudicitia*. To demonstrate that she had resisted, Lucretia had committed a crime by punishing an innocent party, herself, because only the perpetrator was guilty.[42] Augustine's re-framing of Lucretia's exemplarity has received a great deal of scholarly attention, focused primarily on his response to sexual violence rather than self-killing.[43]

In what follows, I want to draw attention to a point that has not received any scholarly attention that I am aware of.[44] All scholarly interventions focus on Lucretia and the broader implications of Augustine's stance on sexual violence against women.[45] Focusing on the laws of war as the structuring element of Book 1 reveals instead that in discussing sexual violence as integral to captivity, Augustine addressed male captives as well as female ones. Just like enslavement, sexual violence affected all captured, so that Augustine – as already indicated in his quote from Sallust, *"rapi virgines pueros . . . matres familiarum pati quae victoribus conlibuisset"* (1.5) – consoled all concerned, men and women: *haec dixi propter eos vel eas* (1.25). Christian Roman boys and men had also killed themselves because they had suffered sexual violence, to avoid having to endure anticipated rape, or because they felt "slaughtered" by the violation of their *pudor* and *pudicitia*.

4 *Pudicitia* and *patientia*

Though addressing sexual violence against women, including consecrated women, as a consequence of Rome's capture, Augustine's main point in Book 1.15–25 was that captivity and its consequences did not justify self-killing. However violent and humiliating, these consequences must be endured. Though earlier exemplars – especially Cato the Younger at Utica – had heralded self-killing as the most appropriate, even as the only appropriate reaction to captivity's humiliation, the sole virtuous response for the true Christian (elite) man and woman was endurance, *patientia* (1.18) and *constantia* (1.17). By emphasizing, first, *pudicitia* as a virtue of

---

42 August. *De Civ. D.* 1.19; Liv. 1.57–60; Webb 2013 rightly argues that Augustine equated sexual violence with torture and hence did not expect anyone to actually enjoy, that is, consent to the act; Evans Grubbs 1995, 203–225.
43 For recent discussions with further bibliography see Trout 1994; Burrus 1999, esp. 192; Webb 2015, 201–205; Bahlbeck and Muehlberger 2018; Barry 2020; Smith 2020.
44 Balberg and Muehlberger 2018, 302 mention sexual violence against men in the context of captivity but do not expand.
45 Barry 2020, 242–243.

the soul rather than the body just like strength, courage, beauty and good health, and next linking it to *patientia*, endurance, Augustine recalibrated both into quintessentially Christian Roman virtues. Here, he made *pudicitia* and *patientia* central Roman Christian virtues for men, including *illustris viri*, and women. To make his point and to effect this transformation Augustine turned to the positive exemplars, Marcus Regulus and Job, in counterpoint to Lucretia, Cato the Younger, and Judas, whose self-killing he no longer considered a virtuous response.[46]

Already Cicero had linked *pudicitia* to liberty and citizenship and applied it equally to men and women. In *his* versions of Catiline's conspiracy, he declared *pudor*, *pudicitia*, and *constantia* virtues his side possessed in abundance, while his opponent Catiline, just vanquished in a civil war, had been a perpetrator of *stuprum*, illicit sexual intercourse or rape. In short, Cicero considered *pudicitia* a core civic virtue.[47] Augustine likewise emphasized that Lucretia should have trusted that he *pudicitia* was undiminished merely because she refused consent. Had she fully grasped that such refusal meant freedom of mind, which preserved *pudicitia*, she would not have killed her innocent self. However, because the virtues her *civitas* embodied and upheld were not yet those of the true *civitas*, that of the Christian God and Christ, Lucretia was not yet able to make the correct decision to endure.

Patientia is noun to *pati*, endure. As Augustine's quote of Sallust indicates – "*pati quae victoribus conlibuisset pati*," endure whatever might be the pleasure of the victors – *pati* also denoted the passive sexual position in which one received as (if one were) a woman. As such, *patientia* captured the external and internal experience of those crushed and taken captive as a consequence of war when, as enslaved person, one was prone to suffer sexual violence.[48] Because of that ambivalence, *patientia* as virtue, much like *pudicitia*, was considered most appropriate for women.[49]

In Book 1.15–25, in response to the reality of sexual violence as part of captivity, Augustine shifted the emotional valance of *patientia* such that it became desirable for elite men as well.[50] To that effect Augustine framed *his* account of Lucretia with

---

46 Cato the Younger was one of Seneca's most important exemplars of a brave man whose bad fortune required self-killing: Sen. *Prov.* 3.4–9; 2.7–9; Dominguez Valdés 2018, esp. 316.
47 Cic. *Part. or.* 86; Cic. *Catil.* 2.25; Langlands 2006, 281–283, 319–363.
48 As made clear for example by Tac. *Agr.* 2.3: Lavan 2011, 131–141.
49 Kaster 2002, 2005, 12, 29, 35–36.
50 Dodaro 2005.

the two positive exemplars of endurance he had already mentioned, Job and Regulus.[51] Both had chosen to endure (*tolerare, ferre*) unimaginable tortures to which they were subjected through no fault of their own (1.15; 1.24). Rejecting twice the example of Judas (1.16, 17) and that of Cato the Younger (1.23), who had killed himself rather than allowing Caesar to pardon him, Augustine fiercely rejected self-killing, the solution championed by so many, in praise of endurance. Endurance, *patientia*, had been Marcus Regulus true virtue. To him Augustine returned after reprimanding those whose weak mind prevented them from "enduring the harsh enslavement of one's own body or the opinion of the vulgar" (1.22).[52]

Cato the Younger and Judas had cowardly killed themselves (1.23) in contrast to Job, "who chose to endure horrendous evils . . . rather than to be rid of his sufferings through self-killing." Regulus had done the same (1.24). Regulus, one of Rome's most *"illustris viri"* (or illuminated man, which denoted by Augustine's time the highest rank in the senate), had won a praiseworthy victory against external foes (*ex hostibus laudandam victoria*) rather than a deplorable one in a civil war (*ex civibus dolendam*); his kudos as a true Roman military man were thus not in doubt. However, when he was subsequently taken captive, he chose twice to endure (*ferre*) enslavement. "Enslaved by the Carthaginians he maintained *patientia* and *constantia* in his love for Rome with an unconquered mind (*animus*)" rather than killing himself, and this was not a man afraid of death. "But if *this* bravest (*fortissimus*) and most shining man (*praeclarissimus vir*)," who had defeated enemies according to all laws of war (*iure belli*), could in defeat choose to endure "whatever tortures his enraged enemies might inflict," and "preferred to be enslaved . . . rather than to inflict death upon [himself]" for the sake of his *patria*, *then* Christians "if they are for any reason subjugated by their enemy" should also endure such humiliation. They should do so all the more willingly to be tried and corrected (*emendare*), because they know that their God who had humbled himself will not desert them "in this humiliation (*in illa humilitate*)." "Who is so grievously in error, then, as to suppose a man may kill himself *(homo se occidat)* because a foe has sinned against him, or for fear that a foe may sin against him . . . in the future?" (1.24; 1.17).

"But we must," Augustine's imagined (male) interlocutors counter, "fear and beware lest the body, when overpowered by the enemy's lust/hostile lust (*libidini hostile*), tempt the soul by a most enticing pleasure (*voluptas*) to consent" (1.25). No, Augustine reiterates "for the sake of the men or women (*propter eos vel eas*)

---

51 For Regulus see e.g. Cic. *Nat. D.* 3.32; *Off.* 3.26.99–32.115; Hor. *Carm.* 3.5; Min. Felix *Oct.* 26.3.37.5; for Job as exemplar of endurance see August. *Urb. Exc.* 3–4; Elm 2017, 73–75.

52 Sen. *Prov.* 1.6 declared self-killing the apex of *patientia* and here Augustine reversed that stance: Dionigi (1991); Kaster (2002) 136–9; Benjamins (2022) 45–59.

who consider inflicting mortal violence on themselves because of another's sin," arousal caused by the violent lust of another does not signify consent. Therefore, no man should kill himself, even if, "to be sure, that lustful disobedience which still dwells in our moribund members sometimes moves itself as if by its own law, apart from the law of our will: when we are asleep, for instance." But just as there is no fault in that involuntary movement of the male member during sleep, there is also none if it moves involuntarily in the context of sexual violence; neither movement indicates consent (1.25).

Because Job and above all "God the Consoler" had been utterly humbled and had endured humiliation out of their own free will, elite male and female Christians should embrace endurance, *patientia*, even more forcefully than Regulus had done. He had endured for the sake of the earthly *civitas*, without any help from his gods, while captured Christian men and women endured for the sake of the eternal *civitas* in the knowledge that Christ will not desert them even in this humiliation, *in illa humilitate non deserit* (1.24). From *gloria belli* to *gloria Dei*.[53]

5 Rejuvenation and Renewal

Book 1, to reiterate, was an overture to the reminder of the massive *City of God*, and Augustine returned to many of its themes in the books that followed. One of Augustine's principal endeavors in the *City of God* was to reorder, to re-found the ideological underpinnings of the most important *civitas terrena*, namely his own: the *imperium Romanum*. That earthly city was intermingled with the *civitas Dei*, and it was Augustine's task to make that intermingling as beneficial as possible for the *peregrini*, the citizens in transit, who inhabited that earthly city so that they might reach the heavenly one if God so chose. At the heart of Augustine' new order were the virtues that had made Rome into an *imperium*, which had led the *corpus imperii* to expand to its dangerously gigantic proportions. Rome's virtues had emerged out of warfare. *Viri*, elite men, had fought with force, *vis*, and fortitude under the command (*imperium*) of their leaders so that they could sue for peace after a war fought victoriously because justly, according to the *ius belli*. Rome's peace then brought *ius* and *iustitia*, laws and justice, to the crushed, as Vergil had so eloquently stated. Such *gloria belli*, such *jour de gloire* granted Rome's eternity, its *imperum sine fine*. Virtue, *vir*-ness, *vis*, demonstrated by slaughtering hostile enemies and defeating bloodthirsty tyrants while sparing the innocent, was

---

53 Conybeare 1999, 73.

thus at the heart of Rome's self-understanding and to change such virtues was a revolutionary undertaking.

Augustine used the "law of war" (*ius belli*) to recast these virtues, because he too was Roman and understood the centrality of war as founding metaphor of Rome's *imperium*. Indeed, as Book 1 makes clear, Augustine resorts to the Roman Republic to re-form Rome's virtues into Christian Roman ones. Capture by foreign enemies and the terrors of civil war are the crucible in which he forged true *pietas vis-à-vis* the sole true God, Christ the Consoler. This new *pietas* required new ways to conduct war, a new *ius* and *mos belli*. Endurance, *patientia* rather than self-killing; *pudicitia* as a matter of will and not of the body; *humilitas*, humility and humiliation as the real *gloria* a Roman Christian should aspire to: *Gloria Dei* rather than *gloria belli*.[54] To teach Rome's inhabitants the true meaning of Roman virtues had been God's intention when permitting the city's sack. God had chosen to correct (*correctio, emendatio*) Rome's Christians through this mild sack because the fate of the eternal city would correct the *imperium Romanum*, that is, the *orbis terrarum*, the entire world. Rome's fate was meant to be a universal correction of Rome's virtues toward the true Christian ones. This correction had been harsh, but that was what was required to make it effective. Indeed, in his mercy, God had been comparatively mild; at least, this had not been a civil war.

Moreover, it was high time. Augustine, like many of his contemporaries, thought that Rome had reached an advanced age, that she had reached *senectus*.[55] In Augustine's words, old age, *senectus*, was "the universal infirmity of the human race," and the inevitable conclusion to a full human life.[56] If Roma, now an elderly lady, was to last for all eternity, she needed rejuvenation. Augustine, like others before him, equated the life of the world with the ages of human life, so that Rome's *senectus*, her decrepit old age, also portended the imminent end of the world; Rome's sack was as good an indicator as any.[57] However, Augustine modelled his conception of the age of man after Genesis and the six days of creation.[58] For him, *senectus* was the last of six ages. In his view that sixth and last stage of man and of the world was an age of immense potential. It was ongoing and would last until the end of the *saeculum*. Then, Christ would return to usher in the final, seventh age, that of perpetual peace and tranquility. Thus, Rome's present moment,

---

54 As Augustine elaborated in Book 5.
55 Parkin 2003, 100–115 also for the distinction between *senior* and *senectus*.
56 Aug. *Ep.* 152.13.
57 Aug. *En. Ps.* 127.15, *serm.* 33A, *serm.* 216.8; Parkin 2003, 86–89 for descriptions of old age's vicissitudes.
58 Aug. *De Civ. D.* 2.29.1; *Gn. adv. Man.* 1.23.29; 1.25.43; 1.24.42; *serm.* 105; Benjamins, *Augustine's Romans*, 91–97.

its *senectus*, represented an unprecedented opportunity for correction and therefore for rejuvenation and renewal. This was the age for potentially renewed *vires* and *virtus*, because it was the age that would witness the coming of Christ. If Rome used this moment of immense revolutionary, or reformatory potential to correct itself, it might restore the vigor of its youth and "take possession of the heavenly country for which you will suffer very little hardship, and then you will reign in it truly and lastingly. For there you will have not the Vestal hearth, not the Capitoline stone, but the one true God who 'sets neither boundaries nor time for your empire; he will give sway without end':" in short, then "the course of history suddenly begins anew."[59]

Bibliography

Arendt, Hannah. *On Revolution*. New York: Penguin Group, 2000 [1963].

Arendt, Hannah. *Der Liebesbegriff bei Augustin. Versuch einer philosophischen Interpretation*. Berlin/Vienna: Philo, 2003.

Azam, Hina. *Sexual Violation in Islamic Law: Substance, Evidence and Procedure*. Cambridge: Cambridge University Press, 2015.

Bahlberg, Mira, and Ellen Muehlberger. "The Will of Others: Coercion, Captivity, and Choice in Late Antiquity." *SLA* 2 (2018): 294–315.

Barry, Jennifer. "So Easy to Forget: Augustine on the Treatment of the Sexually Violated in the *City of God*." *JAAR* 88 (2020): 235–253.

Bartsch, Shadi. *The Aeneid*. New York: Random House, 2021.

Benjamins, Joshua. *Augustine's Romans: Manliness, Empire, and Social Order After 410*. Diss. University of California, Berkeley, 2022.

Burrus, Virginia. "An Immoderate Feast: Augustine reads John's Apocalypse." *History, Apocalypse and the Secular Imagination: New Essays on Augustine's "City of God:" proceedings of a colloquium held at Green College, the University of British Columbia, 18–20 September 1997*. Eds. Allan Fitzgerald, Karla Pollmann, and Mark Vessey. Bowling Green, OH: Philosophy Documentation Center, 1999. 183–194.

Burrus, Virginia. *Saving Shame: Martyrs, Saints, and Other Abject Subjects*. Philadelphia: University of Pennsylvania Press, 2008.

Clark, Gillian. "City of Books: Augustine and the World as Text." *The Early Christian Book*. Eds. William E. Klingshirn and Linda Safran. Washington, D.C.: Catholic University of America Press, 2007. 117–138.

Clark, Gillian. "*Imperium* and the City of God: Augustine on Church and Empire." *The Church and Empire*. Eds. Stewart Brown, Charlotte Methuen, and Andrew Spicer. Cambridge: Cambridge University Press, 2018. 46–70.

Clark, Gillian. *Commentary on Augustine, City of God, Books 1–5*. Oxford: Oxford University Press, 2021.

---

59 Aug. *De Civ. D.* 2.29.1; Arendt 2000 [1963] 21, 27–28, 34–36; Pocock 1975, 31–48.

Conybeare, Catherine. *"Terrarum Orbi Documentum*: Augustine, Camillus, and Learning from History." *History, Apocalypse and the Secular Imagination: New Essays on Augustine's "City of God*:" *proceedings of a colloquium held at Green College, the University of British Columbia, 18–20 September 1997*. Eds. Mark Vessey, Karla Pollmann, and Allan Fitzgerald. Bowling Green, OH: Philosophy Documentation Center, 1999. 59–74.

Conybeare, Catherine. "The City of Augustine: On the Interpretation of *civitas*." *Being Christian in Late Antiquity: A Festschrift for Gillian Clark*. Eds. Carol Harrison, Caroline Humfress, and Isabella Sandwell. Oxford: Clarendon Press, 2010. 139–155.

Dionigi, Ivano. "Il *De Providentia*: Seneca tra Crispio e Agostino." *Seneca e la cultura*. Ed. Aldo Setaioli. Naples: Edizioni Scientifiche Italiane, 1991. 49–66.

Dodaro, Robert J. *Christ and the Just Society in the Thought of Augustine*. Cambridge: Cambridge University Press, 2004.

Dodaro, Robert J. "Augustine's Revision of the Heroic Ideal." *Augustinian Studies* 36 (2005): 141–157.

Dominguez Valdés, Patricio. *"De Civitate Dei* I in Light of Seneca's *De providentia*." *Heythrop Journal* 62.2 (2018): 311–322.

Dyson, Robert W. *Augustine: The City of God Against the Pagans*. Cambridge: Cambridge University Press, 1998.

Elm, Susanna. "Signs Under the Skin: Flogging Eternal Rome." *Unter die Haut. Tätowierungen als Logo- und Piktogramme*. Eds. Iris Därmann and Thomas Macho. Munich: Brill Fink Verlag, 2017. 51–75.

Elm, Susanna. "Books, Bodies, Histories: Augustine of Hippo and the Extraordinary (*civ. Dei* 16.8 and Pliny, *HN* 7)." *Rhetoric and Religious Identity in late Antiquity*. Eds. Richard Flower and Morwenna Ludlow. Oxford: Clarendon Press, 2020. 83–98.

Elm, Susanna. "The Law of War: Augustine of Hippo on (Civil)War, Captured Cities, and Sexual Violence against Men and Women (*Civ. Dei* 1)." *War and Community in Late Antiquity*. Eds. Susanna Elm and Kristina Sessa. Cambridge: Cambridge University Press, forthcoming.

Evans Grubbs, Judith. *Law and Family in Late Antiquity: The Emperor Constantine's Marriage Legislation*. Oxford: Clarendon Press, 1995.

Gordon, Daniel. "The Perplexities of Beginning: Hannah Arendt's Theory of Revolution." *Anthem Companion to Hannah Arendt*. Eds. Peter Baehr and Philip Walsh. London: Anthem Press, 2017. 107–128.

Harding, Brian. *Augustine and Roman Virtue*. London: Bloomsbury, 2008.

Harper, Kyle. *Slavery in the Late Roman World, AD 275–425*. Cambridge: Cambridge University Press, 2011.

van Hooff, Anton J. I. *From Autothanasia to Suicide: Self-Killing in Classical Antiquity*. London: Routledge, 1990.

Järvinen, Hannah O., and Johan Örestig. "Revolution as accelerated modernity: Hannah Arendt and Anselm Jappe on radical social transformation." *Eurozine* August 1, 2019.

Jonas, Friedrich. "Hannah Arendts Theorie der Revolution." *Soziale Welt* 20 (1969): 359–368.

Kaster, Robert A. "The Taxonomy of Patience, or When is *patientia* not a Virtue?" *CP* 97 (2002): 133–144.

Kaster, Robert A. *Emotion, Restraint, and Community in Ancient Rome*. Oxford: Oxford University Press, 2005.

Kenty, Joanna. *"Altera Roma*: Livy's Variations on a Ciceronian Theme." *Illinois Classical Studies* 42 (2017): 61–81.

Kraus, Christina S. "Urban Disasters and Other Romes: The Case of Veii." *Urban Disasters and the Roman Imagination*. Eds. Virginia M. Closs and Elizabeth Keitel. Berlin: De Gruyter, 2020. 17–31.

Langlands, Rebecca. *Sexual Morality in Ancient Rome*. Cambridge: Cambridge University Press, 2006.

Lavan, Myles. *Slaves to Rome: Paradigms of Empire in Roman Culture*. Cambridge: Cambridge University Press, 2013.

Lavan, Myles. "Devastation: The Destruction of Populations and Human Landscapes and the Roman Imperial Project." *Reconsidering Roman Power: Roman, Greek, Jewish and Christian perceptions and Reactions*. Ed. Katell Berthelot. Roma: École française de Rome, 2020. 179–205.

Lowrie, Michèle. "Roman Law and Latin Literature." *The Oxford Handbook of Roman Law and Society*. Eds. Paul J. du Plessis, Clifford Ando, and Kaius Tuori. Oxford: Clarendon Press. 2016a, 70–81.

Lowrie, Michèle. "The Soul, Civil War, and the Cosmos at Seneca, *Thyestes* 547–622: A Tropology." *Wordplay and Powerplay in Latin Poetry, a Festschrift for Frederick Ahl*. Eds. Phillip Mitsis and Ioannis Ziogas. Berlin: De Gruyter, 2016b. 333–354.

Lowrie, Michèle. "Force of Literature." *Roman Law and Latin Literature*. Eds. Ioannis Ziogas and Erica Bexely. London: Bloomsbury, 2022. 25–44.

Lowrie, Michèle, and Barbara Vinken. *Civil War and the Collapse of the Social Bond: The Roman tradition at the Heart of the Modern*. Cambridge: Cambridge University Press, 2022.

MacCormack, Sabine. *The Shadows of Poetry: Vergil in the Mind of Augustine*. Berkeley and Los Angeles: University of California Press, 1998.

Markus, Robert A. *Saeculum: History and Society in the Theology of St. Augustine*. Cambridge: Cambridge University Press, 1970.

Markus, Robert A. "Saint Augustine's Views on the 'Just War'." *Studies in Church History* 20 (1983): 1–13.

Mathisen, Ralph. "*Roma a Gothis Alarico duce capta est*. Ancient accounts of the Sack of Rome in 410 CE." *The Sack of Rome in 410 AD. The Event, its Context and it Impact*. Eds. Johannes Lipps, Carlos Machado, and Philipp von Rummel. Wiesbaden: Reichert Verlag, 2013. 87–102.

Meconi, David V. "Book 1: The Crumbling and Consecration of Rome." *The Cambridge Companion to the City of God*. Ed. David V. Meconi. Cambridge: Cambridge University Press, 2021. 19–38.

Nixon, Barbara, and Barbara S. Rodgers. *In Praise of Later Roman Emperors: The Panegyrici Latini*. Berkeley and Los Angeles: University of California Press, 1994.

van Nuffelen, Peter. "Not Much Happened: 410 and All That." *JRS* 105 (2015): 322–329.

O'Daly, Gerard J. P. *Augustine's City of God. A Reader's Guide*. Oxford: Clarendon Press, 1999.

Parkin, Tim J. *Old Age in the Roman World: A Cultural and Social History*. Baltimore: The Johns Hopkins University Press, 2003.

Paul, G. M. "'Urbs Capta': Sketch of an Ancient Literary Motif." *Phoenix* 36 (1982): 144–155.

Piccaluga, Giulia. "Fondazione della realtà e uscita dalla storia nel Sermo 'de urbis excidio'." *Augustinianum* 53 (1995): 497–510.

Pocock, John G. A. *The Machiavellian Moment: Florentine Political Thought and the Atlantic Republican Tradition*. Princeton: University Press, 1975.

Robert, Frédéric. *La Marseillaise*, Paris: Nouvelles Editions, 1989.

Salzman, Michelle R. "Christian Sermons against Pagans: The Evidence from Augustine's *Sermons* on the New Year and On the Sack of Rome in 410." *The Cambridge Companion to the Age of Attila*. Ed. Michael Maas. Cambridge: Cambridge University Press, 2015. 344–357.

Santangelo, Federico. "The Fetials and their *ius*." *BICS* 51 (2008): 63–93.

Shaw, Brent D. *Sacred Violence: African Christians and Sectarian Hatred in the Age of Augustine*. Cambridge: Cambridge University Press, 2011.

Smith, J. Warren. *Ambrose, Augustine, and the Pursuit of Greatness*. Cambridge: Cambridge University Press, 2020.

Swift, Louis J. "St. Ambrose on Violence and War." *TAPA* 101 (1970): 533–543.

Swift, Louis J. "Pagan and Christian Heroes in Augustine's *City of God.*" *Augustinianum* 27 (1987): 509–522.

Tassin, Etienne. "'. . . *sed victa Catoni*': The Defeated Cause of Revolutions: Hannah Arendt's Centenary." *Social Research* 74 (2007): 1109–1126.

Tornau, Christian. "Book 3: Rome's Woes before Christ: History and Rhetoric in the *City of God.*" *The Cambridge Companion to the City of God.* Ed. David V. Meconi. Cambridge: Cambridge University Press, 2021. 53–80.

Trout, Dennis. "Re-Textualizing Lucretia: Cultural Subversion in the *City of God.*" *JECS* 2 (1994): 53–70.

Tuttle, Darcy. "'Dutifully They were Crucified': The Moral and Legal Redemption of the Sabine Women in Augustine's *City of God.*" *The Late (Wild) Augustine.* Eds. Susanna Elm and Christopher M. Blunda. Leiden: Brill, 2021. 113–137.

Vergerio, Claire. "Alberico Gentili's *De iure belli*: An Absolutist's Attempt at Reconciling the *ius gentium* and the Reason of State Tradition." *Journal of the History of International Law* 19 (2017): 429–466.

Walsh, Peter. *Augustine, De Civitate Dei 1–3.* Liverpool: University Press, 2021 [2005].

Weissenberg, Timo J. *Die Friedenslehre des Augustinus.* Stuttgart: Kohlhammer Verlag, 2005.

Webb, Melanie. "On Lucretia who Slew Herself: Rape and Consolation in Augustine's *De ciuitate Dei.*" *Augustinian Studies* 44 (2013): 37–58.

Webb, Melanie. "Abraham, Samson, and Certain Holy Women: Suicide and Exemplarity in Augustine's *De ciuitate Dei* 1.26." *Sacred Scripture and Secular Struggle.* Ed. David V. Meconi, Leiden: Brill, 2015. 201–234.

Wu, Tianyue. "Shame in the Context of Sin: Augustine on the Feeling of Shame in the *De Civitae Dei.*" *Recherches de theologie et philosophie medievales* 74 (2007): 1–31.

Zwitter, Andrej, and Michael Hoelzl. "Augustine on War and Peace." *Peace Review* 26 (2014): 317–324.

Anselm Haverkamp
Second Romes, and no Sense of an Ending
Tréves/ Trier, Aix la Chapelle/ Aachen, Cologne/ Köln

Quid est enim aliud omnis historia quam romana laus

There were several 'Second Romes' before Paris claimed this title. The aim – to illustrate its imperial ambition and this ambition's universal reach – far surpassed the concept of the translation of power pronounced by the Holy Roman Empire of German succession. The competition for the imperial title of Paris was a far cry from the first of second Romes, and its claim came in a different key. I shall try to identify the historical differences in the translation of second Romes before Paris and against the claims of French nineteenth century politics, in what seems a footnote to the by now outdated continuity of the unique name of Rome and the continuity of its paleonymic uses and discontinuities. As it turns out, it is also a footnote to the forgotten alternatives to the much treated Roman *translatio* as one of *imperii*. There was more to be translated than the notorious brutality – although Brutus was an honourable man – of imperial rule, the humanity of 'city-life' after Rome.

1

The first and rather unobvious, literally second Rome came along without any metaphorical reach. *Roma secunda Augusta Treverorum* or Trèves/ Trier, was the administrative extension of Rome after the division of the empire into Eastern and Western parts. As a second, *Augusta Treverorum* followed in simple continuity from, and even idenitity with, the first, original Rome, which was delegating its power for administrative convenience. As a second Rome, it did nothing but attest to what it was representative of, Rome's extended albeit divided rule. This sounds simpler than it was, since the transfer was enacted in legal terms of legitimacy. The *traditio* occurred as orderly administrative continuity, and the *translatio* was performed *kata poda*, in a step by step, word by word, translation that defined the reach of Roman law from the beginning. Ironically, as Cornelia Vismann has shown and Yan Thomas had elucidated regarding the legal underpinnings, the technical term *kata poda* names in its non-translated Greek form what

https://doi.org/10.1515/9783111334776-003

the standard of Justinian's *Corpus Iuris* in its fixity is about, instead of exemplifying the flexibility of the translation that was guaranteed by its application.[1] I will not go into the metaphorological intricacies of this terminological conundrum, but concentrate on the institutional side of the *institutio,* which defines in Quintilian's handbook, the *Institutio oratoria,* figures and tropes as modes of transfer.

In Georges Dumézil's reconstruction of Roman institutions, emblematized in the triad of *Jupiter, Mars, Quirinus,* the administrative part (Quirinus) like the military part (Mars) are extensions of Jupiter's sovereignty.[2] Thus, Dumézil's master student Michel Foucault began his later political work with a radical response to "Jupiterian history" in the Roman sense. In his first Lecture at the Collège de France in 1975, whose title, "Society must be defended", is deeply ambiguous in its imperative, Foucault aims at an alternative history. He counters every other history as a manifestation of "Jupiterian" sovereignty, beginning with a correction of the modern understanding of the so called "middle ages." As a "discourse of power," Foucault explained, history was "until a very late stage in our society [..] deployed in the function of sovereignty" and "in that sense, there was still a direct continuity between the historical practice of the Middle Ages and the history of the Romans, history as recounted by the Romans".[3] Foucault cited Livy and did not fail to end with Petrarch's famous "Invective" in favor of Rome at the end of the chapter: *Quid est enim aliud omnis historia quam romana laus.*[4] While one might be quite happy about the Roman continuity rediscovered, I disagree with the quick (all too French, too sixties) consequences of the alternative, to which Foucault proceeds without hesitation and almost automatically, it appears, under the attraction of Jupiterian power and its undiminished reach over *omnis Gallia,* however *divisa.* Jupiterian history, Foucault rightly insisted, "enslaves" in that it is "not the history of others" (69). But the "counter-history" he envisaged instead (which "*appears* at this point," he cautiously added) is far too roughly described by the most general of *topoi,* the "history of race struggle." In spite of the striking, undeniable importance of his anti-historical insight, which dissolves history in the counter-move of a generalized anti-Roman resistance, Foucault remains under the spell of what he wishes to discard ("la France insoumise" *ante portas*).

The historical step overlooked and disregarded in Foucault's initiative carries – in spite of the due respect to the factors of war (Mars) and the function of

---

1 Vismann 1997, 156; Thomas 1995.
2 Dumézil 1941.
3 Foucault 2003, 68 f. and 74.
4 See Vinken 2001, 43.

governmentality (Quirinus) – the name of another historian, not forgotten but from a different neck of the woods, the Belgian co-founder, with Marc Bloch and Lucien Febvre, of the *Annales*-School, Henri Pirenne. Already in the famous Pirenne-thesis on *Mahomet et Charlemagne* (1937),[5] Pirenne focused on the domain of Quirinus, economic history, and, more to the point here, on the city as the decisive alternative power-broker, a factor truly counter-historical with respect to the overwhelming Jupiterian nature of sovereigns.[6] It would be tempting to investigate this point in Tacitus's *Histories* and *Annals*, against Livy and his *continuatio* in Augustine's *Civitas Dei*, one of Foucault's first, not as cryptic as it seems, authorities. I restrict myself for the topic at hand to a short glance on the hidden thrust in Tacitus's laconic account, which made him, misleadingly, the pathetic ideal of historical drama rather than analysis. Under the surface of drama, Tacitus concealed his sharpest observations on how the hideous ideosyncracies of the emperors of his time produced, as the flip-side of their tyranny, the arcane routine of administrators like himself.[7]

Tacitus takes Rome as a city for granted, an understanding that was not, no longer, self-evident in the second Romes of *Augusta Treverorum* and her follow-ups, to whom I shall come next. The rise of governmentality (Quirinus's domain) in Tacitus's account, of the structural change that occurred from sovereign power to legal procedure under the umbrella of what one came to name much later a representational monarchy, is counter-balanced by the city as a self-governing body in its own right. In second Romes, the city quality of Rome became apparent. This is evident in the second Romes after Trèves/ Trier. The Merovingian continuation of Roman institutions is an insight we owe to Eugen Ewig, who was the first who managed to bring some plausibility into the obscure history of the Merovingians' relation with the empire, from which Charlemagne's rule originated, and from his work my distinction of types of Roman secondariness proceeds.[8]

Charlemagne's Aix la Chapelle was the first of the next second Romes, the first of a new secondariness. In spite of, or even in accord with, the Christian re-investment of the Roman *civitates*, the cities of medieval history re-defined and pre-figured the concept of a *historia magistra vitae* embedded in city-life. The political format of a *forma vitae* was transposed from its original site, monastic life, to cities, whose economic structure was modelled upon the monasteries outside their limits. These enjoyed their *libertas* from mundane powers, but also, in turn, reformed the life inside

---

5 See Brown 1974, 26 f.

6 Pirenne 1927; Pirenne 1925.

7 See my essay Haverkamp 2018, 44–45.

8 Ewig [1955], 1976–79, I: 409–434. For the technical term of imperial *paternitas*, see Ewig 1983, 57 ff. 60 ff.

cities, and whose part they would soon become. As a supplement, then (in the Derridean sense, of taking over in structure what they complemented in practice, hospitals, schools, welfare), monastic life prefigured modern life-routine. The local continuity between the early Middle Age and so-called Late Antiquity, its Roman predecessor, resided in towns. Their role was a mixed one, if looked upon in Jupiterian terms, but that, I've indicated, is misleading. The oppositional attitude *Contro Roma*, which Italians cultivate up to now, is a dead end: It articulates a 'resistance' against Jupiterian rule and its support by Mars without offering any alternative according to the administrative terms of the third, Quirinus, which is taken for granted – the literary attitude of Tacitus's rhetoric. It is true, that the feudal order of the Middle Ages was eager to translate Jupiter's role into the Divine Right of Kings, but city-related movements like the *Treuga Dei* – "God's peace," strong in communes like Cologne – are underestimated in most historical accounts.[9] The long-term failure of these movements documents, precisely, what Foucault looks for in the failure of the weak against the strong, but whose lure he cannot but prolong in the formulaic pathos of generalized resistance. The continuity in question was and remained beholden to Jupiter primarily in ideological terms, while in the reality of the social order it was the continuity of the cities' self-understanding and their changing luck that worked in Quirinus's administrative key.

2

I turn now to the case of the unequal twin cities Aix la Chapelle/ Aachen and Cologne/ Köln, where the evolutionary potential of a Non-Jupiterian *translatio Romae* was a not an entirely lost hope. The royal Carolingian court chapel, the *capella*, had incorporated the relic of Saint Martin's *capa*, upon which the *capella* was erected. In an intricate turn – the *translatio* from the *imperium* whose second seat had been *Augusta Treverorum* – the newly established Carolingian court's administration, whose seat was the royal chapel (the building as well as the archive with the archive's *capellani* who accompanied the king on his rounds through the kingdom) commemorated a Roman officer's *caritas instead* of the Roman *imperator*. Martin had shared his *capa*, the glorious *signum* of his imperial armor (his red *paludamentum*), with a beggar who turned out to be Christ. In the center of the Carolingian court chapel, the *capa* signified in a double metonymy both a new origin *and* a translation. The court's *capella* (rhetorical diminutive of the *capa* encrypted, i.e. a

---

9 See Hoffmann 1964 in general, and Ennen 1971, 21 f. in particular.

litotes) combined the memory of the constituting act of the *caritas*, as well as the administration of the *imperium* that was revived in the translation.[10] The "Bassenheimer Reiter" of *Moguntiacum*/ Mainz, Cologne's archepiscopal rival further up on the banks of the Rhine, superbly illustrates the translated function of the large sword, from imperial violence to the act of peaceful sharing (Fig. 1).

Fig. 1: *Bassenheimer Reiter* (Mainz 1240)[11] (Photo: Stefan Krabath, NIhK Wilhelmshaven).

I will not go further into the symbolism involved; suffice it to say that the act of imperial usurpation (in Tacitus's *Annals* the *primum facinus* of the imperial *arcana domus* to follow) is replaced by the foundational act of charity, the Roman officer Martin sharing his *capa* with the poor by using his sword – iconographically decisive – to cut the *capa* into truly sym-bolic halves. The institutional origin is reinterpreted not by the take-over of a new *princeps* – in Tacitus through murder in the imperial family – but in the sharing act of the *caritas Romana*, in which the proverbial patriarchal *pietas* is generalized to a cat-holic, i.e. universal, *caritas*.

---

10 See Fleckenstein 1959, 226.
11 Kubach 1981, vol. 16: 70. I owe the reference to Yvonne Pauly (Berlin).

According to the court of Caroligian Renaissance, Aix la Chapelle is *Roma secunda* in this sense.[12] The architectural allusion of the chapel to Byzanthium signified the universal reach of the *pax Romana*. The *Octogon* of Aix la Chapelle carries the learned poet Alkuin's inscription of *lapides vivi pacis* built in into the chapel wall (MGH *Poetae* I, 432). The literary and artistic refinement at Charlemagne's court – of Alkuin, Angilbert and Einhard, to name only the most prominent – is well documented and needs no further elaboration (Fig. 2).[13]

Fig. 2: *Carolingian court intellectuals: The young Rabanus Maurus and his teacher Alkuin, later on abbot of Saint Martin of Tours, dedicating a book to Saint Martin, first bishop of Tours* (Österreichische Nationalbibliothek Vienna, cod. 652, fol. 2v Fulda about 830/40).

---

12 Weishaupt 2020.
13 See here Levison 1946, 155 ff. Like his student Eugen Ewig, Levison is deeply impressed by the catastrophe of the ongoing World War, in which the Jewish emigrant Levison delivered the Ford Lectures in Oxford 1943.

Only at first glance, superficially, the Carolingian refoundation seems to confirm Foucault's design of a tradition of glorification under Jupiter's aegis.[14] But misleadingly so, since it bypasses the re-educative point of the Latin *renovatio* enacted by Alkuin. The revived latinity did not just serve the politics of power, but the educational aim rested on, was restricted by and proceeded from, the new, exemplary role of an "ethical personalism" vis à vis the generalized "lay morality."[15]

As *prima regum curia* of *Karolus, serenissimus augustus*, Aix la Chapelle united the two halves of the West-Roman empire, including the middle Merovingian part, which did not make it into modernity except for being torn apart, again and again, between the modern states of France and Germany.[16] This third part included and, in fact, was ruled by the cities from Basel and Strasbourg down the Rhine and its left bank tributaries, the rivers Maas and Moselle, down to Mainz and Cologne with Aachen, Maastricht, Lièges, Bruxelles, Antwerp in the middle. The point of interest here is the embeddedness of the surviving *forma vitae* in the cities' evolutionary prospect. Their attitude was and remained a shared resilience against Jupiterian claims, fake or authentic. As the capital of France, Paris could not help changing sides, from city to imperial residence with an imperial administration, while Aix la Chapelle, the Carolingian model, was too weak to get beyond the limitations of a residence without empire; she specialized in coronation events of the German kings for over 600 years until Charles V in 1520. Once an exquisite bath of Roman refinement, erected on the premises of a Celtic water-god, the latinized *Granus, Aquisgranum* had also attracted the Merovingian elite but could not compete in the longer run with the city of Cologne whose republican past was no match for an imperial court.

In contrast, *Colonia Agrippina* or, at greater length, *Claudia Ara Agrippinensium* was a *civitas permixta* from the start, with Roman administrative standards and an archbishop in direct succession from the Roman *pontifex maximus*. Cologne and Aix la Chapelle, I said, were unequal twins as second Romes, since the continuity manifested in different degrees: both were similar in the Christian reinvestment of the *pax Romana* in *caritas* and *treuga Dei*, but they remained different with respect to the republican heritage of Cologne as a self-conscious *civitas*. Not feudal lords – in Pirenne's unloved thesis, overlooked by Foucault – but elected bishops in the surviving Roman cities were the main factor of medieval Roman continuity in Cologne.[17] They contradicted the feudal structure of empires new and to come, but guaranteed instead a republican *continuatio* against the

14 As in a recent exhibition in Vienna: Haag (ed.) 2014, chapter III by Franz Kirchweger, 27 ff.
15 Stone 2007, 82.
16 See Ternes 1972; amplified German edition Ternes 1975, 246 f.
17 Pirenne 1936; Pirenne 196 f; Pirenne 1939, vol. I: 171; vol. II: 126.

grain of the salvation-historical *renovatio* of a Jupiterian history, which became the ideological backbone of nation states, eagerly reconstructed as *translationes imperii* in French and German history departments of the nineteenth century.[18] Against the new national projections and their salvation-historical support, the bishops in Cologne as well as in Aix la Chapelle re-invested the Roman past differently, but – in an historical irony familiar as late as Shakespeare's early modern version of *Julius Caesar* – as if they were to repeat ancient Rome's constitutional division.[19]

In competition with the Carolingian chapel, Cologne's republican intention came to fruition in a city-life that included in its Roman heritage the symptoms of questionable moral conduct: *Multiformis Colonia seu mavis Babilonia* was the threat, of which a young man who would continue his studies in Cologne was warned by his tutor Meinhard, head of the cathedral school in Bamberg, later bishop of *Herbipolis/* Würzburg (+1088), and no doubt a witty man: *lubrica bomb-icina Colonidum corpora,* the sweet girls of Cologne, in short, were his fear for the young man, and this fitted into the terrene picture of Saint Augustine's Rome only too well.[20] In this respect, the baths of *Aquisgranum* would have been no better place. In choosing Cologne, the student knew better, what he was after in his academic career. In the early eleventh century, before the Parisian Abaelard's fame, it was Cologne that offered the highest intellectual challenge, in which this city's self-esteem as second only to Rome performed a most remarkable *translatio,* not *imperii* but *studii,* based on the *libertas* of study in the thriving schools of this city of republican descent.[21] The document, to which I want to draw your attention, offers a unique testimony.

3

In the Early Middle High German poem called the *Anno-Lied* (Fig. 3), Cologne's conflict with its arch-bishop Anno is documented and celebrated. Around 1100 this literary work is the earliest piece of city-literature in a European vernacular. What it does, is represent, legitimize as well as pacify, the resistance of the citi-

---

18 For the difference of the nineteenth century see Carl Schmitt's notorious narrative *Nomos der Erde im Völkerrecht des Ius publicum Europaeum*: Schmitt [1950] 2011, 32 f. Schmitt quotes Saint-Simon, Tocqueville, Proudhon, Bruno Bauer and, needless to add, Oswald Spengler.
19 See my chapter on *Julius Caesar*, Haverkamp 2011, 63 f.
20 Erdmann 1930–1932, 360.
21 Tellenbach 1936; Wollasch 1973.

-◦ς(:)ջօ-   ɪ

RHYTHMVS DE S. ANNONE
COLONIENSI ARCHIEPISCOPO.
I.

VVIr horten ie dikke singen Von alten
dingen, Wi snelle helide vuhten, Wi
si veste burge brechen, Wi sich liebin vuini-
siefte schieden, Wi riche Künige al zegien-
gen. Nu ist ciht daz wir dencken Wi wir sel-
ve sülin enden. Crist der vnser héro güt Wi
mantge ceichen her vns vure düt, Alser uffin
Sigeberg havit gedan Durch den diurlichen
man Den heiligen bischof Annen Durch den
sinin willen, Dabi wir vns sülin bewarin
W ante wir noch sülin varin Von disime ellen-
din libe hin cin ewin Da wir imer sülin sin.

Wir horten] Auctor recens Commentarioli in Al-
phabetum Gothicum, à Bonau. Vulcanio editus, ini-
tium huius Rythmi cum se producere asserat, omisso
hoc exordio sequentes tantum tres paragraphos ex-
hibet. Istud itaque à codice illius abfuit.
dikke] sæpè. Retinuerunt Belgæ.
helide] Helden. Cheld, siue aspiratione duplicata
Hheld, idem fuisse veteribus quod nobis Held, asserere
conatur is cui hæ literæ ac Germanum nomen omne
haud parum debent, Melch. Goldastus olim noster.
Quamuis credi possit, quod à Græcis κέλητες, seu per
syncopen κίλται dicti fuerint, quasi desultores, ob
equitandi peritiam. Sed repugnant hæc Cæsaris verba
initio lib.I. de bello Gallico: Gallia est omnis diuisa in
partes tres, quarum vnam incolunt Belga; aliam Aquita-
ni; tertiam qui ipsorum lingua Celta, nostra Galli ap-
pellantur.   A   suten]

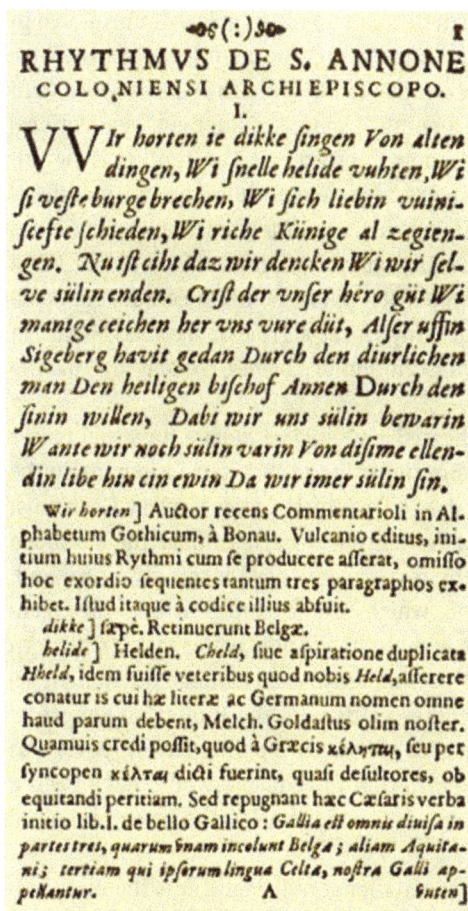

Fig. 3: 1st page of the *Anno-Lied*, critical ed. by Martin Opitz (Breslau 1639),
(Bayerische Staatsbibliothek München).

zens – their senate, in fact – against the bishop's misrule by claiming succession
from the Roman senate. The *libertas senatus* was the freedom par excellence,
which stood in latent contradiction to the imperial imperative of the extended
pax Romana; Tacitus's *Annals* struggle with this inbuilt constitutional problem
that surfaces also here.[22]

Historical background in the *Anno-Lied* is the tyrannical rule of the emperors
after Caesar, and this seems to correlate curiously with the episcopal succession

───────────

22 Wirzubski 1950, 163. Also Arena 2012.

after Constantine. The Early Middle High German text is singularly informative in how it translates the Latin lexicon into Middle High German legal terms. Thus, the Roman term *amicitiae causa*, for example, is rendered in the *Anno-Lied kata poda* as *ci minnin* and addresses the economical sphere of inter-city negotiations, which was endangered by the archbishop's interference. The conflict is significant, not only because of this archbishop's involvement into imperial politics – Anno was also chancelor of the *Reich* – but in view of a whole network of cities mentioned in the text, from Xanten to *Moguntiacum/* Mainz. The *Colonia Ulpia Traiana/* Xanten was of particular exemplarity. Since the ninth century *Ad Sanctos*, it figures in the *Anno-Lied* as 'little Troy', *lüzzele Troie* at the river Sante, in an etymology, which betrays in the transcription of *Colonia Traiana* to *Troie* the onliving Roman tradition at the Rhine.

There is no reason to enter the heated philological debate, in which, after Martin Opitz in the 17th, Johann Jacob Breitinger in the 18th, Karl Lachmann in the 19th, Hugo Kuhn and Walter Haug in the 20th centuries, almost every Germanist with a name took part. Their bone of contention is buried under the stubborn denial of the literary refinement of the text, its advanced ironic structure and, that is, the stamp of the Latin tradition, which had developed as a literary technique after Caesar – and all of this the text seems to know better than its modern critics are prepared to acknowledge. The emphasis on the national monument eclipsed its inbuilt latinity, and that corresponds with the Jupiterian eclipse of cities's other than imperial, like Paris. From Cologne's point of view, Paris was the bad example of a new Rome. The criterion for Cologne would have been a republican Christianity with *libertas* in open opposition to the power-centered translation of empires.[23]

Irony is the worst you could find as a national philologist. It is the most hidden, cryptic figure in Quintilian's assessment, the *figura cryptica* par excellence. In the early medieval state of public affairs in Cologne, the earliest instance of an *Öffentlichkeit* in Habermas's sense, it was imperative to compromise. In the *Anno-Lied*, the bishop Anno's ability to make good in what he found himself forced to admit as the gravest stain – the brutal treatment of his flock and, more to the point here, his interference with the city-merchants' trade – was decisive, and their reconciliation a reason to celebrate. Irony as a means of pacifying a conflict without losing relevant content is the explicit moral of this story: A bishop's office is to forgive where he is wrong, and this not in spite, but because of his power. A

---

23 For an earlier version of this thesis, see Haverkamp 1979, with extensive bibliography on the exemplary role of Cologne for the early history of the medieval city before the late medieval differentiation of "freie Reichsstädte", which secured the immediacy to the Reich against the rule of the bishops, in short, the end of the historical compromise of the *Anno-Lied*.

historical parallel of a similarly violent *coniuratio* in Le Mans at the same time, in 1070, is related in the *History of the Bishops of Le Mans* from the twelfth century; it proves *ex negativo* how unique the solution celebrated in the *Anno-Lied* was. In the retrospect of 200 years later, no comparable Roman traces are remembered in Les Mans, but the sole emphasis is laid on the revolutionary achievement of the commune's *coniuratio*. As the more adequate rhetorical device, the Les Mans text applied a "double perspective," in which the reconciliation that was achieved in the *Anno-Lied* on Cologne's Roman foundation, is absent.[24] Instead, the unbridgable division of interests seems without any alternative from the Merovingian start.

This makes the irony of the *Anno-Lied* a complicated double figure with a specific Roman twist known and named by the text. The sarcasm of a Suetonius is not far and was useful as a repertory for the negative political typologies to come. In Cologne, a Roman irony lived on, self-consciously transposed into the city's vernacular. In irony, the city of Cologne was a true second Rome. The secondary doubling of irony in the *Anno-Lied* worked in both directions, in denial as well as compromise. It enabled an understanding without forcing the understood. The ironic point of the conversion served a conversion to the better. The renewed promise of a latinity *sine fine* (Petrarch) may have had this effect in mind. The Babylonian character of Rome, on the other hand, returned as a commonplace in the nineteenth century. It matched what Augustine had named the *civitas terrena*. It did not capture, however, what the same Augustine had denied to Rome, and Foucault, not the least of his pupils, had overlooked in the Non-Jupiterian impact of the post-Roman cities, the salvific quality of city-life from Anno's Cologne through Dante's Florence to Donne's London – not to speak as yet of the tougher requirements of a *Sentimental Education* in Flaubert's Paris.

4

Let me repeat. Four modes are to be distinguished in the unending paleonym that Rome had become after Rome, the ancient name being hard to replace. Rhetoric, the art of replacing a name in order to have one for everything (Quintilian), helps to evaluate what happened to Rome after it was Rome. At the center of my kaleidoscope of second Romes, I favor Aix la Chapelle with Martin's *capa* in its *capella*, whose republican twin was the city of Cologne, after the administration in *Roma*

---

24 Oexle 2005, 141.

seconda Treverorum had broken down. A telling remnant of the imaginary *trans-latio* from Trèves/ Trier to Cologne is the legendary vino-duct in the *Anno-Lied,* which recalls the remnants of the long aqueduct that lead in ancient times from the direction of Trèves/ Trier through the hills of the Eifel mountains into Cologne. What counts in continuity is conduct. Looking back, the ruins of the vino-duct from *Augusta Treverorum* to *Colonia Agrippina* helped re-imagine Cologne's ancient priority over Trèves/ Trier, which appears in this retrospect as a tributary from republican times: *amicitiae causa* implied that Cologne was in fact the first among second Romes. And indeed, the foundation of Cologne by Agrippa in 19 BC coincides with the finalized imperial title of Augustus in 23 BC, while Trèves/ Trier's foundation occurred only 10 years later in 13 BC. Contemporary with the *Anno-Lied,* the Latin *Gesta Treverorum* took pride in the studied contrast, contrary to its true Roman heritage, of the Assyrian King Ninus's son Trebeta: *ante Romam,* a later inscription of the sixteenth century would claim in the greatest possible forgetfulness, *annis mille trecentis.* Against Cologne's claim, Trèves/ Trier gave up being of Roman descent.

Along the line of second Romes, Trèves/ Trier *Augusta Treverorum,* the first to be called a second Rome, represented the simplest mode of a *continuatio* in factual, administrative terms. It does so by a means, however, that deserves a closer rhetorical examination: *kata poda,* the word by word translation of legal writs. Katachresis seems the underlying trope and, that is – important for the development of European law, by the way – in a productive rather than a reproductive capacity, and thus not as simple as it seems at first glance.

Aix la Chapelle/ Aachen, in contrast, offered (but only partially succeeded in this intention) a ground-breaking paradigm switch with the re-investment of military rule by Christian *caritas* – a truly metaphorical operation, replacing violence by grace. In political reality, this trans-position was not an easy process and only spiritually successful, as the impressive pictorial solution of one particularly precious cult object from the Carolingian chapel in Aix la Chapelle shows (Fig. 4–6), a processional cross crafted, precisely, in Cologne around 985.

The humble front in silver shows Christ's crucifixion in a simple engraving – in highly refined finish, but non-pictorial, like a piece of holy writing, rather, recalling on its glorious back the splendor, in which the *imperator* Augustus's peace had paved the way for the Roman officer Martin's exemplary action: *caritas* performed with an imperial sword, which cut the *capa* in two, a veritable metaphorological paradigm switch, represented by the two sides of this marvellous cross in a translation from image to writing, from imperial representation to a New Testament's testimony. The *cameo* is an original cut of the early first century. In a procession, this marvellous piece looked back over the crowd that followed – under the heading of the crucified whose *signum* led the way.

Fig. 4: *Lotharkreuz*, Domschatzkammer Aachen Inv.-Nr. Gr 022 (© Domkapitel Aachen, Photo: Klaus Bednorz, Augustusseite).

In Cologne/ Köln, unequal twin second, a curious combination of administrative continuity exemplified Rome's paradigmatic role for a *civitas permixta*, "mixing memory and desire" (T.S. Eliot's *Waste Land* remembers, desire confused). Cologne continued Rome's senatorial constitution. At the same time, the city highlighted in the transposition of the *interpretatio christiana* the Carolingian grace, *caritas,* as a bishop's constitutional responsibility. Caesar's historical part, the proverbial *clementia Caesaris,* also cited by the *Anno-Lied,* is a literary achievement, the conflict management of a pacifying irony. As *figura cryptica* (Baumgarten), the latent latinity of modern aesthetics originated in cities like Cologne and Paris. Against the permanent threat of moral corruption, their *forma vitae* was a bi-lingual affair.

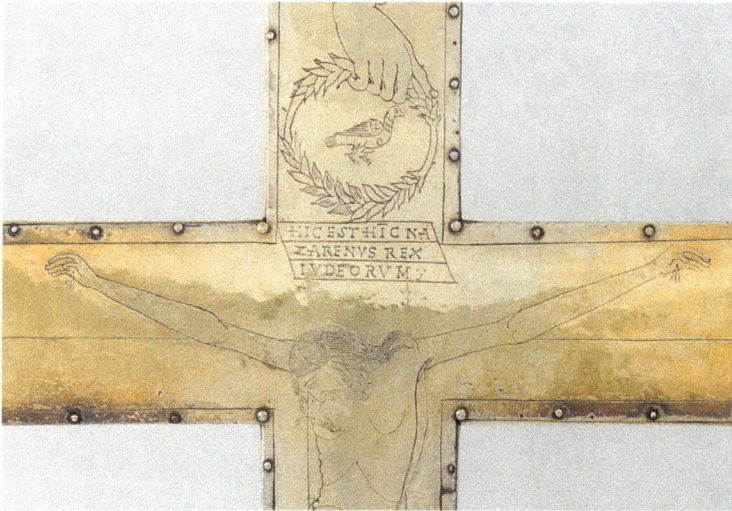

Fig. 5: *Lotharkreuz*, front, Domschatzkammer Aachen Inv.-Nr. Gr 022 (© Domkapitel Aachen, Foto: Klaus Bednorz).

Fig. 6: *Augustus Cameo* (1st century CE) (detail), Domschatzkammer Aachen Inv.-Nr. Gr 022 (© Domkapitel Aachen, Foto: Klaus Bednorz).

Paris, finally, is not part of my presentation, but the perspective of its figuration. Historically conscious of the older uses of the paleonym of power politics, *Roma aeterna*, the fruit of the loom for Paris was literal brutality, the brutal literalness denounced in Flaubert's last legend, *Hérodias* (the third of the *Trois contes*). The last sentence of the last legend carries the heavy weight of John the baptist's head dragged behind by witnesses, who would not qualify as martyrs, after Salomé in her performance had lead to a most frivolous, needless to add, Parisian ending – both, in the oriental technique of the dance and in the revolution's routine of the beheading.

Afterthoughts: Supplementary evidence and the lack thereof

The panorama of secondariness from Trèves to Cologne cannot be but incomplete. Existing historical research is uneven; each of the cities has not only a regional tradition of their own, but a historical focus of local interest in the continuity of that tradition. The lack of an over-arching comparative perspective creates an unfortunate contrast between specialized research on the local level and unanswered questions on the other side of more than local concern. Thus, the second Rome motif enables questions rather than offering answers, questions beyond or underneath the mainstream of historical research, which privileges a sovereign and imperial ideology under the sign of Jupiter in the service of legitimating an otherwise dubious national statehood.

A rather isolated but telling example is the Troy motif in Xanten, which would justify footnotes with a library of secondary references, but without significance beyond Jupiter's prevailing concern. Similarly significant is the historical role of Trèves/ Trier, although more disappointing, if we take the *Gesta Treverorum* as a representative source. Against this unclear backdrop, but also in continuation of the more general propositions, the aim of the present essay is less interested in the doubtful interplay of theo-political ideas, ideals and political developments, but in the tropological relationship of the underlying modes of figuration. Although I do not go into the metaphorological underground of the *translationes Romae*, the gaps in the field of one-sided Jupiter motifs and their historical thrust should be evident and illustrate the open questions. The unequal double of Aix la Chapelle/ Aachen and Cologne/ Köln as twin cities barely covers what deserves a closer inquiry and material supplementation. What looks like a perfect match of Augustan and Carolingian ideology in the traditon of these two cities, the re-established *res publica* of Augustus, celebrated by Livy, is the blueprint for the Carolingian Renaissance, Cologne's republican self-esteem granted.

Unfortunately, the *Anno-Lied* in its singularity does not provide enough of a missing link; it is too late (1100–1110) and the immediate connection seems expired. The history of the bishops of Le Mans relates a *coniuratio* of the citizens for the same time, which proves in the negative the extraordinary, everything but topical character of the *Anno-Lied's* reference to Cologne's Roman constitution, while using two centuries after the event a different, implicitly counter-Roman strategy in the presentation of what happened in the light of what was supposedly intended.

Saint Martin's patronage, on the other hand, was widespread and is celebrated up to now, but the whereabouts of the *capa*, the royal Carolingian treasure, seems no issue anywhere. In this respect, the state of research remains inconclusive. The riddle of how legend and cult of the *capa* became the center piece of a veritable institution is barely recognized as such.[25] The church of Gross Sankt Martin in Cologne was errected on Roman foundations of storage halls of the harbour, in a part of the city that was still an island in the river when the first church there was built in Merovingian times, long before the monastery of Gross Sankt Martin took its place and also long before the *capa's* turn from cult to administration is documented. Its transformational impact lived on in the iconography, encrypted in the performance of the office of the *capella*. What became of the object is unknown; it vanished from the records already in Carolingian times.

As for the *Treuga Dei* peace movement directed against the ongoing feudal feuds and welcomed as initiative in many cities and communes, it too seems to recall from the growing distance of later developments the universal appeal of the *Pax Romana*. The interaction of city life and city politics with the emergence of the newly formatted national ideologies and imperial aims remains an unclear field of negotiation and needs a fresh investigation – if the sources stand up to the questions thus raised.[26]

---

25 Wilhelm Lüders, "Capella: Die Hofkapelle der Karolinger bis zur Mitte des neunten Jahrhunderts", *Archiv für Urkundenforschung* 2 (1909), 1–100: 17 ff.

26 For the current state of the debate see the recent account by Hugo Stehkämper and Carl Dietmar, *Köln im Hochmittelalter 1074–1288* (Köln: Greven 2016), 17 f. and 51 f. Characteristically, the professional historian does not know how to read, and consequently does not include, a literary source like the *Anno-Lied*.

Bibliography

Arena, Valentina. *Libertas and the practice of Politics in the Late Roman Republic*. Cambridge UK: Cambridge University Press, 2012.

Brown, Peter. "'Mohammed and Charlemagne', by Henri Pirenne." *Daedalus* 103 (1974): 25–33.

Dumézil, Georges. *Jupiter Mars Quirinus*: *Essai sur la conception indo-européenne de la société et sur les origines de Rome*. Paris: Gallimard, 1941.

Ennen, Edith. "Europäische Züge der mittelalterlichen Kölner Geschichte." *Mitteilungen des Stadtarchivs Köln* 60 (1971): 1–47.

Erdmann, Carl. "Die Briefe Meinhards von Bamberg." *Neues Archiv der Gesellschaft für ältere deutsche Geschichtskunde* 49 (1930–1932): 332–431.

Ewig, Eugen. "Das Fortleben römischer Institutionen in Gallien und Germanien." *Spätantikes und fränkisches Gallien: Gesammelte Schriften* 1952–1973, I: 409–434. Zürich/München: Artemis, 1976–79.

Ewig, Eugen. *Die Merowinger und das Imperium.* Rheinisch-Westfälische Akademie der Wissenschaften, Geisteswissenschaften 261. Opladen: Westdeutscher Verlag, 1983.

Fleckenstein, Joseph. *Die Hofkapelle der deutschen Könige* I. Stuttgart: Hiersemann, 1959.

Foucault, Michel. *"Society Must Be Defended" Lectures at the Collège de France 1975–1976.* New York NY: Picador 2003.

Haag, Sabine. Ed. *Väter Europas: Augustus und Karl der Grosse.* Wien: Kunsthistorisches Museum, 2014.

Haverkamp, Anselm. *Typik und Politik im Annolied.* Stuttgart: Metzler, 1979.

Haverkamp, Anselm. "The Death of a Shifter." (2008) *Shakespearean Genealogies of Power: A Whisperung of Nothing.* London: Routledge, 2011. 57–71.

Haverkamp, Anselm. "Acta et arcana: Latency Management and the Law." *Law Text Culture* 22 (2018): 39–52.

Hoffmann, Hartmut. *Gottesfriede und Treuga Dei.* Stuttgart: Hiersemann, 1964.

Kubach, Hans Erich. *Die Kunstdenkmäler des Landkreises Koblenz.* Düsseldorf: Schwan, 1981.

Levison, Wilhelm. *England and the Continent in the Eighth Century.* Oxford: Clarendon Press, 1946.

Oexle Gerhard, "Um 1070." Ed. Bernhard Jussen. *Die Macht des Königs: Herrschaft in Europa vom Frühmittelalter bis in die Neuzeit.* München: Beck, 2005.

Pirenne, Henri. *Medieval Cities: Their Origins and the Revival of Trade.* Princeton, NJ: Princeton University Press, 1925.

Pirenne, Henri. *Les villes du moyen âge. Essai d'histoire économique et sociale.* Brüssel: Lamertin, 1927.

Pirenne, Henri. *L'Histoire de l'Europe.* Bruxelles: Nouvelle Société d'Édition, 1936.

Pirenne, Henri. *Les villes et les institutions urbaines,* I-II. Paris/Bruxelles: Alcan, 1939.

Pirenne, Henri. *Geschichte Europas von der Völkerwanderung bis zur Reformation.* Frankfurt/M: Fischer, 1961.

Schmitt, Carl. *Nomos der Erde im Völkerrecht des Ius publicum Europaeum.* Berlin: Duncker & Humblot 1950, 5th ed. 2011.

Stone, Rachel. "Kings are different: Carolingian mirrors for princes and lay morality." *Le prince au miroir de la littérature politique de l'Antiquité aux Lumières.* Eds. Frédérique Lachaud and Lydwine Scordia. Rouen: Publication des Universités de Rouen et du Havre, 2007. 69–86.

Tellenbach, Gerd. *Libertas: Kirche und Weltordnung im Zeitalter des Investiturstreits.* Stuttgart: Kohlhammer, 1936.

Ternes, Charles-Marie. *La vie quotidienne en Rhénanie Romain.* Paris: Hachette, 1972.

Ternes, Charles-Marie. *Die Römer an Rhein und Mosel.* Stuttgart: Reclam 1975.

Thomas, Yan. "Fictio legis: L'empire de la fiction romaine et ses limites médiévales." *Droits* 21 (1995): 17–63.

Vinken, Barbara. *Du Bellay und Petrarca: Das Rom der Renaissance.* Tübingen: Niemeyer, 2001.

Vismann, Cornelia. "Wort für Wort: Übersetzen und Gesetz." *Die Sprache der Anderen: Übersetzungspolitik zwischen den Kulturen.* Ed. Anselm Haverkamp. Frankfurt/M: Fischer, 1997. 147–165.

Weishaupt, Gero P. *Aquisgranum: Descriptio urbis Caroli Magni.* Aachen: Vergangenheitsverlag, 2020.

Wirszubski, Chaim. *Libertas as a political idea at Rome during the late republic and early principate.* Cambridge UK: Cambridge University Press, 1950.

Wollasch, Joachim. *Mönchtum des Mittelalters zwischen Kirche und Welt.* München: Fink, 1973.

II Early Classicisms

Tristan Alonge

Néron et Louis XIV au miroir racinien : *monstre* ou *grand prince naissant* ?

Un grand prince, qui avait dansé à plusieurs ballets, ayant vu jouer le *Britannicus* de M. Racine, où la fureur de Néron à monter sur le théâtre est si bien attaquée, il ne dansa plus à aucun ballet, non pas même au temps du Carnaval (Boileau, « Lettre à Monchesnay, septembre 1707 », 834).

Si la critique racinienne a depuis longtemps deviné derrière les traits du « grand prince » de l'anecdote savoureuse rapportée par Boileau le visage de Louis XIV[1], elle n'a que très ponctuellement et très rarement accordé la moindre vraisemblance à un rapprochement indéniablement surprenant. Certes, quelques passages isolés de la pièce de 1669 peuvent aisément avoir constitué une mise en garde pour le Roi-Soleil, notamment les paroles adressées par Narcisse à Néron à la fin de l'acte IV, lorsqu'il se fait l'écho des prétendues rumeurs circulant dans Rome et reprochant à l'empereur ses excès artistiques qui l'éloignent du statut d'homme d'État[2]. Pourtant, la comparaison semble trop belle pour être vraie, trop choquante surtout. Un jeune dramaturge, dont la carrière théâtrale ne faisait qu'amorcer, timidement et péniblement, les premiers pas de son ascension vers le succès, aurait-il été imprudent et insouciant au point de glisser le premier de ses spectateurs dans les habits du plus cruel et détesté des empereurs romains ? D'ailleurs, Racine n'avait-il pas lui-même pris ouvertement les distances de toute interprétation « innocente » de Néron, dans sa préface de 1669, en insistant sur l'aspect monstrueux du personnage[3] ? Les commentateurs raciniens ont généralement suivi le texte liminaire, reléguant à un poste marginal l'influence potentielle des circonstances du moment. Si des tentatives partielles de lecture à clef ont pu intér-

---

1 Louis Racine (*Mémoires*, 1136) est sans doute le premier à dévoiler explicitement l'identité du « grand prince » : « On sait l'impression que firent sur Louis XIV quelques vers de cette Pièce [. . .]. Ces vers frappèrent le jeune Monarque, qui avait quelquefois dansé dans les ballets ; et quoiqu'il dansât avec beaucoup de noblesse, il ne voulut plus paraître dans aucun ballet, reconnaissant qu'un Roi ne doit point se donner en spectacle ».
2 Racine, *Britannicus*, IV, 4, v. 1468–1476 : « *Néron, s'ils en sont crus, n'est point né pour l'Empire.* / [. . .] / *Pour toute ambition, pour toute vertu singulière, / Il excelle à conduire un char dans la carrière, / À disputer des prix indignes de ses mains, / À se donner lui-même en spectacle aux Romains, / À venir prodiguer sa voix sur un théâtre, / À réciter des chants, qu'il veut qu'on idolâtre* ».
3 Racine, *Britannicus*, préface, 372 : « D'autres ont dit au contraire que je l'avais fait trop bon. J'avoue que je ne m'étais pas formé l'idée d'un bon homme en la personne de Néron. Je l'ai toujours regardé comme un monstre ».

https://doi.org/10.1515/9783111334776-004

esser des figures mineures comme Burrhus[4], ce n'est que pour mieux rappeler la totale décorrélation et l'inconcevable superposition entre Néron et Louis XIV[5], véritable tabou de la critique racinienne que seulement quelques tentatives isolées et datées ont tenté d'aborder[6]. Le but des pages qui suivent consiste à tenter de rouvrir un dossier refermé peut-être un peu trop vite, en accordant du crédit à l'anecdote rapportée par Boileau : et si le visage du monstre naissant racinien cachait effectivement les traits de Louis XIV ?

1 Un grand prince naissant

Si la critique s'est empressé d'écarter toute superposition entre Louis XIV et le Néron racinien, c'est en bonne partie en raison du fait que les deux indices les plus susceptibles d'encourager une telle lecture apparaissent également comme les plus fragiles : les reproches de Narcisse à l'acte IV, ayant découragé le roi danseur, et la mystérieuse retraite chez les Vestales de Junie à l'acte V, interprétée comme une allusion aux amours de jeunesse de Louis XIV, et notamment à la retraite au couvent de La Vallière après la fin de son idylle amoureux avec le monarque. En ce qui concerne l'anecdote de Boileau, les commentateurs raciniens ont préféré y voir une coïncidence fabriquée de toute pièce *a posteriori* : s'il est attesté que Louis XIV – danseur aux qualités indiscutables – avait effectivement renoncé à danser deux mois après la création de *Britannicus*, alors qu'il était attendu dans le ballet des *Amants magnifiques* de Molière[7], pourtant il semble que la raison du renoncement ait été d'ordre médical plus que moral[8]. Par ailleurs, il semblerait que les ap-

---

4 Sur le sujet voir par exemple la tentative de Volker Schröder (1999, 149–150) de deviner derrière les traits de Burrhus une allusion à la nomination d'un militaire comme gouverneur du Dauphin en 1668.

5 Voir entre autres la notice à l'édition de la Pléiade de la pièce dans laquelle Georges Forestier (Racine, *Britannicus*, 1405–1406) considère que le rapprochement est le fruit d'une coïncidence fabriquée *a posteriori*. Pour Jean-Pierre Néraudau (1996, 89–90), malgré les apparences, Louis XIV n'est pas Néron.

6 Voir notamment René Jasinski (1958, 333–347) qui, tout en identifiant un réel parallélisme, considère néanmoins que Racine n'a pas volontairement recherché une lecture à clef.

7 Cf. Robinet, *Lettre en vers à Madame*, 15 février 1670, 3 : « Le Divertissement Royal / Dont la Cour fait son Carnaval, / Est un Balet en Comédie, / [. . .] / Mais c'est tout ce que j'en puis dire, / Sinon que nôtre Auguste Sire / Fait danser, & n'y danse point ».

8 Louis XIV aurait renoncé pour des « vapeurs à la tête ». Cf. la notice introductive de G. Forestier, dans Racine, *Britannicus*, 1406.

paritions du roi danseur s'étaient faites plus rares depuis quelques mois déjà, bien avant la première de *Britannicus*[9]. Ces éléments semblent confirmer, donc, que le rapprochement a été, *a minima*, le fruit d'une simplification des données historiques visant à favoriser l'émergence d'une coïncidence « trop belle pour être vraie » et d'une lecture morale du retrait des scènes. À regarder de près, pourtant, la vérité historique paraît comme le facteur le moins intéressant et le moins significatif de l'anecdote rapportée par Boileau : peu importe que Louis XIV ait effectivement cessé de danser effrayé par la réplique de Narcisse, ce qui compte est plutôt le fait que les contemporains n'hésitèrent nullement à établir un rapprochement entre les deux figures[10]. Ont-ils pu le faire en se fondant uniquement sur la brève mise en garde de l'acte IV, ou faut-il voir dans l'allusion à un monarque qui se donne en spectacle le point le plus éclatant d'un réseau plus large de correspondances entre les deux figures ? Au moment de quitter la tragédie grecque pour venir sur le terrain d'élection du père de la tragédie française, ce n'est pas la Rome exemplaire et héroïque d'Horace ou de l'Auguste de *Cinna* que Jean Racine choisit de peindre, mais bien la Rome maudite du moins vertueux de tous les empereurs. Choix étonnant donc, à moins que le critère de sélection du sujet ait été le même qu'à l'occasion d'*Alexandre le Grand*, à savoir le degré d'allusions potentielles au premier de ses spectateurs. Un souverain qui accède au pouvoir encore très jeune dans un contexte politique complexe et riche en complots, qui se voit contraint de s'émanciper progressivement de la tutelle d'une mère et de ses ministres, qui se prémunit contre son propre frère cadet, de quelques années plus jeune[11], en désamorçant son ambition, qui se distingue en raison d'un intérêt excessif manifesté en faveur du domaine artistique, qui aime se donner en spectacle, qui construit de nouveaux palais, qui organise des naumachies et des ballets en sa présence[12], qui inquiète sa propre mère en raison d'aventures amoureuses extra-conjugales, tout en parvenant à remettre de l'ordre dans la gestion de l'État. Quel autre Empereur romain fournissait à Racine une telle ressemblance avec les premières années du règne de Louis

---

9 Cf. Robinet, *Lettre en vers à Madame*, 9 mars 1669, 3 : « Le Roy, même, par complaisance, / Quoy qu'il n'eust dancé de longtemps, / Dança, comme les autres Gens, / Et s'aquita d'une Courante, d'une maniére tres-galante ».

10 Le rapprochement était sans doute encouragé par le fait que les paroles de Narcisse impliquent une double altération de la réalité historique afin de faciliter la superposition avec Louis XIV : loin de le critiquer, le peuple romain appréciait le visage artistique de Néron (Suétone, *Vie des Douze Césars*, ch. X), et les excès en la matière ne remontaient pas à la jeunesse de l'empereur, mais à après la mort d'Agrippine (Tacite, *Annales*, ch. XIV, 14–16).

11 Il est curieux de remarquer que Racine, en vieillissant Britannicus, réduit l'écart d'âge par rapport à Néron à deux ans au lieu de quatre, précisément l'écart qui séparait Louis Philippe de Louis XIV.

12 Suétone, *Vie des Douze Césars*, ch. XII.

XIV ? À cette liste non exhaustive de rapprochements entre les deux figures, il convient sans doute de rajouter un détail non négligeable : l'un comme l'autre avaient choisi pour symbole le soleil[13]. Peu importe qu'il dépende de la conversion de Néron à la religion de Mithra plutôt qu'à des croyances égyptiennes[14], le culte du soleil de la part du fils d'Agrippine est indéniable, au vu des monnaies frappées pendant son règne, du colosse placé devant la *Domus aurea*, sans parler des vers de Lucain promettant à l'empereur qu'il montera aux cieux sur le char du Soleil, ainsi que ceux de l'*Apocoloquintose* de Sénèque, comparant Néron à un soleil levant. Compte tenu de l'accumulation impressionnante de correspondances, sommes-nous vraiment obligés d'interpréter la superposition suggérée par l'anecdote de Boileau comme le fruit d'une coïncidence fabriquée *a posteriori*, ou faut-il se rendre plutôt à l'évidence que Racine a sans doute choisi d'écrire une tragédie sur l'empereur romain qui présentait le plus de points de contacts avec Louis XIV ?

Si la coïncidence suggérée par ce premier indice semble donc difficilement pouvoir être le fruit du hasard, elle ne constitue toujours pas une preuve décisive, contrairement au deuxième indice qui se situe sur un tout autre plan : imaginer que Racine ait pu modifier l'histoire romaine pour faire place à une retraite chez les Vestales qu'aucune source n'attestait, relève d'une catégorie de preuves qui ne se cantonne plus à souligner des correspondances entre figures historiques. Cette fois le texte racinien ne pourrait s'expliquer qu'en référence au vécu réel du monarque français, et en particulier à son amour malheureux pour La Vallière. Si les commentateurs se sont méfiés du rapprochement de Boileau avec le roi danseur, ils ont repoussé ce deuxième indice de façon bien plus radicale, en lui reprochant son anachronisme flagrant[15] : comment Racine aurait-il pu modifier le récit de Tacite dans sa pièce de 1669 afin de faire allusion à un événement historique – la retraite de La Vallière au couvent des Carmélites – qui s'était produit plusieurs années après la représentation de la pièce ? L'objection, par son évidence, semble clore définitivement le débat en montrant la nature totalement artificielle de tout rapprochement entre la figure de Louis XIV et celle de Néron. Pourtant, un regard plus attentif à la relation entre le Roi-Soleil et son amante oblige à reconsidérer radicalement la question, du moins selon le récit qu'en fait un témoin de l'époque, Madame de La Fayette.

> Le Roi se mit dans une colère épouvantable, elle ne lui avoüa point ce que c'étoit, le Roi se retira au desespoir contre elle. Ils étoient convenus plusieurs fois, que quelques brouilleries qu'ils eus-

---

13 Certains ont voulu voir dans le Néron racinien un détournement de la symbologie royale, avec l'idée d'un « soleil noir ». Cf. Eigeldinger 1969, 48–53 ; Delmas 1999, 217–226.
14 Voir en particulier Grimal 1972, 225–230.
15 Voir entre autres Dubu 1995, 93.

sent ensemble, ils ne s'endormiroient jamais sans se racommoder & sans s'écrire. La nuit se passa sans qu'elle eût de nouvelles du Roi, & se croyant perdue, la tête lui tourna; elle sortit le matin des Tuilleries; & s'en alla, comme une insensée, dans un petit Couvent obscur, qui étoit à Chaillot. Le matin on alla avertir le Roi qu'on ne sçavoit pas où étoit la Valiére. Le Roi qui l'aimoit passionnément fut extremement troublé; il vint aux Tuilleries, pour sçavoir de Madame où elle étoit; Madame n'en sçavoit rien, & ne sçavoit pas même le sujet qui l'avoit fait partir.[16]

L'épisode en question, contrairement aux apparences, n'est pas la célèbre retraite définitive, mais une première retraite temporaire intervenue le 25 février 1662, c'est-à-dire des années avant que Racine n'entreprenne l'écriture de *Britannicus*. Si nous n'aurons jamais la certitude que cet événement historique joua un rôle crucial dans la création racinienne, la coïncidence est, tout de même, troublante, la chronologie ne constituant, en tous les cas, plus du tout un obstacle. Une lecture à clef redevient donc possible et encourage de nouvelles interrogations autour du personnage de Junie, figure totalement inventée par Racine et plutôt atypique au sein de sa production[17]. Dans des circonstances comparables, les héroïnes raciniennes mettent fin à leur présence scénique par le suicide, comme l'attestent le cas d'Antigone dans *La Thébaïde* ou celui d'Hermione dans *Andromaque*. Les excuses que le dramaturge de La Ferté Milon s'empresse d'évoquer dans sa préface afin de justifier à la fois le retour sur scène de Junie à l'acte V[18] et l'invraisemblable retraite chez les Vestales, contestable sur le plan historique[19], cachent mal le malaise suscité chez les spectateurs, et chez Racine lui-même probablement, par ces entorses à la dramaturgie et à l'histoire. Des entorses qui ne trouvent aucune explication satisfaisante si non dans le souhait de suggérer au public une allusion à la situation réelle des amours de Louis XIV. Une lecture à clef classique faisant de Junie le double de La Vallière s'avère pourtant insuffisante devant la richesse du personnage et de l'opération racinienne, qui a visiblement voulu résumer en une seule figure féminine plus d'une femme de Louis XIV : la duchesse délaissée certes, mais également et peut-être surtout Henriette d'Angleterre[20]. Comment expliquer autrement la tenace volonté de Racine de faire de Junie la femme de son frère, tout comme Henriette était la femme du duc d'Orléans, et de faire en sorte que Néron en soit fasciné, tout comme Louis

---

16 Madame de La Fayette, *Henriette d'Angleterre*, 88–89.

17 Malgré la maladroite tentative de Racine, dans sa préface de 1675, de lui trouver une origine historique, en jouant sur l'homonymie avec une certaine Junia Calvina (cf. Racine, *Britannicus*, « préface 1675 », 445), il est évident que ni Tacite ni aucun historien n'avaient jamais évoqué l'existence d'une Junie, femme de Britannicus et convoitée par Néron.

18 Racine, *Britannicus*, « préface », 373–374. Malgré sa défense acharnée du retour de Junie à la scène 6 de l'acte V, il finira par y renoncer dans la deuxième édition (1675), preuve ultérieure du malaise de Racine.

19 Racine, *Britannicus*, « préface », 375.

20 Jasinski (1958, 341–342) préfère y voir une allusion à La Vallière et à Montespan.

l'était de sa belle-sœur, au point de susciter les préoccupations de sa mère[21] ? Tout laisse croire que Racine s'est laissé entraîner par sa volonté de créer une symétrie avec les amours de jeunesse du roi au point d'imposer deux entorses supplémentaires à ses sources. D'une part, si Tacite prêtait bien une amante à Néron, qui avait provoqué la colère de sa mère Agrippine, il ne s'agissait pourtant pas du tout d'une prétendue femme de Britannicus, mais tout simplement de l'esclave Acté. À la recherche d'une source de conflit passionnel entre les deux frères, le dramaturge, sans besoin de lui prêter une fiancée, aurait beaucoup plus aisément pu imaginer que Britannicus aussi était épris d'Acté et que celle-ci était une jeune femme de l'aristocratie romaine et non pas une esclave, de sorte à respecter la bienséance. Racine voulait visiblement introduire à tout prix un double de cette même Henriette qui était devenue sa muse et à laquelle il venait de dédier sa dernière tragédie. Par une curieuse coïncidence, si la Vallière avait initialement été utilisée comme « paravent » pour cacher l'affection de Louis pour Henriette, Tacite précise, au chapitre 13 du livre XIII que l'entourage de Néron s'était empressé également de voiler les débuts de la passion de l'empereur pour Acté en ayant recours à un « paravent ». Dans la réécriture racinienne, Junie joue ainsi à la fois le rôle de « paravent » et de celle qui est censée s'abriter derrière le « paravent », résumant ainsi sur le plan symbolique en un seul personnage tous les amours de jeunesse du roi, interdits ou mal perçus à la cour. La présence en filigrane d'Henriette d'Angleterre derrière le visage de Junie semble d'ailleurs confirmée par un autre détail textuel sur lequel Racine s'attarde de façon curieuse au moment du récit du rapt, lorsqu'il insiste sur le fait que Junie était éloignée de la cour pendant ses jeunes années, raison pour laquelle Néron ne fait que découvrir à l'instant ses qualités et sa beauté. Alors qu'aucun indice historique ne pouvait avoir conduit le dramaturge dans cette direction, c'est précisément le destin qu'avait connu la jeune Henriette : tenue à l'écart des pompes royales dans sa jeunesse, elle avait été redécouverte par la Cour[22] et par le roi en particulier[23] à l'occasion de son mariage avec le duc d'Orléans.

---

21 Madame de La Fayette, *Henriette d'Angleterre*, 53 : « L'attachement que le Roi avoit pour Madame, commença bientôt à faire du bruit, & à être interpreté diversement. La Reine Mere en eut d'abord beaucoup de chagrin, il lui parut que Madame, lui ôtoit absolument le Roi, & qu'il lui donnoit toutes les heures, qui avoient accoutumé d'être pour elle. La grande jeunesse de Madame lui persuada qu'il seroit facile d'y remedier ».

22 Madame de La Fayette, *Henriette d'Angleterre*, 48–49 : « Il n'y eut personne qui ne fût surpris de son agrément, de sa civilité, & de son esprit : comme la Reine Mere la tenoit fort près de sa personne, on ne la voyoit jamais que chés elle, où elle ne parloit quasi point. Ce fut une nouvelle découverte de lui trouver l'esprit aussi aimable que tout le reste ; on ne parloit que d'elle, & tout le monde s'empressoit à lui donner des louanges ».

23 Madame de La Fayette, *Henriette d'Angleterre*, 52 : « Après quelque séjour à Paris, Monsieur & Madame s'en allerent à Fontainebleau. Madame y porta la joye, & les plaisirs. Le Roi connut en la

Bien que cela puisse paraître étonnant et malgré l'absence d'un jeu de correspondances univoque et d'une traçabilité précise entre figures de la cour versaillaise et personnages raciniens, le faisceau d'allusions que nous venons de rassembler semble rendre moins absurde l'hypothèse selon laquelle c'est bien avec en tête le premier de ses spectateurs que Racine aurait non seulement choisi son sujet et sélectionné son empereur romain, mais surtout modifié l'histoire antique pour faire place à des entorses susceptibles d'éveiller chez le public une partielle lecture à clef avec au centre les amours de jeunesse du roi.

2 Climat frondeur à la cour de Néron

Si les deux principales objections soulevées par la critique pour nier toute lecture à clef semblent donc fragiles, et si la proximité entre Néron et Louis XIV pouvait difficilement échapper à la sensibilité des spectateurs de la cour, il existe un deuxième faisceau d'indices tout aussi important, qui semble confirmer la volonté, de la part de Racine, de plier les sources pour mieux coller au contexte de ses spectateurs, et surtout du principal d'entre eux. La réécriture racinienne ne se contente pas de glisser quelques allusions à la jeunesse du monarque français, elle comporte surtout un retournement de perspective par rapport au récit de Tacite, qui finit par présenter Néron comme la victime d'une conspiration tentant par tous les moyens de réaffirmer son autorité légitime. Si le dramaturge a été amené, dans sa préface, à recourir à la formule curieuse de « monstre naissant » pour justifier le caractère de son empereur, c'est parce que ce dernier apparaît indéniablement bien moins méchant que le Néron historique ou que celui peint habituellement par les dramaturges[24]. Alors que chez Tacite, l'épisode de l'assassinat de Britannicus s'inscrivait dans un processus de progressive émancipation de l'empereur, souhaitant se libérer de l'emprise de sa mère pour se plonger plus librement dans le crime, chez Racine Néron se trouve immédiatement sur la défensive. C'est Agrippine qui est à l'initiative et qui tente par tous les moyens de freiner les ambitions du fils, en encourageant le mariage entre Britannicus et Junie afin de faire émerger un rival légitime, candidat à l'empire, et en conspirant chez Pallas avec les aristocrates romains. En d'autres termes, Racine a transformé en réalité ce qui ne relevait chez Tacite que de menaces

---

voyant de plus près, combien il avoit été injuste, en ne la trouvant pas la plus belle personne du monde. Il s'attacha fort à elle, & lui témoigna une complaisance extrême ».

24 Il suffit de penser au Néron de l'*Octavia* de Sénèque, de *La mort de Sénèque* de Tristan L'Hermite, ou d'*Arie et Pétus* de Gilbert. Comme le remarque Schröder (1999, 76–77), toutes les pièces de l'époque portent en scène un monstre abouti.

virtuelles, inutilement invoquées par la mère de l'empereur. C'est ainsi que pendant les trois premiers actes, aux yeux des spectateurs, le danger ne pèse pas tant sur le destin du jeune Britannicus mais plutôt sur celui d'un empereur contraint de casser l'encerclement dont il est victime, en faisant arrêter d'abord Junie – pour en empêcher un mariage dangereux sur le plan dynastique et se réserver ainsi le droit d'épouser une aristocrate à la filiation trop prestigieuse –, puis Pallas – le puissant ministre que Racine a fait survivre pour le mettre à la tête de la conspiration alors qu'il disparaissait bien plus tôt dans le récit historique –, et enfin Britannicus et sa propre mère, outré par une désobéissance qui risque de s'étendre à l'armée[25]. Plusieurs modifications apportées aux données historiques semblent confirmer que le dramaturge a ouvertement œuvré afin de minorer la monstruosité de l'empereur et de le présenter au moins partiellement comme la victime d'un complot. Si Tacite avait peint Britannicus comme un pauvre enfant innocent, empoisonné après avoir été violé par Néron, plus aucun détail scabreux ne figure dans le récit de sa mort à l'acte V ; par ailleurs, Racine l'a volontairement vieilli de quelques années, comme il le précise dans sa préface, de sorte à en faire un rival crédible et menaçant à la fois sur le plan dynastique et sur le plan amoureux. Confronté à un complot qui se trame dans l'ombre pour le destituer, rongé par la jalousie envers le bonheur d'un couple qui échappe à son contrôle et qui n'hésite pas à se retrouver dans son propre palais[26], défié par l'impertinence effrontée de son demi-frère à l'acte III, Néron dispose donc de plusieurs conditions atténuantes dans sa décision finale de suivre les conseils fratricides de Narcisse, pourtant longtemps repoussés[27].

Sans pour autant que ces transformations suppriment totalement le caractère monstrueux de l'empereur, il est pourtant évident que Racine en a ouvertement adouci les traits et excusé partiellement l'ordre d'empoisonnement, rendant mécaniquement moins ignoble une potentielle identification de la part du Roi-Soleil. Ce n'est pas tout. Si Racine a voulu renforcé la situation de danger dans laquelle verse l'empereur, peut-être en souvenir des dangers courus pendant la Fronde par le jeune Louis XIV, il a, par un même mouvement, renforcé la redoutable capacité de Néron à s'en sortir, et cela notamment grâce à un réseau d'espionnage bien huilé, dont les sources ne faisaient aucune mention ou presque[28]. Si

---

25 Sur l'intérêt dramaturgique d'une telle transformation du sujet voir Alonge 2022.
26 À l'acte III, scène 8, Néron surprend Britannicus aux genoux de Junie, ce qui ne peut qu'exacerber sa colère et sa jalousie.
27 Jusqu'à l'acte IV, comme l'attestent les mots adressés à Narcisse. Cf. Racine, *Britannicus*, IV, 4, v. 1412–1413 : « C'est prendre trop de soin. Quoi qu'il en soit, Narcisse, / Je ne le compte plus parmi mes Ennemis ».
28 Tacite (*Annales*, XIII, 15) évoque le fait que Néron avait placé des « gens sans foi ni loi » dans l'entourage de son demi-frère Britannicus.

lui-même n'hésite pas à espionner Junie et Britannicus, caché derrière un rideau dans la célèbre scène 6 de l'acte II, il se sert surtout de Narcisse pour contrôler les mouvements et les pensées de son rival. Racine en a fait le gouverneur du jeune prince, alors que chez Tacite il mourait bien avant les faits et n'entretenait aucun lien avec le fils de l'empereur Claudius. Si dans la pièce Néron a donc mis « sous écoute » son demi-frère, cela est peut-être vrai aussi pour sa mère Agrippine, comme semblent le suggérer deux mystères textuels passés inaperçus. Le premier concerne une information primordiale – la tenue d'une réunion des conjurés chez Pallas au premier entracte – dont l'empereur semble déjà au courant dans les premiers vers de l'acte II alors que Narcisse n'a pas encore eu le temps de l'informer, ce qu'il fera à la scène suivante. Si l'allusion de Néron (v. 365–366) peut paraître une simple intuition, c'est curieusement une intuition qui lui suggère une décision extrême – le bannissement de Pallas. Il serait étonnant qu'il prenne une décision d'une telle ampleur à la légère, à partir d'une pure suspicion. L'absence de réaction à la scène suivante, lorsque Narcisse l'en informe officiellement, semble confirmer que Néron était, en réalité, déjà au courant. Mais comment ? Si les hypothèses peuvent se multiplier (Néron écoutant derrière le rideau tout au long de l'acte I, Néron disposant d'espions chez Pallas, etc.), il y en a pourtant une beaucoup plus simple et que le texte n'interdit pas. Au moment où Agrippine invite officiellement Britannicus à s'unir à la réunion secrète à l'acte I, scène 3, quatre personnages seulement se trouvent sur scène. Or de ces quatre personnages, le texte contraint de blanchir de tout soupçon d'espionnage Narcisse pour les raisons susmentionnées, ainsi que le jeune prince et la mère de l'empereur pour des raisons évidentes ; il reste pour autant la mystérieuse Albine, figure silencieuse et ignorée par la critique[29]. Or, si elle parle peu, cette étrange madame Albine parle curieusement toujours en défense de l'empereur : c'est le cas à l'ouverture de la pièce dans un long et animé échange avec sa maîtresse, au cours duquel elle tente en vain de défendre les vertus du Prince (v. 25–30), s'émeut du complot que trame Agrippine (v. 59 : « Vous leur appui, Madame ? »), souligne ouvertement les délicatesses de Néron envers sa mère (v. 79–87) et invite enfin à s'éclaircir avec lui (v. 115–117). Son attitude ne change pas à l'acte III, lorsqu'elle reproche sans fard à sa maîtresse de vouloir contraindre « César jusque dans ses amours » (v. 878). Ce sera enfin toujours elle qui mystérieusement a suivi les pas précipités de Junie à la fin de l'acte V (v. 1746), et qui reviendra sur scène pour appeler au secours, pour tenter de sauver la vie de l'empereur (« Venez sauver César de sa propre fureur », v. 1738). Si les critiques les plus avertis pourraient conjecturer que Racine ne dis-

---

29 « A peine plus qu'une figurante » à en croire Malachy 1995.

posait de personne d'autre pour assurer le récit qui remplit la dernière scène[30], il n'était, en tous les cas, pas obligé de rendre Albine si fidèle à l'empereur tout au long de la pièce. Si on allie à cet indice, le fait que Tacite évoquait dans la personne de Junia Silana, au chapitre 19 du livre XIII, une proche d'Agrippine l'ayant trahie et dénoncée à Néron, il n'est pas invraisemblable de penser qu'Albine constitue bien la solution à ce premier mystère textuel qui ouvre l'acte II. C'est sans doute en elle aussi qu'il faut identifier la solution au deuxième mystère textuel, à l'acte IV cette fois : confronté à sa mère, Néron l'accuse ouvertement d'avoir voulu se rendre au camp et présenter Britannicus aux armées (v. 1256–1257), information réelle qu'Agrippine n'avait reconnue qu'une seule fois sur scène, à Burrhus (v. 839–854). Or Burrhus ne peut pas en avoir informé l'empereur car tout au long de l'acte III et de l'acte IV il est, d'une certaine façon, tombé en disgrâce aux yeux du prince. Ce dernier le soupçonne en effet de conjurer avec sa mère, comme il le lui suggère à la fin de l'acte III (v. 1094–1098), et lui confesse ouvertement à la fin de l'acte IV (v. 1310–1312). Si Burrhus, qui est d'ailleurs occupé à rapprocher les parties et qui n'aurait donc aucun intérêt à livrer une telle information, avait révélé ce secret à Néron entre temps, ce dernier n'aurait nullement pu le soupçonner de complicité avec Agrippine. Il faut donc se tourner vers le seul autre personnage qui avait assisté aux menaces de la femme de Claude à l'acte III : Albine, comme par hasard. Les deux informations essentielles, dont Néron dispose mystérieusement dans la pièce et qui lui permettent d'une certaine façon de déjouer le complot qui se trame contre lui, ont pour point commun l'étrange présence de la muette Albine, qui peut donc vraisemblablement être considérée comme le troisième agent du réseau d'espionnage mis en place par un empereur soucieux de se défendre par ses propres moyens.

À la lumière de toutes ces modifications apportées au récit historique, il apparaît donc d'autant plus vraisemblable que Racine a bien retravaillé ses sources avec en tête si non à proprement parler des allusions précises à des faits contemporains, du moins le climat qui régnait à la cour de Louis XIV, ou en tous les cas celui qui avait régné pendant la jeunesse du roi. Un climat fait de suspicions, de complots, et naturellement d'espions susceptibles de déjouer toutes les tentatives de renverser le pouvoir, y compris au sein de sa propre famille.

---

30 À vrai dire, des alternatives existaient pourtant : il aurait, par exemple, pu changer la disposition pour transformer Burrhus en messager.

3 L'ambiguïté du plaisir théâtral

Si à la fois les traits du prince et le contexte dans lequel Racine le fait évoluer rappellent fortement la jeunesse du règne de Louis XIV, si effectivement derrière le monstre naissant le dramaturge a voulu renforcer les allusions au monarque de son temps, il reste à comprendre les raisons d'une telle audace. À première vue, le fait de glisser des allusions au souverain n'a rien d'exceptionnel pour le théâtre du XVIIe siècle et en particulier pour la dramaturgie de Racine : le premier de ses succès, celui d'*Alexandre*, n'avait-il pas été le fruit justement de l'identification entre le roi et le conquérant macédonien ? Que dire de la tragédie qui suivra de quelques mois *Britannicus* ? L'idée d'un roi qui renonce à une passion personnelle pour le devoir de régner dans *Bérénice* n'était-elle pas une allusion explicite au renoncement du jeune Louis XIV à ses amours sous la pression de la reine mère et de Mazarin ? Et que dire plus tard d'*Esther*, pour laquelle les lectures à clef se multiplieront en devinant derrière le triomphe de la reine juive sur Vasthi celui de Madame de Maintenon sur les maîtresses précédentes. Rien de bien surprenant donc pour un auteur, et cela a été montré depuis longtemps, qui s'est servi de la littérature, de la poésie dès son plus jeune âge, et surtout du théâtre, pour gravir les échelons de la société de l'époque[31], qui avait débuté sa carrière littéraire par un long poème encomiastique à l'occasion du mariage de Louis XIV et de Marie-Thérèse d'Autriche, et qui terminera son parcours dans le cercle versaillais le plus restreint, d'abord en tant qu'historiographe officiel, puis en qualité de gentilhomme ordinaire de la chambre du roi. Si la volonté de montrer le monarque sur scène répond donc à un réflexe courtisan finalement assez attendu, il n'est pas étonnant non plus que Louis XIV ait apprécié la démarche. Dans ses *Mémoires pour l'instruction du Dauphin*, n'avait-il pas pris le temps de préciser que pour un souverain les plaisirs des spectacles ne constituent pas uniquement une occasion de repos et divertissement, mais également un instrument de puissance et de contrôle ? Le peuple français se distinguant à ses yeux de tous les autres peuples dans sa recherche systématique d'une proximité avec le roi[32], il devient politiquement nécessaire de lui montrer une « honnête familiarité » en se ren-

---

31 Cf. notamment Viala 1990.

32 Louis XIV, *Mémoires pour l'instruction du Dauphin*, 134 : « s'il y a quelque caractère singulier dans cette monarchie, c'est l'accès libre et facile des sujets au prince. C'est une égalité de justice entre lui et eux, qui les tient pour ainsi dire dans une société douce et honnête, nonobstant la différence presque infinie de la naissance, du rang et du pouvoir ».

dant au théâtre et en se prêtant, pendant quelques heures, à un plaisir partagé[33]. En d'autres termes, en acceptant et en approuvant un spectacle rempli d'allusions à sa personne, le roi montre qu'il trouve du plaisir à s'identifier aux personnages, comme n'importe quel autre spectateur, et à se retrouver associé à des figures historiques majeures, en compagnie de ses sujets.

Si le procédé appliqué dans *Britannicus* semble s'inscrire dans une mouvance globale du théâtre racinien, la pièce de 1669 est pourtant porteuse d'une spécificité étonnante, à savoir la nature choquante du rapprochement proposé. Il ne s'agit plus de suggérer une identification élogieuse avec un monarque exemplaire comme Alexandre, ou comme l'Auguste cornélien ; dans l'imaginaire collectif, Néron n'a rien d'un empereur louable, il s'apparente au contraire à un contre-modèle tyrannique. Comment expliquer donc que Racine ait pu porter sur scène un monstre, bien que naissant, en renforçant les allusions qui permettaient une identification au roi Louis XIV ? Comment expliquer le décalage avec des règles de bienséance qui imposaient depuis des décennies aux auteurs de théâtre de faire particulièrement attention au rôle attribué aux rois, de peur justement de froisser la sensibilité du premier des spectateurs ? Comment expliquer surtout que Louis XIV se soit prêté au jeu au point d'apprécier la pièce, alors même qu'il ne pouvait pas ignorer le jeu de miroir suggéré par le dramaturge ? Une lecture morale reste possible. Il est évident que les temps ont changé, au lieu de louer ouvertement, comme il l'avait fait dans *Alexandre*, Racine loue cette fois par prétérition, comme déjà montré par la critique[34] : Néron n'est pas ce que Louis devrait être, mais ce qu'il aurait pu devenir s'il n'avait pas disposé d'une nature vertueuse. Un autre passage des *Mémoires pour l'instruction du Dauphin*, remontant à 1662, semble pourtant suggérer peut-être une autre explication encore, avec en filigrane une réflexion autour de la mise en scène de la personne du roi bien plus complexe et énigmatique. En se référant au Grand Carrousel, donné justement en l'honneur de la naissance de son fils, Louis XIV précise au Dauphin que le souverain, tout en participant aux cérémonies, ne doit pas « réussir au-delà du commun » dans les exercices dans lesquels il s'engage.

> Toutes ces considérations, mon fils, quand mon âge et mon inclination ne m'y auraient pas porté, m'obligeaient à favoriser des divertissements de cette nature, et vous y doivent obliger de même, sans aller pourtant à un excès d'attachement qui ne serait pas louable ; car alors,

---

33 Louis XIV, *Mémoires pour l'instruction du Dauphin*, 135 : « Cette société de plaisirs, qui donne aux personnes de la cour une honnête familiarité avec nous, les touche et les charme plus qu'on ne peut dire. Les peuples, d'un autre côté, se plaisent au spectacle, où au fond on a toujours pour but de leur plaire ; et tous nos sujets, en général, sont ravis de voir que nous aimons ce qu'ils aiment, ou à quoi ils réussissent le mieux. Par là nous tenons leur esprit et leur cœur, quelquefois plus fortement peut-être que par les récompenses et les bienfaits ».

34 Jaouen, 1995, 109.

mon fils, quelque gravité que vous puissiez d'ailleurs affecter dans vos autres actions, ne vous y trompez pas, vous ne tromperiez point le public. Sous la couronne, quand vous l'auriez toujours en tête, et au travers du manteau royal, on aurait bientôt reconnu que vous faites de vos plaisirs vos affaires, et passez par-dessus les affaires comme il faut passer par-dessus les plaisirs. Pour cette raison, il est quelquefois dangereux aux jeunes princes de réussir au delà du commun à de certains exercices, et de ce genre surtout ; car ce fonds inépuisable d'amour-propre qui nous est si naturel nous porte toujours à cultiver, estimer et aimer sans mesure toutes les choses où nous pensons exceller au-dessus des autres [. . .] Vous savez le mot de ce roi d'autrefois à son fils : N'as-tu point de honte de jouer si bien de la lyre ? Souffrez qu'en toutes ces sortes de choses, il y ait parmi vos sujets des gens qui vous surpassent, mais que nul ne vous égale, s'il se peut, dans l'art de gouverner, que vous ne pouvez trop bien savoir, et qui doit être votre application principale (Louis XIV, *Mémoires pour l'instruction du Dauphin*, 135–136).

Tout en se référant probablement aux exercices équestres ou de danse, Louis XIV semble pourtant esquisser une réflexion plus globale autour de la fonction et de la posture qu'un souverain doit adopter lorsqu'il se met en scène pendant un divertissement. Ce qui amène logiquement à inclure dans ce schéma également les personnages qu'il est appelé à incarner lors de représentations théâtrales, et pourquoi pas les personnages dans lesquels le public est censé le reconnaître, comme c'est le cas pour le Néron de *Britannicus*. Loin d'exiger la perfection sur scène, Louis XIV revendique au contraire la nécessité de se montrer en défaut, plus faible que certains sujets ou professionnels du spectacle, afin de rappeler constamment au peuple que l'essentiel de ses efforts est consacré à l'art de gouverner. D'une certaine façon, les deux corps du roi doivent s'opposer aux yeux du spectateur afin de faire ressortir le décalage entre l'homme privé, qui se prête aux divertissements communs à ses sujets avec des qualités moyennes, et l'homme public, le souverain qui ne connaît d'égal dans l'exercice du pouvoir. Il suffit alors de relier ce passage des *Mémoires* avec celui susmentionné qui incitait à instrumentaliser la « société de plaisirs » afin d'affecter une égalité apparente et temporaire entre le roi et ses sujets, pour s'apercevoir de la nature foncièrement politique que Louis XIV attribue aux divertissements : conscient du danger de la Fronde, qu'il mentionne explicitement, il a compris que le peuple a besoin par moments de se sentir proche, voire supérieur à son roi[35]. S'il lui reconnait une supériorité dans l'art de gouverner, il doit pourtant « prendre sa revanche » ailleurs, et le théâtre fait peut-être partie de cet « ailleurs » justement. Pourquoi ne pas faire l'hypothèse alors que le fait de voir le roi montrer un visage cruel, injuste, imparfait sur la scène peut permettre de mieux gérer le rapport au pouvoir, l'acceptation de la supériorité du monarque dans la vraie vie ? En d'autres termes, le roi

---

[35] Il est curieux de remarquer que Louis XIV ne dédaigna pas, dans certains ballets, de tenir des rôles sans gloire (ex. : un berger, un Egyptien, un Maure, une Heure, etc.). Sur le sujet cf. Néraudau 1986, 121–122.

accepterait de se voir « dégradé » sur scène, pour revendiquer encore plus fort à la sortie du théâtre son statut exceptionnel dans la vie réelle. Le paradigme tradition-nellement employé par les dramaturges consistait à se servir de la scène comme d'un miroir pour le monarque, afin de l'éduquer sur le plan moral, soit en exaltant la grandeur exemplaire de son double, soit en le mettant en garde à travers la représen-tation d'un monstre tyrannique. Paradigme visiblement dépassé dans la réflexion de Louis XIV, qui encourage au contraire à briser le miroir, à confondre illusion et réa-lité, et à transcender une logique purement morale. Si Corneille distinguait encore le roi qui paraît sur la scène « comme Roi seulement, quand il n'a intérêt qu'à la conser-vation de son Trône [. . .] sans avoir l'esprit agité d'aucune passion particulière » et celui qui paraît « comme homme seulement, quand il n'a que l'intérêt d'une passion à suivre ou à vaincre, sans aucun péril pour son État »[36], Racine semble avoir compris qu'il est désormais possible, sans danger, de brouiller les pistes en présen-tant un roi qui peut être en même temps pleinement homme et pleinement roi, sus-ceptible de mettre en danger son État pour une passion particulière, comme c'est le cas pour Néron. Si cela est possible c'est parce que Louis XIV n'attend pas nécessaire-ment du spectacle un enseignement moral, mais plutôt une possibilité de défoule-ment thérapeutique, cathartique pourrait-on dire, à la fois pour lui et pour ses sujets. Si une enquête systématique mériterait d'être conduite afin de valider une telle hypo-thèse, force est de constater que c'est bien ce genre de mécanisme qui semble être à l'œuvre quelques années avant *Britannicus*, lors des divertissements organisés à Ver-sailles en 1664, ceux des *Plaisirs de l'île enchantée*, dont Félibien résume magistrale-ment l'essentiel.

> Il prit pour sujet le Palais d'Alcine, qui donna lieu au Tiltre des Plaisirs de l'Isle Enchantée ; puis que selon l'Arioste le brave Roger et plusieurs autres bons Chevaliers y furent retenus par les doubles charmes de la beauté, quoy qu'empruntée, et du sçavoir de cette Magi-cienne ; et en furent délivrez apres beaucoup de temps consommé dans les delices, par la bague qui destruisoit les enchantemens (*Les plaisirs de l'île enchantée*, 5).

Sur l'île d'Alcine, au cœur de la troisième journée des Divertissements, les cheva-liers festoient, font l'amour et ne s'inquiètent guère de leur devoir héroïque, empri-sonnés dans une bulle de pur plaisir. Malgré le contexte peu édifiant, Louis XIV accepte d'y prendre part et de jouer le rôle ambigu de Roger[37], coupable, dans le poème d'Arioste, d'avoir abandonné son amante Bradamante pour fuir avec la ma-

---

36 Corneille, *Clitandre ou l'Innocence délivrée*, « Examen », 102–103.
37 *Les plaisirs de l'île enchantée*, 8–9 : « Le Roy representant Roger les suivoit, montant un des plus beaux chevaux du monde, dont le harnois couleur de feu esclattoit d'or, d'argent et de pierreries ».

gicienne. Comme déjà rappelé par la critique[38], le roi-acteur s'autorise ainsi devant la cour une évasion temporaire, littéraire et donc sans conséquence dans l'hédonisme, et libère par un même mouvement le roi-homme d'État de toute tentation de répliquer cette quête de jouissance dans la vie réelle. L'effet collatéral recherché est de rassurer les courtisans quant à son investissement total dans l'art de gouverner, à la tombée du rideau, tout en leur ayant permis de prendre une revanche symbolique pendant quelques heures, à la vue d'un homme fragile et pécheur comme eux tous.

4 Rome, *the bad Paris* ?

Nous pouvons maintenant revenir à notre point de départ en portant un regard différent sur le témoignage « invraisemblable » de Boileau : peu importe que le roi ait cessé de danser avant ou après avoir vu *Britannicus*, l'anecdote en elle-même est déjà révélatrice du succès de l'opération racinienne, visant à pousser au rapprochement paradoxal entre Néron et Louis XIV, ce que les contemporains n'ont pas pu s'empêcher de faire. À commencer par le roi lui-même qui, selon les chroniques de l'époque, apprécia la pièce, visiblement moins choqué que les commentateurs modernes par un ambigu jeu de miroirs, suggéré en filigrane sans jamais qu'une lecture à clef radicale et univoque ne s'impose. S'indigner devant l'idée tabou d'un Louis-Néron c'est sous-estimer la complexité et l'ambiguïté du plaisir théâtral, c'est oublier que c'est sur cette ambiguïté qu'avaient été bâties les fêtes de l'île enchantée de Versailles cinq ans plus tôt à peine, c'est ignorer que la relation du roi au spectacle et à l'histoire évolue dans le temps : tout comme l'image de Louis XIV servira en 1673 à Desmarets à charpenter celle de Clovis[39], pourquoi refuser de voir une opération similaire dans la création de ce Néron de 1669, si machiavélique et si peu monstrueux ? Si la mythistoire de la monarchie française s'est bâtie, entre autres, sur une appropriation de l'antiquité impériale comme modèle de référence susceptible d'anoblir le présent d'un prestige ancien, en faisant de Paris une nouvelle Rome, pourquoi ne pas imaginer que cette même Rome, par moments, ait pu jouer un rôle diamétralement inverse ? Qu'elle ait pu constituer le réceptacle des désirs indicibles d'un « grand prince naissant », en projetant dans ce passé lointain le côté obscur et caché de la cour, celui des complots et des empoisonnements, des trahisons et des adultères, de la

---

38 Sur le sujet voir notamment les pages consacrées à l'ambiguïté du plaisir pendant les divertissements de 1664 par Apostolidès 1981, 98–101.
39 Sur le sujet voir Apostolidès 1981, 118–119, et Néraudau 1986, 75.

vengeance de clan et de la cruauté familiale ? Si Louis XIV apprécia autant *Britannicus*, c'est peut-être parce que le désespoir libérateur de Néron dans les derniers vers de la pièce fut aussi le sien au moment de se réveiller d'un songe théâtral qui lui avait permis, pendant quelques heures, une évasion coupable.

Bibliography

Alonge, Tristan. « *Britannicus*, tragédie cornélienne ? ». *XVIIᵉ siècle* 297 (2022) : 719–739.

Apostolidès, Jean-Marie. *Le roi-machine. Spectacle et politique au temps de Louis XIV*. Paris : Les éditions de Minuit, 1981.

Boileau, Nicolas. « Lettre à Monchesnay, septembre 1707 ». *Œuvres complètes*. Éd. Françoise Escal. Paris : Gallimard (Bibliothèque de la Pléiade), 1966.

Corneille, Pierre. *Clitandre ou l'Innocence délivrée*. *Œuvres complètes I*. Éd. Georges Couton. Paris : Gallimard (Bibliothèque de la Pléiade), 1980.

Delmas, Christian. « Néron, soleil noir ». *Racine et la méditerranée. Soleil et mer. Neptune et Apollon*. Nice : Université de Nice-Antipolis, 1999. 217–226.

Dubu, Jean. « *Britannicus*. politique et théâtralité de l',invisible présence' ». Racine, Jean. *Britannicus*. Éd. Pierre Ronzeaud. Paris : Klincksieck, 1995. 85–96.

Eigeldinger, Marc. *La mythologie solaire dans l'œuvre de Racine*. Genève : Droz, 1969.

Félibien, André. *Les plaisirs de l'île enchantée*. Paris : Ballard, 1665.

Grimal, Pierre. « Le *De Clementia* et la royauté solaire de Néron ». *Comptes rendus des séances de l'Académie des Inscriptions et Belles-Lettres* 1 (1972) : 225–230.

Jaouen, Francoise,« *Britannicus* ou l'éloge de la cruauté ». *Op. cit.* 5 (1995) : 103–110.

Jasinski, René. *Vers le vrai Racine*. Paris : Armand Colin, 1958.

Louis XIV. *Mémoires pour l'instruction du Dauphin*. Paris : Imprimerie Nationale, 1992.

Madame de La Fayette. *Histoire de Madame Henriette d'Angleterre première femme de Philippe de France, duc d'Orléans*. Amsterdam : 1720.

Malachy, Thérèse. « Y-a-t-il un statisme racinien ? Une lecture de *Britannicus* ». Éd. Michel Autrand. *Statisme et mouvement au théâtre : actes du colloque organisé par le Centre de recherches sur l'histoire du théâtre, Université de Paris IV, 17–19 mars 1994*. Poitiers : Université de Poitiers, 1995. 191–196.

Néraudau, Jean-Pierre. « Mais où sont ces Romains que fait parler Racine ? ». *Littératures classiques* 26 (1996) : 75–90.

Néraudau, Jean-Pierre. *L'Olympe du Roi-Soleil*. Paris : Les Belles lettres, 1986.

Racine, Jean. *Britannicus*. *Œuvres complètes I*. Éd. Georges Forestier. Paris : Gallimard (Bibliothèque de la Pléiade), 1999.

Racine, Louis. *Mémoires*. Racine, Jean. *Œuvres complètes I*. Éd. Georges Forestier. Paris : Gallimard (Bibliothèque de la Pléiade), 1999.

Robinet, Charles. *Lettre en vers à Madame*. Paris : Chenault, 15 février 1670.

Robinet, Charles. *Lettre en vers à Madame*. Paris : Chenault, 9 mars 1669.

Schröder, Volker. *La Tragédie du sang d'Auguste : politique et intertextualité dans « Britannicus »*. Tübingen : Narr, 1999.

Suétone. *Vie des Douze Césars*. Paris : Les Belles Lettres, 1967.

Tacite. *Annales*. Paris : Les Belles Lettres, 1990.

Viala, Alain. *Racine : la stratégie du caméléon*. Paris : Seghers, 1990.

Larry F. Norman
Versailles, A New Rome? Perrault and the Quarrel of the Ancients and Moderns

In the second half of seventeenth century, just as French political and cultural power was largely being transferred from Paris to Versailles, so too was the traditional parallel between France and Rome undergoing an equally striking displacement, with the sparkling new palace superseding the longtime capital city as the privileged locus for sweeping historical comparisons. It is no surprise, then, that the author of one of the first guide books to Versailles, published in 1681 – that is, roughly two decades after the earliest phases of radically transforming Louis XIV's father's old hunting lodge into what would become, in 1682, France's seat of government – should exclaim in wonderment to the reader, "There you will see the ancient and the new Rome" ("Vous y verrez l'ancienne et la nouvelle Rome").[1]

While the parallel between Versailles and Rome has long interested historians, and particularly art historians, of the palace,[2] my aim in the following pages is to situate this commonplace comparison in the broader context of the historical imagination of the time. We might start by asking what exactly Sieur Combes means by "ancient" and "new" Rome. What is the relation between the Rome of Augustus and the Rome of Bernini, and how do each of these "Romes" shape seventeenth-century France's understanding of its own place in history? More broadly, how do "ancient" and "modern" Rome inform early-modern French paradigms of historical understanding (or regimes of historicity, to use François Hartog's formula[3]), conceptualizations of distinct national or cultural identities, and elaborations of the history and periodization of the arts?

To probe these questions, I will situate the relationship between Rome and Versailles in the framework of the quarrel of the ancients and the moderns.[4] That

---

1 Published under the name of Sieur Combes, a pseudonym of Laurent Morellet 1681, 4. See Cornette 2006, 275.
2 Indeed, my title reprises in interrogative form that given to a chapter by Alexandre Maral ("Versailles et la Nouvelle Rome") in the superb exhibition catalogue and essay collection, *Versailles et l'antique* Maral and Milovanovic 2012, 23–45.
3 See Hartog 2003. His later application of the concept to the French quarrel of the ancients and moderns (and to Perrault's *Parallèle*) has been crucial to my analyses Hartog 2005.
4 In the following pages I expand upon some earlier reflections on the quarrel Norman 2011. While the bibliography concerning this debate is too massive to cover here, the reader may con-

https://doi.org/10.1515/9783111334776-005

explosive debate over the relative merits of antiquity and modernity had already been long brewing when the 1681 guidebook labeled Versailles as the "new Rome." Although prepared by two earlier decades of polemical skirmishes, the quarrel was officially inaugurated with the 1687 public reading by modern party champion Charles Perrault of his royal encomium in verse, "Le Siècle de Louis le Grand." And that poem begins precisely with Perrault, in the opening lines, not only comparing the reign of Louis XIV with that of Augustus, but furthermore suggesting that modern France is indeed superior to Rome's ancient golden age.

> Beautiful antiquity was always venerable,/But I never believed it was adorable./I see the Ancients without bending a knee,/They are great, yes, but men just as are we./And one can compare, without injustice,/The Age of Louis with that of Augustus.

> [*La belle Antiquité fut toujours vénérable,/Mais je ne crus jamais qu'elle fût adorable./Je vois les Anciens, sans plier les genoux,/Ils sont grands, il est vrai, mais hommes comme nous ;/Et l'on peut comparer, sans craindre d'être injuste,/Le siècle de LOUIS au beau siècle d'Auguste.*][5]

Perrault spent the following years developing his comparison (or more often, contrast) between Roman antiquity and modern France through the massive four volumes of his *Parallèle des anciens et des modernes*, successively published from 1688 to 1697. But Perrault's historical analyses, like those of most of his allies (and opponents) in the quarrel, reveal a much more complex, and much more multipolar, understanding of history than a simple binary opposition between ancient Rome and modern France, between the Age of Augustus and that of Louis. New theories of continuous human progress, indebted to Francis Bacon, Descartes and Pascal, led thinkers to take in a much broader sweep of their civilization's evolution: pre-classical Greek antiquity, the Middle Ages, and the now already historicized Renaissance of the sixteenth century constitute other important historical players in the quarrel – and have starring roles in what we might call Perrault's non-binary parallel. Indeed, Perrault considers Versailles itself less as a stable site, or fixed moment in time, than as a kind of emblem a of modern France that

---

sult an excellent recent survey of scholarship on the quarrel Taylor 2020; recent important overviews include Bullard and Tadié 2016, Bos and Rotmans 2021, and Bahier-Porte and Reguig (2022).
5 "Le Siècle" was included as an appendix in the first volume of the *Parallèle* Perrault 1688–1697; the poem is non-paginated. All quotations from Perrault are from the 1688–1697 edition and will be referenced with page and volume number alone. All translations from French texts are my own, unless otherwise indicated; I have throughout modernized seventeenth-century French spelling.

is itself ever evolving and progressing in the more than two decades since Louis XIV began the reconstruction and expansion of the palace and gardens.[6]

> Versailles is [. . .] an image of our century, which, since a certain number of years, has so changed its face that, if we were to have been blinded for twenty-two years to the progress made in the arts and sciences, we would be no less astonished [to see this progress] than those who, arriving here [i.e., at Versailles] after having been away for the same period of time, are surprised by the new beauties they find before them.

> [*Versailles est [. . .]une image de notre siècle, qui depuis un certain nombre d'années a telle-ment changé de face, que si nous avions pu pendant vingt-deux ans ne point voir le progrès qui s'est fait dans les Arts et dans les Sciences, nous n'en serions pas moins étonnés que ceux qui arrivent ici après avoir été ce temps-là sans y venir, sont surpris des nouvelles beautés qu'ils y trouvent.*] (2.2)

1 The Fluid Temporalities of Multiple "Romes"

Just as Versailles serves as a kind of dizzying metonymy for the ever-shifting progress of modern France,[7] unrecognizable in its cascading advances from just two decades earlier, so too the recourse to Rome, as a comparative term, proves to be dynamic and multivalent. To illustrate this point, consider a text written shortly after Combes's labeling of Versailles as a "new Rome," in this case, an evo-cation of Paris as usurper of Rome in a 1682 anonymous article in the *Mercure galant*, the leading periodical of the day:

> To return to the paintings, busts, and ancient sculptures with which the king has filled his royal estates since he chose to govern the State by himself, one can say that Italy is in France and that Paris is a new Rome, not only due to every rare object consecrated by antiquity that his Majesty has brought from everywhere in the world, but also due to the great num-ber of French people who come back every day from foreign lands after having made them-selves expert in the particular arts of each nation.

> [*Pour revenir à tous les tableaux, bustes et figures antiques dont le roi a rempli les maisons royales depuis qu'il a pris le soin de gouverner son État lui-même, on peut dire que l'Italie est en France et que Paris est une nouvelle Rome, non seulement pour tout ce que Sa Majesté y a fait venir de curieux et qui était consacré par l'antiquité dans toutes les parties du monde,*

---

6 Perrault's focus on (even obsession with) Versailles is no surprise given his important role in advising the regime on the massive project. See Rabinovitch 2013.

7 On Versailles as universal symbolic representation of modern France and the absolutist re-gime, see Marin 1991 and Pommier 1998.

mais encore par le grand nombre de Français qui reviennent tous les jours des pays étrangers, après s'être rendus savants dans ce que chaque nation a de particulier pour les arts.][8]

The passage hints at several meanings given to the name "Rome." (I won't dwell on the equal polyvalence of the term "Paris", interchangeable here with "France" itself and its many "royal estates," of which of course Versailles was now the most important). The first references to Rome appear to designate the ancient city – or more generally the Empire and its artworks: ("ancient sculptures," "every rare object consecrated by antiquity"). Yet even these references are temporally ambiguous, since the greatest part of the "ancient" sculptures referred to here were either modern adaptations of ancient works, or copies or plaster casts.[9] (I'll return below to the problem of the "faux-antique.") But the second part of the passage gives a very different meaning to Rome, referring to it as the modern, cosmopolitan capital of the arts, the place where people throughout the world come to practice their craft. Here today's Paris (or modern France and the King's "estates," which it represents) is seen as the most recent destination of a long-term displacement of cultural capital, once again conceived in the westward movement of *translatio studii*, continuing the previous trajectory from Athens to Rome.[10] The relocation of cutting-edge modernity from Paris to suburban Versailles would, according to this scheme, represent one last westward (if geographically miniscule) shift.

The Rome in question in these late seventeenth-century debates is thus strikingly multifaceted and multidimensional; far from being a univocal marker of the "golden age" of Augustus, Rome, in its contemporaneity, is also the living rival to modern France's cultural ambitions. Indeed, if we consider the whole of Perrault's writing (as well as that of other authors engaged in the quarrel), we find that three distinct periods emerge: 1) *ancient Rome*, most frequently indicating the early Roman Empire; 2) *Renaissance Rome*, which is generally referred to as the Rome of "the past century" or that of the "time of Raphael, of Titian"; and 3) *contemporary Rome*, the baroque Rome of Bernini, the home of the "Académie de France à Rome" recently founded (1666) by Louis XIV (precisely as work continued on Versailles), and the city generally considered the capital of European art –

---

8 *Mercure galant*, juillet 1682, 138–139; cited in Maral and Milovanovic 2012, 25.

9 See Haskell and Penny 1981, and Maral and Milovanovic 2012, 105–114.

10 Pommier 1998 also places Versailles's competition with Rome in the context of the linguistic rivalry between ancient and modern tongues, as the monarchy leaned further into its program of replacing Latin with French as the universal language of learning and historical commemoration. On this linguistic turn of the quarrel, see Ferrier-Caverivière 1981.

but now, Perrault and his modern partly allies claim, challenged and perhaps superseded by Versailles.

Each of these three periods are furthermore themselves complex, and indeed increasingly complexified under the lens of historical examination as it was then being filtered through new paradigm of infinite human progress. If we simply take the "Age of Augustus," so central to the debates, as an example, we can see that it was itself seen within a history of antiquity in which it represented, for Perrault and Modern partisans at least, the culmination of millennial progress. That is to say that in relation to the Greek past, Imperial Rome represented a first 'modernity' and thus a model for all future modernities. It is thus that Perrault – speaking through his mouthpiece in the dialogues of the *Parallèle*, the Abbé – proclaims the astonishing modernity of the Roman Virgil in relation to the Greek Homer:

> I find a great difference between the works of Homer and those of Virgil. To the same degree that the first [. . .] seem full of vulgarity, puerility, and foolishness, so the second seem to me filled with refinement, seriousness, and reason; all of which is explained by the different time periods in which they wrote, and that Virgil is more modern than Homer by eight or nine hundred years.

> [*Je mets une grande différence entre les ouvrages d'Homère et ceux de Virgile. Autant que ceux du premier [. . .] me paraissent pleins de grossièreté, de puérilité, et d'extravagance; autant ceux du dernier me semblent remplis de finesse, de gravité, et de raison : ce qui ne vient que de la différence des temps où ils ont écrit, et de ce que Virgile est plus moderne qu'Homère de huit ou neuf cents ans.*] (3.126).[11]

Perrault repeats the same line of argument to praise Cicero's modernity:

> I have great esteem for Cicero; since he is a Modern in comparison to Demosthenes, he better understood the craft in which he dealt [. . .] and he came into a century that had made many new discoveries in the art of eloquence.

> [*J'estime fort Cicéron ; comme il est un Moderne à l'égard de Démosthène, il a su aussi beaucoup mieux que lui le métier dont il se mêlait, [. . .] et il est venu dans un siècle où il s'était fait beaucoup de nouvelles découvertes dans l'art de bien dire.*] (2.185)

Perrault represents here a larger trend among modern partisans in the Quarrel: he openly embraces a positive self-identification with classical Rome, roughly from the time of Cicero to that of Hadrian. As self-proclaimed champions of today's "moderns," these authors deeply sympathized with the "moderns" of the

---

11 On the relation between Virgil, the quarrel of the ancients and moderns, and Versailles, see Goupillaud 2005.

past, in this case, with the Romans who had to contend with the irrational worship of the Greek past. In his 1688 *Digression sur les Anciens et les Modernes,* Perrault's ally in arms, Fontenelle, beautifully typifies this conflation of ancient Roman modernity and contemporary France when he asserts, "There was a time when the Romans were moderns, and they complained of the infatuation that people had for the Greeks, who were then the ancients" [*Un temps a été que les Latins étaient modernes, et alors ils se plaignaient de l'entêtement que l'on avait pour les Grecs, qui étaient les anciens.]* (Fontenelle 1990, 2.428). Fontenelle's identification with the avant-garde of ancient Rome suggests that the Modern party was indeed a kind of Augustan party, and that the comparison between Versailles and ancient Rome can at times be one between two relative modernities, separated though they be by a millennium and a half.

This first foray into the manifold temporalities and multiple valences assigned to ancient Rome can be applied to the two other "Romes" evoked above, those of the Renaissance and of the subsequent seventeenth century. To probe the consequences and the resonances of this rich interplay of temporalities and cultural categories, I will focus in the following pages on the treatment of the arts in Perrault's second dialogue of the *Parallèle,* where the central sites evoked are Versailles and Rome. The dialogue is roughly divided into three principal sections covering architecture, sculpture, and painting (with concluding reflections on landscape design). Perrault assigns to each of these arts their own historical trajectories; an examination of these varying paths of progress will help illuminate something of the complex layering and interpenetration of historical periods at play. But Perrault does not simply adumbrate here various histories of Roman and French art; he more fundamentally probes the problem of what we might call the "preference for the ancient," the idealization of the Roman past which, he claims, blinds contemporaries to Versailles's manifest superiority over ancient models. I will consider this analysis of cultural nostalgia before turning, in conclusion, to the ancient party's response to Perrault's critique – and to their own radical decentering of Rome, not in favor of modern France, but instead in praise of a more ancient Greek past, thus announcing the philhellenism to prevail in the coming eighteenth century.

2 Perrault's Comparative Histories of the Arts, between Rome and Versailles

The four volumes of Perrault's *Parallèle* present a dialogue between three interlocutors touring Versailles. I will be principally examining here the remarks of the Abbé, whose artfully reasoned praise of the modern superiority makes him a spokesman for Perrault; his counterparts are a more playfully witty comrade in arms for the modern cause, the Chevalier, and, in the opposing camp, a rather dimwitted and reactionary champion of antiquity, the Président. The second dialogue, entitled "en ce qui regarde l'architecture, la sculpture et la peinture," opens with three continuing the tour of Versailles that began in the first dialogue. The very first line of the second dialogue, spoken by the Abbé, explicitly references as points of comparison the "palace of Augustus" and "the gardens of Lucullus," and thus makes immediately clear what the measuring stick of Versailles' beauty is to be: ancient Rome.[12]

Yet, as we have seen, Rome is rarely strictly defined as merely ancient. The fundamental temporal ambiguity of Rome, it's hybridity of ancient and modern, was indeed already firmly established in the opening lines of the first dialogue, when the comparison between Versailles and Rome is first raised. Here the stodgy ancient apologist, the Président, is reprimanded by the Abbé for his prejudices against modern France:

> Le Président: You can say all you want, but I doubt that Versailles will ever match Tivoli or Frascati.
> L'Abbé: I'm astonished at your bias. It's been more than twenty years since you've been to Versailles, and you boldly declare yourself in favor of the beautiful buildings of Italy; wait until you've seen it! But I'm wrong. Even though Versailles contains more beauties than fifty Tivolis or as many Frascatis put together, it will always lose out in your mind.

> [Le Président: *Vous me direz tout ce qu'il vous plaira, mais je doute que Versailles vaille jamais Tivoli ni Frascati.*
> L'Abbé: *J'admire votre prévention. Il y a plus de vingt ans que vous n'avez été à Versailles, et vous prononcez hardiment en faveur des belles maisons d'Italie, attendez que vous l'ayez vu. Mais j'ai tort. Quoique Versailles renferme seul plus de beautés que cinquante Tivoli et autant de Frascati mis ensemble, il perdra toujours sa cause dans votre esprit.*] (1.6)

Tivoli and Frascati present richly layered comparisons with Versailles: both, like the French palace, are homes to splendid countryside residencies outside the capital city, and were prized in Roman antiquity by both the cultural elite (Horace for Tivoli, Cicero for Frascati) and political power (Augustus and famously Hadrian for the first, Cicero again for the second). But the references to the beauties of the ancient sites draw as much upon their modern repurposing for magnificent Renaissance villas as upon the remains of their classical prestige. Indeed, the comparison to the gardens and extensive waterworks of the Renaissance Villa

---

12 Comparisons to classical antiquity, and specifically Rome, characterize the earliest written description of Versailles from the 1660's; see Berger 2008.

d'Este seem to be first and foremost in mind in the reference to Tivoli. And in the case of Frascati, the choice of the modern name to designate the ancient town of Tusculum clearly indicates that Perrault targets here more the town's famed six-teenth-century Villa Aldobrandini (whose innovative "water theater" Versailles emulated) than Cicero's Tusculum villa. Perrault, however, makes no effort to dis-tinguish between the ancient and modern in these references; the temporal con-fusion appears almost willful. He furthermore conflates throughout the political and cultural: an amalgamation, it must be said, deeply congruent with these sites themselves, and perfectly emblematized by Hadrian's mixture of gigantic outdoor museum and *de facto* suburban seat of government in Tivoli, making it the most resonant ancient model for Versailles's politico-artistic ambitions.

As the second dialogue advances from one art to another, Perrault slowly and sinuously develops a more theoretical framework for what often appears to be a haphazard accumulation of conversational commentary and critique. The overall aesthetic principle driving the dialogue is one of rational idealism, the promotion of ordered design above sensorial or emotional effect as the hallmark of true artistic greatness. This aesthetic position is also deeply historicized. As we have seen with the above assertions concerning Virgil's superiority over Homer (or Cicero's over Demosthenes), the perfection of rational design – and its atten-dant qualities such as order, clarity, and propriety – can only be achieved after centuries of accumulated learning and refinement.[13] But different arts, Perrault asserts, require different levels of such intellectual sophistication. And it is here that the chronological order of the arts considered in the dialogue reveals its se-cret thread. For Perrault, in a proto-Hegelian move, considers architecture the most readily perfected art, sculpture as representing a later stage of artistic devel-opment, and painting as the most complex, and thus most slowly perfected, art.

When the dialogue turns to the first art, architecture, the Abbé sketches its early progress from Egypt to Rome, stressing its increasing complexity across the centuries:

> There are two things to consider in a building, the greatness of its mass, and the beauty of its structure. Massive size may do honor to the princes or people who have who have made the expenditure. But it is only the beauty of the design and aptness [*propreté*] of the execu-tion that one must truly attribute to the architect; otherwise, we would have to esteem more highly the person who designed the least of the Egyptian pyramids, which only consists of a simple triangle, than the architects of Greece and Rome.

---

13 Perrault's importance in the transnational history of aesthetic thought was first established by Paul Oskar Kristeller 1951. On Perrault's approach to the visual arts, see also Lavezzi 2016 and Cojannot-Le Blanc 2022.

[Il y a deux choses à considérer dans un bâtiment, la grandeur de sa masse, et la beauté de sa structure ; la grandeur de la masse peut faire honneur aux Princes ou aux Peuples qui en ont fait la dépense. Mais il n'y a que la beauté du dessin et la propreté de l'exécution dont il faille véritablement tenir compte à l'Architecte, autrement il faudrait estimer davantage celui qui a donné le dessin de la moindre des Pyramides d'Égypte, qui ne consiste qu'en un simple triangle que tous les Architectes Grecs et Romains.] (1.173–174)

Here again, Perrault lauds the relatively "modern" ancient Romans (and even the classical Greeks) when viewed in chronological relation to pharaonic Egypt. The progress is considered not in technological terms, but instead in terms of abstract notions of complex composition ("beauty of design") and the propriety of the execution of the architect's overall conception. In addition, this idealization of art tends to isolate the evaluation of the work from its political context – which proves something of a paradox from an author who spills much ink in royal encomium. The pyramids may show the Pharaohs had fantastic wealth and power, but that, Perrault suggests, is irrelevant to the structures' value as art objects.[14]

When Perrault moves on to sculpture, he is, however, considerably less indulgent with ancient Roman art. The key distinction here is between, one the one hand, single-figure statuary, or sculpture in the round [*ronde-bosse*], and, on the other, the more complex art of compositional bas-relief narrative groupings. Perrault first concedes that in what he considers the more primitive art of statuary the Greeks and Romans excelled. Rendering a single human body in sculpture requires, he claims, no advanced art of perspective or sophisticated translation from three to two dimensions. It is, he claims, just a matter of mindless replication of reality in marble: "You just have to choose a beautiful model, find a good pose, and then copy it exactly" [*Il n'y a qu'à choisir un beau modèle, le poser dans une attitude agréable, et le copier ensuite fidèlement*] (1.188–189).

While the Romans could thus vaunt their triumph in the art of statuary, they were miserable failures at the more complex art of compositional and narrative sculpture, a form only perfected in modern times. Here Perrault turns to that canonical marvel of Rome, Trajan's Column, as key example:

The ancients thus excelled in statuary and did not have the same advantage in the works of other, more compositional [*plus composé*], arts that require a great amount of reflection and precepts. They did not know an infinite number of secrets of this part of sculpture even in the times when they made Trajan's Column, where there is no [knowledge of] perspective.

[Les Anciens ont donc pu exceller dans les figures de ronde-bosse, et n'avoir pas eu le même avantage dans les ouvrages des autres Arts beaucoup plus composés et qui demandent un

---

14 On Perrault's approach to architecture, and his relation to his architect brother, Claude Perrault, see Cojannot-Le Blanc 2014.

plus grand nombre de réflexions et de préceptes [. . .] Ils ignoraient une infinité de secrets de cette partie de la Sculpture dans le temps même qu'ils ont fait la colonne Trajane où il n'y a aucune perspective.] (1.189)

Perrault's choice of Trajan's Column as illustration was no accident. As part of the massive work of plaster casts produced under the auspices of the French Academy in Rome, sectional copies of the Column were molded and then transported to France and displayed in Paris; Perrault takes advantage of the public interest in the event to deride the crudity of the Roman work – and to assert that the disappointed Parisian viewing public is on his side.[15]

When the bas-reliefs [i.e., casts of Trajan's Column] were unpacked and spread out in the hall of the Palais Royal, everyone eagerly ran to see them [. . .]. It is true that people noticed some beautiful profiles and happy poses, but almost no art in the composition of the whole, no subtlety in the relief, and a great ignorance of perspective. Two or three connoisseurs [*curieux*], still full of what they had heard in Rome, broke out in loud praise of the excellence of these works; everyone else tried to be of the same opinion, since there is such honor in being charmed by all things antique, but it was no use, and everyone left unsatisfied.

[*Lorsque les bas-reliefs furent déballés et arrangés dans le Magasin du Palais Royal, on courut les voir avec impatience [. . .]. On y remarqua à la vérité de très beaux airs de tête et quelques attitudes assez heureuses, mais presque point d'Art dans la composition, nulle dégradation dans les reliefs, et une profonde ignorance de la perspective. Deux ou trois Curieux pleins encore de ce qu'ils en avaient ouï dire à Rome, s'épanchaient en louanges immodérées sur l'excellence de ces Ouvrages, le reste de la Compagnie s'efforçait d'être de leur avis ; car il y a de l'honneur à être charmé de ce qui est antique, mais ce fut inutilement et chacun s'en retourna peu satisfait.*] (1:193–194)

It is of course when he turns to the third, and culminating, art of painting that Perrault identifies the media whose sophisticated visual "compositions" can allow the imitative arts to attain their ultimate goal, in conformity with Perrault aesthetic idealism, of pleasing the mind more than the mere senses or emotions:[16]

[The ancients] never understood, unless it was very imperfectly, th[e] last part of painting which regards the composition of the picture [. . .]. The attractive order of a composition that is judiciously organized pleases our reason, and makes us feel a joy that is admittedly less intense, but more intellectual and spiritual, and thus more worthy of a man.

---

15 On the French Academy in Rome's mission to copy sculptures to be sent to Versailles and Paris, see Macsotay 2014, 147–161 and Bresc-Bautier 2002.
16 For Perrault's tripartite distinction concerning art's effect on the senses, emotions, and intellect, see Norman 2014 and Lavezzi 2016.

[Les anciens] n'ont jamais connu, si ce n'est très imparfaitement, cette troisième partie de la peinture qui regarde la composition d'un tableau [. . .]. Le bel ordre d'une composition judicieusement ordonnée plaît à la raison, et lui fait ressentir une joie moins vive à la vérité, mais plus spirituelle et plus digne d'un homme.] (1.211–214)

This long trajectory toward the ultimate intellectual triumph of painting cannot, however, be inscribed within the tight bounds of a Rome versus Versailles polarity. First of all, Perrault assigns to Greece, and not Rome, the initial (but later far surpassed) summit of painting; all the ancient painters that he names are from the Greek world.[17] Even more importantly, a third term, the Italian Renaissance, here disrupts the strict dichotomy between ancient and modern (that is, late seventeenth-century France). It is thus that Perrault adumbrates a three-staged history of painting:

> Since we are now considering the art of painting, we must begin by making the distinction, according to the various ages when it has flourished, between three periods [*classes*]: that of the time of Apelles, of Zeuxis, of Timanthes [. . .]; that of the time of Raphael, of Titian, of Paul Veronese and several other excellent Italian Masters; and that of the century in which we live. If you follow common opinion, which judges merit based on its antiquity [*ancienneté*], we would put the Age of Apelles far above that of Raphael, and that of Raphael far above our own, but I do not agree at all with this arrangement, particularly in regard to the preference given to the Age of Apelles over that that of Raphael.

> *[Puisqu'il s'agit présentement de la Peinture, il faut commencer par la distinguer suivant les divers temps où elle a fleuri, et en faire trois classes : Celle du temps d'Apelle, de Zeuxis, de Timante [. . .] ; Celle du temps de Raphaël, du Titien, de Paul Véronèse, et de plusieurs autres excellents Maîtres d'Italie, et celle du siècle où nous vivons. Si nous voulons suivre l'opinion commune qui règle presque toujours le mérite selon l'ancienneté, nous mettrons le siècle d'Apelle beaucoup au-dessus de celui de Raphaël et celui de Raphaël beaucoup au-dessus du nôtre, mais je ne suis nullement d'accord de cet arrangement, particulièrement à l'égard de la préférence qu'on donne au siècle d'Apelle sur celui de Raphaël.]* (1.197–198)

The tremendous respect that Perrault gives to the "age of Raphael" is quite an extraordinary concession in view of his general preference for all things "modern" and French. Indeed, he suggests that the art of painting was largely perfected beginning in the early sixteenth century. The opposition between Renaissance Italy and classical Greece constitutes in this field, and this field alone, the battle-

---

17 His brief consideration of ancient Roman painting dismisses it as following the "same manner" as the Greeks, although Perrault follows his usual preference for the more modern by nevertheless asserting that Roman painters, "being a little less ancient might have known something more" [*étant un peu moins anciens pourraient avoir su quelque chose davantage*] about the art than the earlier Greeks (1:219).

ground between ancients and moderns. Perrault thus devotes most of the argument regarding painting to proving the superiority of Renaissance Italy over antiquity. France seems here to be sidelined.

Perrault, however, is not yet ready to entirely abandon modern French painting, and he devotes considerable energy to a comparison between Paulo Veronese and the French painter Charles Le Brun, who was Perrault's contemporary and chief artist of Versailles. Here again the rivalry between Italy and France is perfectly incarnated by the décor of Versailles. Perrault thus undertakes an extended comparative analysis of two paintings intentionally hung side-by-side in the palace's *grands appartements*: Veronese's *The Pilgrims of Emmaus* (c.1559) and Le Brun's *The Tent of Darius* (1660–1661).[18] Although Perrault finds in Veronese's canvas certain infractions against the rules of art – and in particular against the neo-Aristotelian "unities" which neoclassical theory applied to history painting and which he contends contemporary French painters alone follow perfectly – he concludes by stating that the Italian Renaissance masters might still by many "be preferred to those of today" [*être préférés à ceux d'aujourd'hui*] (1.233). But the reasons for such a preference for the Italian past, Perrault argues, are not, if one scratches the surface, grounded in dispassionate analysis, but instead based on merely sensorial and emotional factors, and prove thus unsuitable for a truly rational and objective examination of comparative value.

3 The Lure of the Ancient

What exactly produces this adoration of a remote and foreign past? Perrault adumbrates a number of causes for the bias in favor of the ancients, all of which share fundamentally non-rational sources. Even though modern times have happily seen artists attain the judicious method and intellectual refinement necessary to lift the beholder's mind by complexly arranged compositions, Perrault must admit that, despite all the advances of the new age, the cruder pleasures of the senses and passions, which were the only ones available to primitive antiquity, are still today the most commonly appreciated. The enlightened moderns are always but a happy few among the backward *peuple*:

> In order to be admired by the whole earth, it sufficed for Apelles and Zeuxis to have charmed the eyes and touched the heart, without it being necessary for them to possess this third part of the art of painting, which aims only to please our reason; this is because the

---

18 On this pairing, see Milovanovic and Habert 2004.

third part, far from charming the great majority of common people, often impedes it from doing so, and only ends up displeasing them.

[*Il a suffi aux Apelle et aux Zeuxis pour se faire admirer de toute la terre d'avoir charmé les yeux et touché le cœur, sans qu'il leur ait été nécessaire de posséder cette troisième partie de la peinture, qui ne va qu'à satisfaire la raison; car bien loin que cette partie serve à charmer le commun du monde, elle y nuit fort souvent, et n'aboutit qu'à lui déplaire.*] (1.214)

In short, most people, including the mass of uneducated moderns, prefer the vulgar pleasure of recognizing a lifelike portrait to the more arduous task of appreciating the "intellectual" complexity of methodically designed narrative painting.

But other of antiquity's lures prey upon not just the masses, but even the most learned critics – including, one supposes, Perrault's erudite opponents in the ancient party. Among these, we may distinguish three snares that entrap even the most educated and sophisticated of critics. The first of these is purely material and sensorial: the ever seductive and suggestive varnish of time. Old paintings, even those of the more recent Renaissance masters, have benefited from the mellowing brush of time, for "time alone can cook and soften by tempering that which is too vivid [. . .] and by diluting the extremities of the colors" [*le temps seul peut cuire et adoucir en amortissant ce qui est trop vif* [. . .] *et en noyant les extrémités des couleurs les unes dans les autres* (1.235). Although Perrault claims this pleasant effect of aging colors is entirely independent of the true value of the artwork in itself, he cannot deny the "real and effective beauty that this ancientness gives" to paintings [*la beauté réelle et effective que cette ancienneté leur donne*] (1.234). He makes the same argument in regard to sculpture concerning the seductive patina of age, mocking the counterfeiters of ancient statuary who soak their freshly-made bright modern copies in manure [*fumier*] in order to fool connoisseurs with a faux varnish signaling antiquity (1.184). The glamour of the faraway past is thus revealed to be, quite literally, nothing but a coat of muck.

The second non-rational basis for the love of the ancients is more mental than sensorial, and it lies in a moral flaw that preys upon the scholarly: pride in learning. We have already seen this critique of vanity at work in the final line of Perrault's description of the Parisian exhibition of the Trajan's Column copies, where he derides the self-proclaimed connoisseurs who, "full of what they had heard in Rome" believe that there is great "honor in being charmed by all things antique." In parallel, Perrault repeatedly affirms that the champions Roman literature are simply smugly defending a dead language, Latin, that it took so much time for them to master. There appears to be no greater fuel for the preference for the past than pedantry.

But Perrault's condemnation of vain learning goes beyond, and indeed deeper, than this denunciation of pretentious erudition. Beyond moral analysis, he attempts to uncover what we might call an experiential grounding for the prejudice in favor of Roman antiquity. This is the third and final bias that Perrault tackles. The intimate and personal experiences that promote a love for ancient Rome – its literature and artworks – are double: the exotic pleasure of tourism and the irresistible appeal of nostalgia for one's own youthful reading of the classics.

In regard to the specious attractions of travel, Perrault takes aim at the secular pilgrimage to Rome and Italy, the Renaissance Humanist voyage south that will of course spread well beyond a select few scholars and connoisseurs in the next century's growing passion for the Grand Tour. (One can imagine Perrault rolling over in his grave at Goethe's enthusiasm in his *Voyage to Italy*.) Perrault thus unmasks the purely accessory and material attractions of the trip to Rome that falsely magnifies in the viewer's imagination the value of an artwork such the Capitoline equestrian statue of Marcus Aurelius:

> If the title of "ancient" is of great weight and merit for the work of a sculptor, then so too is the circumstance of being in a faraway country – one that it costs a voyage of three or four hundred leagues to see – which contributes no less to make it highly prized and of great reputation. Back when you had to go to Rome to see the Marcus Aurelius, nothing could equal this famous equestrian statue, and nothing was more enviable than the happiness of those who had seen it. Now that we have it [i.e., the copy] in Paris, it is unbelievable how people neglect it, even though it is perfectly cast, and [has] has the same beauty and grace as the original.

> [*Si le titre d'ancien, est d'un grand poids et d'un grand mérite pour un ouvrage de sculpture, la circonstance d'être dans un pays éloigné, et qu'il en coûte pour le voir un voyage de trois ou quatre cents lieues, ne contribue pas moins à lui donner du prix et de la réputation. Quand il fallait aller à Rome pour voir le Marc Aurèle, rien n'était égal à cette fameuse figure équestre, et on ne pouvait trop envier le bonheur de ceux qui l'avaient vue. Aujourd'hui que nous l'avons à Paris, il n'est pas croyable combien on la néglige, quoi qu'elle soit moulée très exactement, et qu['] elle ait la même beauté et la même grâce que l'Original.*] (1.185–186)

The dematerialized nature of Perrault's approach to art, in which the "circumstances" of its viewing are entirely discounted, extends to book-learning as well. "We no longer believe that a young man must travel to make himself eloquent" since, thanks to the invention of the printing press, a well-furnished library in Paris provides more knowledge "than Cicero could learn in all his voyages" [*l'on ne s'avise plus de faire voyager un jeune homme pour le rendre Éloquent [. . .] ; il y a plus de choses à apprendre dans une Bibliothèque [. . .] que Cicéron n'en pouvait apprendre dans tous ses voyages*] (1.273). The pleasures of embodied travel, the escape from familiarly modern France, are a source of bias that inevitably – and Perrault argues, unjustly – favor Rome.

Finally, Perrault's critique is broadened to another form of travel, affection for one's faraway and lost youth, the nostalgia for childhood. We have already seen that Perrault attacks the alleged pedantry of the lovers of antiquity, who prize the Latin they learned at school above the grace of modern languages. But the critique goes well beyond a moral condemnation of shallow vanity; Perrault plumbs the psyche of his opponents to understand the affective basis for their unreasoned passion for Latin works: "Others maintain a love for the authors they read when they were young, like for the places where they spent the first years of their lives, because these places and authors bring back to their mind pleasant ideas of their childhood." [*Les autres conservent un amour pour les Auteurs qu'ils ont lus étant jeunes, comme pour les lieux où ils ont passé les premières années de leur vie ; parce que ces lieux et ces Auteurs leur remettent dans l'esprit les idées agréables de leur jeunesse*] (1.100). Perrault thus locates in the subconscious of the ancient partisan a kind of Bovarysme *avant la lettre*: a desire, powered by youthful literary reading, to escape prosaic modernity and find refuge in an exalted and faraway past.

4 Decentering Rome: The Ancient Party Response

Whatever truth there may be (and there is certainly some) in Perrault's critique of the irrational love for antiquity, his opponents in real life of course laid out their own rationales for their position. But if we limit ourselves here to the ancient party position specifically concerning Rome, we will find little direct contradiction of Perrault's overall criticism. Why? Because, simply put, ancient partisans in the quarrel were concerned first and foremost with Greece, and not Rome. Homer was their hero, not Virgil. Deeply attached to antiquity, they homed in on the most ancient of the ancients, and not the "moderns" among the ancients preferred by Perrault and Fontenelle. Thus when the leader of the ancient party, the poet and critic Nicolas Boileau, wrote a letter directly to Perrault during a 1690s cease-fire in the debate, he can in good faith assure his opponent that their disagreement on the score of Rome is in fact minimal:

> You and I are not so far apart in our thinking as you think [. . .]. Your intention is to show that [. . .] the Age of Louis the Great [i.e., XIV] is not only comparable but superior to all the most illustrious ages of antiquity and even to the Age of Augustus. You'll be quite surprised when I tell you that I am entirely of your opinion on this matter.

> [*Nous ne sommes pas même vous et moi si éloignés d'opinion que vous pensez. [. . .] Votre dessein est de montrer que [. . .] le siècle de Louis le Grand est non seulement comparable, mais supérieur à tous les plus fameux siècles de l'Antiquité, et même au siècle d'Auguste. Vous allez donc être bien étonné, quand je vous dirai, que je suis sur cela entièrement de votre avis.*] (Boileau, *Lettre à Perrault*, 1966, 571)

Boileau then devotes several pages to a nuanced catalogue of comparisons, covering a wide gamut of fields, between Augustan Rome and seventeenth-century France. In the political domain, Boileau is ready to entertain French advances over imperial Rome, affirming by understatement that the moderns are by no means deficient in this area, and that "the Roman Augustus would not triumph over the French Augustus" (meaning Louis XIV) [*l'Auguste des Latins ne l'emporte pas sur l'Auguste des Français*] (Boileau 1966, 573). As for the sciences, the defender of the ancients emphatically proclaims himself delighted to "triumph with Perrault" over the defeated Roman naturalists (Boileau 1966, 572). He likewise concurs with Perrault on contemporary superiority in philosophy, elevating far above the Romans both Descartes and Gassendi.

Turning to literature and the arts, Boileau fully agrees with Perrault that in the domain of tragic drama "we are superior to the Romans," and proceeds to trash – with a disdain that would delight the most ardent of modern partisans – the "pompous" plays attributed to Seneca (Boileau 1966, 572). As for the visual arts, Boileau also finds every reason to believe in France's superiority over classical Rome.

> [One cannot] name a single talented [*habile*] architect, a single talented sculptor, a single talented painter among the Romans. Those who became famous in Rome in each of the arts [were] Greeks of Europe and Asia, who came to Rome to practice the arts that the Romans, so to speak, did not know; while today the whole world recognizes the reputation of the works of our Poussins, our Le Bruns, our Girardons, our Mansarts.

> [[*On ne peut*] *nommer un seul habile architecte, un seul habile sculpteur, un seul habile peintre Latin. Ceux qui ont fait du bruit à Rome dans tous ces arts, étant des Grecs d'Europe et d'Asie, qui venaient pratiquer chez les Latins des arts que les Latins, pour ainsi dire, ne connaissaient point : au lieu que toute la terre aujourd'hui est pleine de la réputation et des ouvrages de nos Poussins, de nos Le Bruns, de nos Girardons, et de nos Mansards.*] (Boileau 1966, 573)

Boileau's numerous concessions to Perrault prove, however, to be artfully circumscribed. For the ancient partisan shrewdly reminds the reader at various points that he is delimiting his parallel to one between modern France and the Rome of *only* the Augustus age. When, for example, he asserts the superiority of modern French comedy to that of the time of Augustus, he wryly notes that the Roman emperor reigned well *after* the apogee of Latin comedy, for under Augustus "there was not a single comic playwright whose name is worth remembering: the Plautuses, Ceciliuses and Terences were dead a century before." In typical ancient partisan style, the praise here goes not to the Augustan but to the pre-Augustan, not to the more modern imitator but to the more ancient inventor.

Here lies the secret of Boileau's parallel. It may operate through a comparison of two highly civilized (thus essentially "modern") periods, imperial Rome and absolutist France; but it does so by explicitly contrasting these two with earlier, more creative, and more ancient periods. Hence the regressive detour by way of Plautus and Terence. The most powerful oppositional figure to the "Roman Augustus"/ "French Augustus" dyad, however, is not found in an earlier Latin antiquity, but in the Greek world. So it is that we have seen that when Boileau turns to the visual arts, he deprecatingly notes that the only successful artists in ancient Rome were imported from the Hellenized east, "the Greeks of Europe and Asia, who came to Rome to practice the arts that the Romans, so to speak, did not know." Exploiting the fractures dividing the Greco-Roman past, Boileau privileges Greece at Rome's expense. Indeed, the whole exercise of Boileau's letter aims to subvert the notion of a "parallel" as practiced by Perrault, to undermine any binary opposition between antiquity and modernity.

Yet we have also seen that in his own history of the visual arts, Perrault as well frequently subverts the binary comparison; one might say he thus laid the groundwork, paradoxically enough, for Boileau's riposte. Whereas Perrault's complexification of the parallel tends to layer in supplementary historical periods in order to valorize a more "modern" past (Italian Renaissance above Roman antiquity, Roman antiquity above classical Greece), Boileau's operates in the opposite direction, revealing a Roman golden age that simply gilds a previously existing antiquity that is more vital, authentic, and inventive. It is a lesson that will prove invaluable to the next century and its rising philhellenism, to the considerable loss of Rome.[19]

Bibliography

Bahier-Porte, Christelle, and Delphine Reguig. Eds. *Anciens et Modernes face aux pouvoirs: l'Église, le Roi, les Académies (1687–1750)*. Paris: Honoré Champion, 2022.

Berger, Robert W. "The earliest literary descriptions of the gardens of Versailles." *Studies in the History of Gardens & Designed Landscapes* 28.3–4 (2008): 456–487.

Boileau, Nicolas [Boileau-Despréaux]. *Œuvres complètes*. Ed. Françoise Escal. Paris: Gallimard (Bibliothèque de la Pléiade), 1966.

Bos, Jacques, and Jan Rotmans. Eds. *The Long Quarrel: Past and Present in the Eighteenth Century*. Leiden: Brill's Studies in Intellectual History, 2021.

---

19 On the impact of the quarrel on eighteenth-century philhellenism, see among others, Décultot 2000, Norman 2011, 213–226, and Robertson 2016.

Bresc-Bautier, Geneviève. "Les transports vers Paris de sculptures de l'Académie de France à Rome." *L'Idéal classique: Les échanges artistiques entre Rome et Paris au temps de Bellori, 1640–1700*. Ed. Olivier Bonfait. Paris: Simogny, 2002. 327–362.

Bullard, Paddy, and Alexis Tadié. Eds. *Ancients and Moderns in Europe: Comparative Perspectives*. Oxford: Voltaire Foundation, 2016.

Cojannot-Le Blanc, Marianne. "Les artistes privés de l'invention? Réflexions sur les 'desseins' de Charles et Claude Perrault pour les Bâtiments du roi dans les années 1660." *Dix-septième siècle* 264.3 (2014): 467–479.

Cojannot-Le Blanc, Marianne. "Charles Perrault et l'Académie royale de peinture et de sculpture." *Anciens et Modernes face aux pouvoirs: l'Église, le Roi, les Académies* (see supra). 167–177.

Cornette, Joël. "Le Versailles des contemporains de Louis XIV." *Versailles: Le pouvoir de la pierre*. Ed. Joël Cornette. Paris: Tallandier, 2006. 251–321.

Décultot, Elisabeth. *Johann Joachim Winckelmann: Enquête sur la genèse de l'histoire de l'art*. Paris: Presses Universitaires de France, 2000.

Ferrier-Caverivière, Nicole. *L'image de Louis XIV dans la littérature française, de 1660 à 1715*. Paris: PUF, 1981.

Fontenelle, Bernard Le Bovier de. *Œuvres complètes*. Ed. Alain Niderst. 9 vols. Paris: Fayard, 1990–2001.

Goupillaud, Ludivine. *De l'or de Virgile aux ors de Versailles: Métamorphoses de l'épopée dans la seconde moitié du XVIIᵉ siècle en France*. Geneva: Droz, 2005.

Hartog, François. *Régimes d'historicité: Présentisme et expériences du temps*. Paris: Seuil, 2003.

Hartog, François. *Anciens, modernes, sauvages*. Paris: Galaade, 2005.

Haskell, Francis, and Nicholas Penny. *Taste and the Antique: The Lure of Classical Sculpture, 1500–1900*. New Haven: Yale University Press, 1981.

Kristeller, Paul Oskar. "The Modern System of the Arts: A Study in the History of Aesthetics." *Journal of the History of Ideas* 12.3 (Oct. 1951): 496–527; part 2, 13.1 (Jan. 1952): 17–46.

Lavezzi, Elisabeth. "Painting and the Tripartite Model in Charles Perrault's *Parallèle des Anciens et des Modernes*." *Ancients and Moderns in Europe: Comparative Perspectives* (see supra). 155–170.

Macsotay, Tomas. *The Profession of Sculpture in the Paris Académie*. Oxford: Voltaire Foundation, 2014.

Maral, Alexandre, and Nicolas Milovanovic. Eds. *Versailles et l'antique*. Paris: Artlys, 2012.

Marin, Louis. "Classical, Baroque: Versailles or the Architecture of the Prince." Trans. Anna Lehman. *Yale French Studies* 80 (1991): 167–182.

Milovanovic, Nicolas, and Jean Habert. "Charles Le Brun contre Paul Véronèse: la *Famille de Darius* et les *Pèlerins d'Emmaüs* au château de Versailles." *Revue du Louvre et des musées de France* 5 (2004): 63–72.

Morellet, Laurent [alias Sieur Combes]. *Explication historique de ce qu'il y a de plus remarquable dans la maison royale de Versailles et en celle de Monsieur à Saint-Cloud*. Paris: C. Nego, 1681.

Norman, Larry F. *The Shock of the Ancient: Literature and History in Early-Modern France*. Chicago: University of Chicago Press, 2011.

Norman, Larry F. "La pensée esthétique de Charles Perrault." *XVIIᵉ siècle* 264.3 (2014): 481–492.

Perrault, Charles. *Parallèle des Anciens et des Modernes, en ce qui regarde les arts et les sciences*. 4 vols. Paris: Coignard, 1688–97. Online critical edition: https://parallele-anciens-modernes.huma-num.fr/corpus/PAM0106 (26 June 2023)

Pommier, Edouard. "Versailles, the Image of the Souverain." *Realms of Memory: The Construction of the French Past*. Trans. Arthur Goldhammer. Eds. Pierre Nora and Lawrence D. Kritzman. New York: Columbia University Press, 1998. 293–323.

Rabinovitch, Oded. "Versailles as a Family Enterprise: The Perraults, 1660–1700." *French Historical Studies* 36.3 (2013): 385–416.

Robertson, Ritchie. "Ancients, Moderns and the Future: the *Querelle* in Germany from Winckelmann to Schiller." *Ancients and Moderns in Europe: Comparative Perspectives* (see *supra*). 257–275.

Taylor, Helena. "État présent: The Quarrel of the Ancients and Moderns." *French Studies* 74.4, (2020): 605–620.

III Classicism Enlightened and Revolutionized

Philip Hardie

Translatio laudum. Rubens' Maria de' Medici cycle, and Voltaire's *Henriade*

Classicizing, and more specifically Romanizing, imagery was a central strategy of representations of the early modern French monarchy, in texts and images both contemporary with kings and their political and military programmes, and those created at a distance in time. Best known is the vast amount of classicizing imagery constructed around the person of Louis XIV, in the media of architecture, sculpture, painting, medals, court entertainments and music, and texts in poetry and prose.[1] The sun king, after all, is an idea and an image deeply rooted in classical precedents. The emperor Nero, for example, used solar and Apolline imagery to project his power; a modern biography of Nero by a leading ancient historian, which attempts to rehabilitate the reputation of this notorious Roman emperor, argues that Nero exploited this imagery in a consistent policy of imperial self-fashioning.[2]

My chief exhibits are a cycle of paintings, and a poem, on Louis XIV's grandfather, Henri IV. As a preliminary example of a Roman image of Henri IV that was created to make a statement about the king and his achievements shortly after his assassination in 1610, and that developed different political meanings long after his death, I take the equestrian statue of Henri IV on the Pont Neuf.[3] It was erected in 1614, indirectly commissioned by Henri's widow Maria de' Medici, from the leading Italian sculptor Giambologna, and completed by his pupil Pietro Tacca. It was the first free-standing equestrian statue of a monarch in a public place in France, and was modelled, like many other equestrian statues of rulers, on the equestrian statue of Marcus Aurelius in Rome.[4] 'The pedestal, designed by Pietro Francavallia, highlighted Henri's contribution to the glory and well-being of the French by commemorating his battles and his entry into Paris, which marked the end of the French wars of religion.[5] The statue was destroyed during the French Revolution, in 1792, and a recreation was finished by 1818, 'simultaneously symboliz[ing]', according to Victoria Thompson, 'the legitimacy of the re-

---

1 See Néraudau 1986.
2 See Champlin 2003, esp. ch. 5 'Shining Apollo'.
3 See Thompson 2012.
4 See Stewart 2012. After c. 1480 a consensus emerged that it was a statue of Marcus Aurelius, rather than Constantine the Great.
5 Thompson 2012, 8.

https://doi.org/10.1515/9783111334776-006

stored monarchy, reconciliation following a long period of civil conflict, and the legitimate authority of the crowd.'[6]

But my main exhibit from the visual arts is Rubens' cycle of paintings on the life of Maria de' Medici. This was executed between 1622 and 1625 for a gallery in Maria's Palais de Luxembourg, and now hangs in the Louvre. The cycle illustrates Maria de' Medici's relationship to two French kings, her husband Henri IV, and their son, Louis XIII, for whom Maria acted as regent, subsequently becoming dowager queen. Maria's relationship with her son, once he became king in his own right, was marked by the familial discord of repeated fallings-out and reconcilations. The centrepiece of Rubens' 24-canvas cycle, placed at the far end of the gallery, marks the turning point of Maria's life, on the death of her husband.[7] A single canvas pairs the death of Henri IV, shown ascending to the heavens in a Roman imperial apotheosis, with the proclamation of the regency of Maria. Typical of the cycle as a whole is the combination in this single canvas of, on the one hand, the mythological and allegorical, the elevation of Henri by the figures of Jupiter and Saturn to a heaven populated by the classical gods, and, on the other, the historical, the proclamation of Maria's regency in the monastery of the Grands-Augustins. The mythological and allegorical components of the cycle are steeped in Rubens', and his advisors', scholarly study of the iconography of antiquity, both through direct access to ancient coins, medals, cameos, and larger works of art, and through the mediated form of Renaissance iconologies and emblems. In celebrating a queen and her royal husband and son, Rubens draws extensively on the iconography of ancient Roman imperial panegyric.

My text is Voltaire's ten-book epic the *Henriade*, on Henri IV's war with the Catholic Ligue, given Aristotelian unity by taking for its main narrative the single action of the siege of Paris in 1590.[8] Voltaire (François-Marie Arouet, as he was before 1718) conceived the project when he was a very young man, in the years 1715–1717. It was first published in 1723 in nine books, with the title *La Ligue, ou Henry le Grand*; the first edition of an expanded ten-book version with the title *La Henriade* was published in 1728. Voltaire continued to make alterations to the text until the edition of 1757.[9] In the eighteenth century, and well into the nineteenth,

---

6 Thompson 2012, 5.

7 My numbering of the 24 canvases follows that of Millen and Woolf 1989; ibid. 20–21 for a hypothetical reconstruction of the plan of the Luxembourg gallery.

8 A single action created through the poetic licence of taking the siege of 1590 as continuous with Henri of Navarre's conversion to Catholicism in 1593, and his welcome into Paris in 1594.

9 References to and quotations from the *Henriade* are from the 1757 text as printed in Taylor 2005, unless otherwise specified.

the *Henriade* enjoyed a fame and success that most modern readers find hard to understand.

The *Henriade* brings Rome to Paris through its ambition of achieving the status of a French *Aeneid*, Virgil's Roman national epic, whose structure, plot, and characters the *Henriade* tracks, at points very closely, in an imitation that is at the same time a 'correction' of major aspects of the *Aeneid*. The structural imitation of the *Aeneid* is particularly close in the first three books. Book 1 launches the reader *in medias res*, as we find Bourbon (Henri king of Navarre, the future Henri IV of France) and Valois (Henri III) already besieging Paris. Bourbon is sent on a secret mission to ask for support from Elizabeth I of England, undertaking a sea-journey in which he survives a storm, to land in a foreign country and there meet with a foreign queen, all as in *Aeneid* 1. In a flashback narrative in books 2 and 3, corresponding to Aeneas' narrative to Dido of his sufferings and adventures so far in *Aeneid* 2 and 3, Bourbon narrates to Elizabeth the evils of the wars of religion in France. In book 2 a vivid account of the St Bartholomew's Day Massacre in 1572 reworks Aeneas' narrative to Dido of the Sack of Troy in *Aeneid* 2. Virgil's death of Priam is replayed in the death of Admiral de Coligny.

The reworking in the encounter of Bourbon and Elizabeth of the Dido and Aeneas episode swerves from the Virgilian plot of a meeting that will lead to future undying enmity between two nations once joined by ties of hospitality and love. Instead England becomes a model of peace and constitutional government, reflecting Voltaire's admiration for England. The absence of an erotic encounter between the virtuous Henri and the English virgin queen is the reason why the *Henriade* ceases to follow the plot of the *Aeneid* so closely when we get to the fourth book of the epic. The hero does succumb to erotic infatuation and enervation, but much later in the poem, in the penultimate book 9, in a self-contained episode without further consequences. There Henri (notorious for his many mistresses) is recalled from his liaison with the irresistible Gabrielle d'Estrées by his Achates, the sternly stoic Du-Plessis-Mornay, in an episode that owes more to the rescue of Ruggiero from Alcina in *Orlando furioso*, or the rescue of Rinaldo from Armida in *Gerusalemme liberata*, than it does to Aeneas' abandonment of Dido in the *Aeneid*. The *Henriade* ends not with the angry killing of the enemy leader in a duel,[10] but with Henri's humanity in relieving the effects of famine in the be-

---

10 A reworking of the final duel in the *Aeneid* between Aeneas and Turnus is displaced on to the encounter of Turenne and d'Aumale in the climactic siege action of book 10, and preceded by another version of the final Virgilian duel in the encounter of Egmont and Henri at 8.364–92, with an imitation of the final line of the *Aeneid* at 391–2 'Et son âme en courroux s'envola chez les morts, | Où l'aspect de son père excita ses remords': cf. *Aen.* 12.952 *uitaque cum gemitu fugit indignata sub umbras.*

sieged Paris, and the final recognition of Henri as king by the leader of the Ligue, the Duke of Mayenne.

In producing a French national epic, Voltaire brought to completion something that Ronsard had failed to achieve with the *Franciade*, begun in the 1540s for Henri II, but of which only four of a planned 24 books were finally published in 1572 for Charles IX. The *Franciade*, like the *Aeneid*, tells of the legendary Trojan origins of a nation, in the person of a Trojan ancestor, Francion, who travelled from the sack of Troy to a new foundation in Gaul. Voltaire chose to write an epic on an episode in relatively recent history, rather than from the remote legendary past. Unlike the unfinished *Franciade*, the *Henriade* is unambiguously a panegyrical epic, entirely in keeping with an ancient and post-classical definition of epic as poetry of praise, and one would be very hard put to it to hear two voices in the poem.

Voltaire limited the scope for drawing on the vocabulary of Roman imperial panegyric through his elimination of the divine machinery of Homeric and Virgilian epic. In this he follows the precedent of Lucan's historical epic on the Roman civil war. Voltaire does deploy a cast of personifications, in addition to the historical actors, but replaces the Olympian gods with the Christian God and his intermediary between heaven and earth, St Louis, ancestor and protecting saint of Henri Bourbon.

Notwithstanding the avoidance of classical mythology, other than in some of the similes, there are a number of areas in which productive comparisons may be made between the classicizing of Rubens' cycle of paintings, and of Voltaire's epic. One general consideration that might predispose one to look for parallels between the creations of Rubens and Voltaire is the fact that Rubens' visual celebration of Maria de' Medici takes the rather unusual form of a pictorial biography, a narrative cycle, for which one model might be epic as the premier literary narrative form.[11] I leave aside the question of any more direct connection between the subject-matters of Rubens' cycle and Voltaire's epic. I would assume that Voltaire is at least quite likely to have seen the cycle of paintings. I point to three areas in particular where commonalties might be sought:

---

11 For suggestive reflections along these lines see Cojannot-Le Blanc and Prioux 2018, 210, pointing out that the spatial and temporal dilation of the cycle, and the theme of apotheosis, give it the amplitude of an epic; that 24 canvases is the same number as the books of both the Homeric epics, and of Ronsard's projected *Franciade*, which inspired a gallery for Henri IV at the chateau of Saint-Germain-en-Laye, and that the proposed Luxembourg gallery on the life of Henri IV was probably also intended to have 24 canvases. The bust of Homer on the ground in the canvas of *The education of the princess* hints that the whole cycle on the life of Maria is grounded in the fountainhead of epic.

1. The connections between heaven and earth, and, descending deeper, hell, and travel up and down the vertical axis of the universe. A moralized and divinized spatial hierarchy provides the armature of much imperial panegyric of ancient Rome, with the final legitimation and sanctification of an emperor, as a Divus, through the fiction of an ascent from the funeral pyre in apotheosis. The plot of Virgil's *Aeneid* is one of horizontal geographical displacement, in a journey from Troy to Italy, from east to west, but on this is overlaid a plot of travel along the vertical axis, with the final, Fate-driven, destination of translation to the skies of Aeneas, and of his descendants, future rulers of Rome, Romulus, Julius Caesar, and Augustus. That will happen after the defeat of forces of evil and chaos, which have been summoned up from the Underworld.

2. Discord. In the *Aeneid*, the most dangerous and disruptive of these forces of disorder is Allecto, the Fury whom the goddess Juno calls up from the Underworld to sow all-out war between Trojans and Italians. Allecto is a supernatural embodiment of Discord, or in Latin *Discordia*. The war in Italy, between Italians and ancestors of the Romans, is an image of Roman civil wars that will break out in much later, historical, time. Civil war is a central theme of post-Virgilian Roman epic: Lucan's *Civil War*, on the historical war between Pompey and Julius Caesar, and Statius' *Thebaid*, on the legendary war of the Seven against Thebes, the warriors who supported Oedipus' son Polynices in his dispute with his brother Eteocles, who had usurped sole rule of Thebes for himself. Statius' legendary epic, like that of Virgil, is also a commentary on the events and ideology of Roman history. Civil war, and wars of religion, ran through the reign of Henri IV. Discord is a major theme of both Rubens' Maria de' Medici cycle and Voltaire's *Henriade*, and in both cases extensive use is made of classical texts and images.

More generally, plots and imagery of civil war process the abstract opposition of order and disorder, of cosmos and chaos. This is the theme of Michel Jeanneret's *Versailles, ordre et chaos*,[12] a study of the anxieties of the Grand Siècle, including extensive discussion of the iconography of the landscaped gardens of Versailles, and of the plots and imagery of the ballets de cour and operas at the court of Versailles. All of these productions draw very heavily on classical sources. One question to which I do not know the answer, is how seminal the iconography of Rubens' Maria de' Medici cycle was for subsequent developments of political and panegyrical art under Louis XIII and Louis XIV.

---

12 Jeanneret 2012.

3. A smaller topic is the role of Vérité, Truth, both as it relates to the desire to arrive at the historical truth of the events that form Rubens' and Voltaire's subject-matters, and as it relates, self-reflexively, to the awareness and anxiety of the painter and the poet as to the truthfulness of the forms of representation that they have chosen for the historical content of, respectively, their paintings and their poetry.

1 Heaven and Earth, Gods and Men

A standard device in the Roman representation of imperial power, with precedents in the Roman Republic and in the panegyric of Hellenistic Greek monarchs, is the association or identification of the emperor with a god: Jupiter, Apollo, the sun god, Mars, Mercury. By the end of the *Aeneid*, Aeneas has moved closer to wielding the power of Jupiter, hurling his spear with the force of a thunderbolt. Suetonius (*Life of Augustus* 70) tells of a scandalous dinner put on when Augustus was still Octavian, the dinner of the twelve gods, at which the guests appeared in the guise of gods and goddesses, Octavian taking the part of Apollo. Such identifications are particularly common in the small-scale, and more private, media of gems and cameos,[13] a passion for which Rubens shared with his close friend and advisor, the antiquary Nicolas-Claude Fabri de Peiresc.[14] One example is a cameo of Claudius and Messalina as Jupiter and Ceres, of which there is a drawing by Rubens.[15] There are already examples in sixteenth-century French royal iconography of the identification of earthly rulers as celestial gods, at Fontainebleau and Tanlay.[16] At the eighth station of the procession in Paris in 1610 celebrating Henri IV's newly crowned queen Maria, abandoned after the assassination of Henri, the royal couple were to be represented in the guise of Jupiter and Juno; the emblematic association of Maria and Juno has a longer history, before and after 1610.[17] In early modern France, as in England, there was also a wider fashion for mythological portraiture, the portrayal of the sitter in the guise of a classical god or hero.[18]

I preface my detailed commentary on Rubens' approximations and equations of the human and the divine with a late antique example from the panegyrical

---

13 For a comprehensive survey of early imperial cameos see Smith 2021.
14 The importance of ancient cameos as sources for the iconography of the Maria de' Medici cycle is explored exhaustively in Cojannot-Le Blanc and Prioux 2018.
15 Discussed and illustrated by Cojannot-Le Blanc and Prioux 2018, 130–131.
16 Millen and Wolf 1989, 77. On the classicizing iconography of François I see Tauber 2009.
17 Millen and Wolf 1989, 77–79.
18 For France see Bardon 1974.

epics of Claudian, a poet more widely read in the early modern period than today, in part precisely because of his usefulness as a source for themes and topics of royal and imperial praise.[19] This is the elegiac *praefatio* to *On the sixth consulship of Honorius*, recited, it is to be assumed, at the inauguration of Honorius as consul on 1 January AD 404 (lines 11–26):

> Me quoque Musarum studium sub nocte silenti
>   artibus adsuetis sollicitare solet.
> namque poli media stellantis in arce videbar
>   ante pedes summi carmina ferre Iovis;
> utque favet somnus, plaudebant numina dictis   15
>   et circumfusi sacra corona chori.
> Enceladus mihi carmen erat victusque Typhoeus:
>   hic subit Inarimen, hunc gravis Aetna domat.
> quam laetum post bella Iovem susceperat aether
>   Phlegraeae referens praemia militiae!   20
> Additur ecce fides nec me mea lusit imago
>   inrita nec falsum somnia misit ebur.
> en princeps, en orbis apex aequatus Olympo!
>   en quales memini, turba verenda, deos!
> fingere nil maius potuit sopor, altaque vati   25
>   conventum caelo praebuit aula parem.

Me too in the silence of the night devotion to the Muses commonly troubles with my accustomed craft. For I seemed to find myself in the very heart of the citadel of the starry heavens, bringing my songs before the feet of Jupiter the Most High. And, such is the flattery of dreams, the gods applauded what I sang, and so also all the sacred throng that stood around Enceladus was my theme, and Typhoeus conquered (one lies beneath Inarime, the other weighty Etna holds in subjection); and how joyful was Heaven when, the war concluded, it welcomed Jupiter, receiving the spoils of battle on the fields of Phlegra! See how confirmation is now granted me, and my vision has not played me false, nor has the deceitful Gate of Ivory sent dreams that come to nothing. Behold our Prince, behold the world's pinnacle made level with Olympus! Behold the gods as I remember them, a venerable host! Sleep could imagine nothing greater, and this lofty hall has shown the bard a gathering that is the peer of heaven. (Trans. M. Dewar)

Here the identification of Olympus and the imperial court in Rome is made through the medium of a dream, a dream that turns out to be true. There is a self-conscious playfulness here about the fictions and hyperboles of imperial panegyric that we might do well to bear in mind when reading Rubens' canvases. It should also be remembered that Claudian deploys the vocabulary of pagan my-

---

19 On the importance of Claudian's panegyrics for the conception of the Maria de' Medici cycle see Saward 1982.

Fig. 1: Rubens, *Maria de' Medici cycle*. 'The Fates spin the destiny of the future queen', photo © RMN-Grand Palais (musée du Louvre) / Christian Jean / Hervé Lewandowski.

thology in praise of a thoroughly Christian emperor without any friction between the pagan and the Christian, something that is equally true of the use of pagan imagery to praise the Christian monarchs of the early modern period.

I turn now to the Rubens cycle, in order trace the progressive association and identification of the royal couple on earth, Maria de' Medici and Henri IV, with the pagan gods of Olympus. At the top of the canvas that inaugurates the life history of Maria, even before her birth,[20] *The Fates spin the destiny of the future queen* (3) (Fig. 1), is seated the loving matrimonial pair of Jupiter and Juno, in a pose that echoes that in a cameo, the Gemma Constantiniana, now in Leiden and of which a drawing was made in the studio of Rubens, which shows (probably) the emperor Constantine and his wife Fausta seated in a triumphal chariot, in the likeness of the thunderbolt-bearing Jupiter and Ceres, holding a ear of wheat. The supreme god and his wife preside over (literally) the spinning of Maria's destiny, and, in their conjugal closeness, anticipate the future happy marriage of the royal couple on earth.

In *The presentation to Henri of the portrait of Maria* (6) (Fig. 2), Henri appears as the viewer of work of art The 'real' Henri, in a painting, looks at a painting of the 'real' Maria, so at a second degree of removal from the extra-pictorial world. At a third level, these two historical personages are framed by personifications, as the helmeted figure of France holds Henri to a steady gaze at the portrait, which is held up by a winged Hymen, symbolizing the marriage which will follow from this first encounter through image. A Cupid, pointing to the painting, personifies or embodies the desire stimulated in Henri by the image of Maria. Above, Jupiter and Juno, holding hands with again greater mutual affection than they often display in Greek mythology, gaze down on the scene on earth, anticipate the now imminent conjugal bliss to which Henri and Maria can look forward. We, as the outmost level of viewers, are invited to reflect on the way in which history, allegory, and the classical gods interact and merge into one another.

That merging reaches the point of identification in (9) *The marriage consummated at Lyons* (9) (Fig. 3). On earth reality and allegory are still kept separate: in the background there is a small topographical depiction of the real city of Lyons, while, in the foreground, there is a much larger image, a personification of the city, in a chariot drawn by lions, in the guise of the Magna Mater. In heaven we see, again, Jupiter and Juno, with, respectively, their divine attributes of eagle and peacock, but with the faces of Henri and Maria, who are now fully embodied, and portraited, in a *hieros gamos* of the supreme divine couple. But this painting looks further still into the future history of the divinized couple. The six-pointed star above the head of Jupiter/Henri is of the kind reserved for deceased emperors made gods. Henri's assassination on 14 May 1610 took place the day before Maria's

---

Fig. 2: Rubens, *Maria de' Medici cycle*. 'The presentation to Henri of the portrait of Maria',
© RMN-Grand Palais (musée du Louvre) / René-Gabriel Ojeda / Thierry Le Mage.

planned entry into Paris as crowned queen. At the eighth station of the procession the married couple were to be imaged in the likenesses of Jupiter and Juno as gods who preside over marriage.[21]

---

21 Millen and Wolf 1989, 77.

Fig. 3: Rubens, *Maria de' Medici cycle*. 'The marriage consummated at Lyons', photo © RMN-Grand Palais (musée du Louvre) / Hervé Lewandowski.

In the somewhat mysterious canvas to which is given the title of *The consignment of the regency* (11) (Fig. 4), Henri and Maria appear as their literal selves, clasping right hands over the head of the Dauphin, in a composition that reproduces that on a medal minted in 1603 to a design by Guillaume Dupré, with the legend PROPAGO IMPERII, to mark Henri's giving Maria a seat in the Council of State, and in which the three figures are the divinities Mars and Minerva, and the infant

Fig. 4: Rubens, *Maria de' Medici cycle*. 'The consignment of the regency', photo © RMN-Grand Palais (musée du Louvre) / Thierry Le Mage.

Amor. Viewers who know the medal might see an allusion to, and so quasi-identification with, the divine figures there represented, but this is perhaps to stretch the model of 'intertextuality' too far.

In the central canvas of *The death of Henri IV* and *The proclamation of the regency* (13) (Fig. 5) we watch the physical elevation of Henri from earth, which he leaves in death, to the heavens, as Jupiter, with Saturn, takes hold of the king

Fig. 5: Rubens, *Maria de' Medici cycle*. 'The death of Henri IV' and 'The proclamation of the regency', photo © RMN-Grand Palais (musée du Louvre) / René-Gabriel Ojeda / Thierry Le Mage.

to bear him up. This is a scene of Roman imperial apotheosis, with specific reference to the apotheosis of Julius Caesar after his assassination.[22] Henri is physically transported to the place that he had previously reached only in allegorical representation. In keeping with his full integration into a classical apotheosis, Henri is a cuirassed and sandalled figure *all'antica*. The first of the gods to confront him on his journey up through the zodiac is the deified Hercules (Gallicus), a local variety of the hero who, as a mortal who earned divinity through his exploits on earth, is a ubiquitous figure for the ruler with celestial aspirations, both in classical antiquity and in the Renaissance.

The main actors in the apotheosis are male. The female gods are shunted off to the far right of the segment of the zodiac towards which Henri is travelling, while, in the foreground and, merely reacting in shock and grief to the death of the king, are what are probably to be identified as two winged Victories. In the paired scene, on the right, of *The proclamation of the regency*, the main actors are all female: the historical queen, attended by personifications of France, Providence, and Prudence, and by an Olympian divinity, the armed goddess Minerva, behind the throne. Corresponding to the grieving Victories on the left, in the right foreground are the male figures of five nobles, from the world of historical real-

---

22 On the equation of the assassinated Henri with the deified Julius Caesar see Millen and Wolf 1989, 127.

Fig. 6: Rubens, *Maria de' Medici cycle*. 'The queen triumphant', photo © RMN-Grand Palais (musée du Louvre) / Jean Schormans.

ity, who acclaim the queen-regent, and placed at a lower level than the group of female figures surrounding Maria, spectators rather than main actors.

What is new in Rubens' cycle is the adaptation for a female ruler of the ancient iconography of imperial panegyric of male rulers. One consequence of this is the potential for a different relationship between the subject of panegyric and the personifications that proliferate in the imagery of praise. That is to say, a female ruler can appear in the likeness of a female personification. In *The Felicity of the regency* (17) Maria appears as Justice, holding her scales. The final painting in the cycle, standing outside the narrative sequence itself, is *The queen triumphant* (24) (Fig. 6), facing the pivotal *The death of Henri IV and the proclamation of the regency* at the other end of the gallery. Maria appears in the likeness of another Olympian goddess, Minerva Victrix. In the earlier canvases of *The education of the princess* (5) and *The proclamation of the regency* (13) Minerva had appeared as an attendant of Maria, but now as one of her embodiments. But there are also allusions to female personifications, as well as to a female Olympian. Maria-Minerva holds a golden Victory, as ancient images of Minerva sometimes do; on a 1599 medal of Henri with the legend ΑΠΤΕΡΟΣ ΝΙΚΗ, a 'wingless Victory' holds a statuette of a winged Victory.[23] The message is perhaps that Maria is, as it were, a 'personification' of the achievements of her dead husband, the military victories that would have been celebrated in Maria's plan for a second gallery dedicated to Henri IV, including 'les triomphes desdites victoire en la façon des triomphes des Romains . . .' That plan was thwarted by Maria's exile in 1631. Maria/Minerva Victrix stands in front of a pile of weapons and pieces of armour. In an earlier sketch the figure is seated on a pile of arms, an 'idea [that] comes directly from a great many Roman coins stamped with the image of Roma . . .'[24] If that idea continues to glimmer through the standing figure, as finally executed, the implication is perhaps that Maria is nothing less than a personification of the nation itself. That might be supported by the fact that in her left hand she bears the sceptre of France, the only time that she is given this attribute in the cycle; and she is clad in a dark mantle with golden fleur-de-lys. Maria-Roma-France – the ultimate Rome on the Seine!

In *The council of the gods* (14) (Fig. 7), the globe of the world is divided between France and Spain, in a conference of gods concerning the reciprocal marriages of France and Spain, producing the (marital-political) concord of the personification holding a bundle of arrows below Maria. The central figure is an etherealized Maria, the earthly Juno, in the final stage of an elevation that has taken place over the three large canvases, *The coronation of Maria* (12), *The proclamation of the regency* (13), and now raised to the skies in *The council of the gods*.[25] Maria bows towards the Jupiter, besides whom is seated Juno herself. Juno and Maria both wear diadems, hinting at a quasi-identification, while Maria is lit up by the radiations from the aureoled head of Jupiter, alluding to emblems of

---

23 Millen and Wolf 1989, 225.
24 Millen and Wolf 1989, 225.
25 See Millen and Wolf 1989, 140.

Fig. 7: Rubens, *Maria de' Medici cycle*. 'The council of the gods', Louvre, Paris, France / Bridgeman Images.

Maria which show her reflecting or being nourished by the rays of the sun. In the lower register of *The council of the gods*, larger through perspective than the figures above, is the sun-god himself, Apollo, in the pose of the Apollo Belvedere, his aureoled head in the likeness of the Dauphin, the future Louis XIII, son of Henri as Apollo is the son of Jupiter.[26] Apollo/Louis shoots at Fury-like figures, personifications of Vices, so banishing the hell of war and discord which are overtaken by the concordant peace and prosperity of Henri's and Maria's policy of alliances through marriage.

The last two canvases in the narrative sequence, however, introduce Christian models for the approximation of the earthly to the divine. In *The return of the mother to her son* (Louis XIII) (22) (Fig. 8), Maria is 'Maria Assumpta elevated by grace of her now beatifically godlike son'; 'light streams from his head in the shape of a rayed golden crown: thus King of France, Apollo, and, unabashedly, Christ the King.'[27] Upwards movement is balanced by a female St Michael-like (so Christian) figure blasting a many-headed leonine Hydra monster (so classical) down to hell with a thunderbolt. In the final canvas, *Time unveils the truth* (23) (Fig. 9), Queen Mother and King are seated against a radiant sky, glorified and apotheosed, in a composition that alludes to the Coronation of the Virgin. The

---

26 Louis was typified as a boyish Apollo in numerous media after his father's death.
27 Millen and Wolf 1989, 216.

Fig. 8: Rubens, *Maria de' Medici cycle*. 'The return of the mother to her son', photo © RMN-Grand Palais (musée du Louvre) / Christian Jean / Hervé Lewandowski.

crown that mother and son hold between them, however, is a Roman military garland of laurel, enclosing a classical emblem of *fides* 'trust, loyalty', a pair of clasped hands. A Christian(ising) closure to the sequence is perhaps felt to be appropriate, while the audacious equivalence of Louis and Maria with Christ and the Virgin is perhaps licensed by that same space for panegyrical free play that

Fig. 9: Rubens, *Maria de' Medici cycle*. 'Time unveils the truth', photo © RMN-Grand Palais (musée du Louvre) / Christian Jean / Hervé Lewandowski.

has been established by the self-evidently fictional masking of the human rulers as pagan gods.

I turn now to the handling of heaven and earth, god and man in Voltaire's *Henriade*. As I said above, the 'Romanization' of Henri IV in Voltaire's *Henriade* is effected not through the direct appropriation of the imagery of ancient imperial panegyric, but through the assimilation of Virgil's national Roman epic, the charter for the newly founded Augustan principate.

Faithful to the Virgilian model, the *Henriade* also plots the relationship between the divine and the human, but within a strictly Christian framework. The intermediary between heaven and earth is St Louis, introduced near the beginning (1.79–90), 'Le père des Bourbons, du sein des immortels, | Louis, fixait sur lui ses regards paternels . . .' – as Jupiter and Juno look down benignly at the start of the Rubens cycle in *The Fates spin the destiny of the future queen*; and as Jupiter looks down, with rather less concern, on earth and sea at the beginning of the *Aeneid*, when he is approached by Venus, distraught about the chances of survival of her son, Jupiter's grandson, Aeneas. On earth, Aeneas, recently escaped from the storm, has no knowledge of what part he has to play in the script of Fate that Jupiter reads out to Venus. Similarly, *Henriade* 1.87–90 'Louis du haut des cieux lui pretât son appui; | Mais il cachait le bras qu'il étendait pour lui, | De peur que ce héros, trop sûr de sa victoire, | Avec moins de danger n'eût acquis moins de gloire.'

St Louis only reveals himself to his descendant in an apparition at the end of book 6, where he checks Henri's reckless determination to press on with the storming of Paris. The following book, book 6 in the first version of the epic, relates a dream in which Henri is taken up by St Louis into the skies in a chariot of light, for an eschatological vision of post-mortem punishments and rewards, concluding with a vision of his unborn descendants. This is a large-scale, celestial, reworking of Aeneas' journey to the Underworld in book 6 of the *Aeneid*.

The final sequence of the poem returns to heaven (10.411–506), in a series of epic ascents to and descents from the skies. They begin with an ascent of the hero, not however in a personal apotheosis, but through the proxy of his (not fully personified) virtue, 412 'La vertu de Henri pénétra dans les cieux.' This prompts St Louis to an interview with God enthroned on high, an interview that corresponds to that between Venus and the supreme Olympian god Jupiter in the first book of the *Aeneid*. Louis prays for the 'enlightenment' of Henri, that is to say the conversion to Catholicism of the Protestant Henri that will bring an end to the divisions of the wars of religion. A fully personified Vérité descends to effect the enlightenment, followed in short order by the descent, firstly of Christ to his altars on earth to reveal to Henri (492) 'un Dieu sous un pain qui n'est plus', and secondly, of St Louis holding an olive branch, to open the gates of Paris to Henri.

2 Discord and Furies

The full span of the Virgilian vertical axis encompasses heaven, earth, and hell. St Louis' entry in the *Henriade*, looking down on earth 'du sein des immortels' (79–90), forms a pendant to the preceding introduction of the personification of Dis-

corde (57–66), 'On voyait dans Paris la Discorde inhumaine, | Excitant aux com-
bats et la Ligue et Mayenne . . .' Discorde, as we learn in a later book, is a child of
Hell, (3.103 'O fille de l'enfer, Discorde inexorable'); she is virtually a personification of civil war. Discorde plays a major role in motivating several of the actions
of the *Henriade.*[28]

Voltaire's personification Discorde is a demythologized version of the Virgilian Fury Allecto, summoned up in *Aeneid* 7 by Juno to unleash war between Trojans and Italians. This is the ultimate model for the multiple interventions of
Discorde in the plot of the *Henriade.* I take just one example of a more specific
allusion to Virgil: at the end of book 5 of the *Henriade,* Discorde, frustrated by
Henri's successes, decides to adopt a different strategy, 512 'Si je n'ai pu le vaincre,
on le peut amollir', adapting Juno's change of plan at *Aeneid* 7.312, *flectere si ne-
queo superos, Acheronta mouebo* ('If I cannot persuade the gods above, I will stir
up hell'), whereupon she resorts to Hell to summon up Allecto.

Virgil's Fury, Allecto, is herself virtually a personification of *discordia*, a word
which in Latin has particular reference to the strife of civil war. She has an extensive progeny in the Furies of later Latin epic, and then post-classical epic, and
also in the visual arts.

Furies, and related monsters, feature recurrently in the dramatization of the
struggle between good and evil, order and disorder in the Rubens cycle. In *The
Council of the Gods* (14) Apollo Belvedere ~ sun-king Louis XIII drives off Furies
(Fig. 7). In *The Queen opts for security* (21), a composition modelled closely on
Rosso Fiorentino's fresco at Fontainebleau of *Francis I overcoming the evils of ignorance*, a blind masculine Fury brandishes a viper. In *The return of the mother
to her son* (22), the penultimate canvas in the narrative cycle, a female figure of
vengeance blasts a hydra monster of sedition, doubling up as the Beast of Apocalypse, down to the underworld with a thunderbolt (Fig. 8).

Both Rubens' cycle and the *Henriade* reach a point of closure with the restoration of concord after repeated resurgences of discord. At the end of the *Henriade* the sainted King Louis IX, holding the olive of peace descends to lead Henri
into Paris, where 'all the people' recognise him as 'son vrai roi, son vainqueur, et

---

28 3.157 ff. Discorde's flight to Rome to enlist Politique; 4.96 ff. Discorde's defence of d'Aumale;
5.57 ff. Discorde incites Jacques Clément to assassinate Henri III, summoning up Fanatisme from
Hell; 8.29 ff., following a simile of Gigantomachy, Discorde encourages the Duke of Mayenne and
his men; at the end of book 8, 505 ff., frustrated by Henri's successes, Discorde decides to adopt a
different strategy, 505 ff., followed at 9.1 ff. with the set-piece of Discorde's approach to Amour to
seduce Henri from his commitment to the war; at 10.510 'La Discorde rentra dans l'éternelle
nuit'.

son père.' The Duke of Mayenne, leader of the Ligue, is led to recognizing Henri as king, and, in the last line of the poem, 'Fut le meilleur sujet du plus juste des princes.' Three lines earlier, 10.511 'La Discorde rentra dans l'éternelle nuit', as the monster of sedition is despatched to Hell in *The return of the mother to her son*.

In *Time unveils the truth* (23), the final canvas of the narrative cycle (Fig. 9), another Louis, Louis XIII, offers his mother, as we have seen, a Roman emblem of *fides*, clasped hands within a laurel *corona militis*, a conclusion of reconciliation and concord.

3 What is Truth?

Is it coincidence that a personification of Truth also provides closure in the *Henriade*? As we have seen, the personification of Vérité plays a major role in the divine machinery with which Voltaire ends his epic. She descends from God to the camp of Henri, hidden at first from human sight in a thick veil, the shadows of which then give way to a brilliant, but not blinding, light. Henri 'sees, knows, loves' her eternal light, and confesses, in faith, that religion exceeds human reason, and gives himself up – paradoxically? – to the holy mysteries of the catholic faith. This is the last appearance in the poem of Truth, a key theme of the poem, and one which raises the question of what kind of truth is at stake.[29] In the main narrative and character speeches of the poem, Vérité is above all religious Truth, but she is also the spirit whom the poet Voltaire addresses in the opening invocation, 1.7–20, which replaces an invocation to a very Virgilian Muse in the 1723–1724 editions:

> Descends du haut des cieux, auguste Vérité!
> Répands sur mes écrits ta force et ta clarté:
> Que l'oreille des rois s'accoutume à t'entendre.
> C'est à toi d'annoncer ce qu'ils doivent apprendre;
> C'est à toi de montrer aux yeux des nations
> Les coupables effets de leurs divisions.
> Dis comment la Discorde a troublé nos provinces;
> Dis les malheurs du peuple et les fautes des princes:
> Viens, parle; et s'il est vrai que la Fable autrefois
> Sut à tes fiers accents mêler sa douce voix;
> Si sa main délicate orna ta tête altière,
> Si son ombre embellit les traits de ta lumière,

---

29 On the replacement of the more Virgilian invocation of the Muse, and on the wider role of Vérité in the *Henriade see* Rieks 2010.

Avec moi sur tes pas permets-lui de marcher,
Pour orner tes attraits, et non pour les cacher.

Truth will show kings and peoples the errors of their ways, and more particularly teach the ills brought about by Discorde. She is also called upon to provide a more personal service for the poet, in allowing him to combine Fable and Truth, using fable, or fiction, to adorn, without concealing, truth, and adding shadow to set off the light of truth, mingling her sweet voice in the way in which Tasso uses the Lucretian image of the honeyed cup at the beginning of the *Gerusalemme Liberata* (I. 3.5–8). One of these touches of 'fable' is indeed the fiction that there is such a thing as a personification of Truth who will give ear to the poet's invocation.

Is there a comparable self-awareness in Rubens' deployment of the personification of Truth (a very different female figure from Voltaire's proud celestial creature) at the end of his Medici cycle, prompting the viewer to reflect on exactly what truth status there is in the twenty-four canvases?[30] Is she even a little reluctant to be dragged by Time towards an image that could be seen as a dissonant amalgamation of the classical and the Christian? Does she believe that the final reconciliation of mother and son is true? Do the meanings of the cycle as a whole all stand revealed to the eyes of the beholder. Time has revealed that, from the earliest commentaries on the paintings to modern scholarship, there has been no unanimity as to how to read individual paintings, or the cycle as a whole. It may be that this is a deliberate strategy on the part of the artist. Elizabeth McGrath[31] argues that allegory is used precisely to avoid the unambiguous representation of historical events, and that Rubens' own preference was for allegory over the 'historical truth' on which at times his patron insisted. In a letter to his scholarly adviser Peiresc, Rubens reported on Louis XIII's first visit to the Palais du Luxembourg, where Claude Maugis explained the pictures to the King 'con una diversione e dissimulatione del vero senso molto artificiosa.' The symbolism of Roman imperial iconography can be at once a means of communication, and a veil.

And finally, who is the ideal viewer of Rubens' cycle on the life of Maria de' Medici, with its elaborate apparatus of classical myth and allegory in the service of a Christian monarchy? One answer might be Maria herself, formed as just such an ideal viewer in *The education of the princess* (5) (Fig. 10). The figure of the girl bending over the book of her female instructress echoes the compositional type of St Anne teaching the Virgin to read, but this is no St Anne, but rather Minerva,

---

30 For suggestions as to the metaliterary and metapictural meanings of the cycle see Cojannot-Le Blanc and Prioux 2018, 212–213.
31 McGrath 1980.

Fig. 10: Rubens, *Maria de' Medici cycle*. 'The education of the princess', photo © RMN-Grand Palais (musée du Louvre) / René-Gabriel Ojeda / Thierry Le Mage.

goddess of wisdom as well as of military victory (in the final painting of the sequence, Maria as Minerva Victrix (24)). The three Graces confer the beauty which will win her a royal husband, and also symbolize concord, another lesson that she may learn. The musician playing the viola da gamba is perhaps best taken as Orpheus rather than Apollo, but Maria will know. Hurtling down from above is Mercury, offering the gift of his caduceus. Immediately this may be the gift of eloquence, but it is also the symbol of peacemaking and concord. To read this, and the other symbolisms of the picture, aright requires a quick intelligence, of which Mercury is also the god. Mercury-Hermes is also the god of interpretation, hermeneutics, the god of messages and how to read them. At the bottom of the canvas, as it were grounding the composition as a whole and the sum of its messages, is a bust of Homer, the foundation of Greek and Roman literature and culture, the formation necessary for the full understanding of the cycle of which Maria is the subject.

Bibliography

Bardon, Françoise. *Le Portrait mythologique à la cour de France sous Henri IV et Louis XIII*. Paris: Picard, 1974.

Champlin, Edward. *Nero*. Cambridge, Mass: Harvard University Press, 2003.

Cojannot-Le Blanc, Marianne, and Évelyne Prioux. *Rubens. Des camées antiques à la galerie Médicis*. Paris and New York: LePassage, 2018.

Jeanneret, Michel. *Versailles, ordre et chaos*. Paris: Gallimard, 2012.

McGrath, Elizabeth. "Tact and Topical Reference in Rubens' 'Medici cycle'." *Oxford Art Journal* 3.2 (1980): 11–17.

Millen, Ronald Forsyth, and Robert Erich Wolf. *Heroic Deeds and Mystic Figures. A New Reading of Rubens' Life of Maria de' Medici*. Princeton: Princeton University Press, 1989.

Néraudau, J. P. *L'Olympe du roi-soleil, ou comment la mythologie et l'Antiquité furent mises au service de l'idéologie monarchique sous Louis XIV à travers la littérature, la peinture, la musique, les fêtes, la sculpture, l'architecture et les jardins, à Vaux-le-Vicomte, Meudon, St Cloud, Sceaux, Marly, St Germain et Versailles*. Paris: Belles Lettres, 1986.

Rieks, Rudolf. "Zu Voltaires Vergilrezeption in der Henriade." *Vestigia Vergiliana. Vergil-Rezeption in der Neuzeit*. Eds. Thorsten Burkard, Markus Schauer, and Claudia Wiener. Berlin: De Gruyter, 2010: 269–298.

Saward, Susan. *The Golden Age of Marie de' Medici*. Ann Arbor: UMI Research Press, 1982.

Smith, R. R. R. "*Maiestas serena*: Roman Court Cameos and Early Imperial Poetry and Panegyric." *Journal of Roman Studies* 111 (2021): 75–152.

Stewart, Peter. "The Equestrian Statue of Marcus Aurelius." In *A Companion to Marcus Aurelius*. Ed. Marcel van Ackeren. Oxford: Blackwell, 2012: 264–277.

Tauber, Christine. *Manierismus and Herrschaftspraxis. Die Kunst der Politik und die Kunstpolitik am Hof von François I*. Berlin: De Gruyter, 2009.

Voltaire. *La Henriade*. Ed. O.R. Talyor. 2nd ed. Oxford: Voltaire Foundation, 2005.

Thomas, Danièle. *Henri IV. Images d'un roi entre réalité et mythe*. Pau: Héraclès, 1996.

Thompson, Victoria. E. "The Creation, Destruction and Recreation of Henri IV: Seeing Popular Sovereignty in the Statue of a King." *History & Memory* 24 (2012): 5–40.

Wehlen, Bernhard. *"Antrieb und Entschluss zu dem was geschieht". Studien zur Medici-Galerie von Peter Paul Rubens*. Munich: Scaneg, 2008.

Christine Tauber
Jacques-Louis David's Roman Revolutions in Paris

Jacques-Louis David's art production had to take a back seat to his political commitment between 1792 and 1794.[1] It shifted increasingly to ephemeral genres such as festive decorations or to projects for monuments in public space (for example, for a 50-meter-high monumental statue of the *peuple*, which was to rise on the ruins of the royal gallery of Notre-Dame and, in a less colossal form, came to stand for a short time next to the temporary *montagne* at the Feast of the Supreme Being on June 8, 1794; (Fig. 1).[2] In this turbulent period, there are only three paintings in which the painter commemorated the so-called revolutionary martyrs as his murdered 'brothers':[3] at the beginning of 1793 Louis-Michel Le Peletier de Saint-Fargeau, who had been murdered by a member of the royal body-

Fig. 1: Pierre-Antoine de Machy, La fête de l'Etre Suprême, au Champs de Mars, ca. 1794. Paris, Musée Carnavalet, wikimedia, public domain.

---

1 On this and the following cf. Tauber 2016; Bordes 1996b. Bordes 1993 against the more legitimistic approach in Dowd 1948. Cf. also Michel and Sahut 1988; Clark 1994.
2 Ozouf 1987; Ehrard and Viallaneix 1977; cf. also Crow 1985.
3 Cf. Clarke 2007, ²2011.

https://doi.org/10.1515/9783111334776-007

guard because of his vote for the execution of the French monarch; then the ultra-revolutionary Jean-Paul Marat, who was stabbed to death in his bathtub by the royalist Charlotte Corday on July 13, 1793. Finally, the 13-year-old horse-servant Joseph Barra, who had fallen victim to a brigand attack during fighting in the Vendée in 1793, was transfigured into a martyr. In David's depiction, the gender-ambiguous child martyr was to be stylized as the exemplary brother of France's youth.

In David's design for the stage curtain of the Opéra in the spring of 1794[4] (Fig. 2) we can once again observe a group of revolutionary martyrs behind the triumphal chariot of the French people with their 'saintly attributes' held up accusingly: the blade of the guillotine, a vial of poison, and prison chains. In the first row, Marat ostentatiously exposes his chest disfigured by scrofula. This "allégorie de la Terreur"[5] unites contemporary regicides and historical virtue heroes in a triumphant procession that transcends time and is bound together solely by the suggestion of heroism – the *régicide* itself is depicted on the left in its utmost drasticness.[6]

Fig. 2: Jacques-Louis David, Le Triomphe du Peuple français, 1794. Paris, Musée Carnavalet.

---

4 Schnapper 1988; Schnapper 1989, cat.no. 123, 124; Stein 2022, cat.no. 55, 194–196. Philippe Bordes connects the opera curtain with the fall of Danton and David's involvement in it: Bordes 1993, 334–338.

5 Bordes 1993, 340.

6 Cf. the detailed description of the *Triomphe de la liberté et du peuple* in Lenoir 1835, 7–8; De Baecque 1987.

1 Making steel hard and swearing in the republican body

As master of the pageants in the revolutionary period, David employed aesthetic principles in these republican stagings of a new, autonomous and egalitarian fraternal communion beyond the monarchical-patriarchal order that characterize large parts of his pictorial œuvre. These secularized processions followed a choreography planned down to the last detail, which was modeled on ancient Roman triumphal processions which David adopted again in 1794 in his design for the stage curtain of the Opéra with the triumphal chariot of the French people: the masses of people performing publicly in the revolutionary festivals for the first time ever were subjected on the one hand to physical conditioning of their movements,[7] and on the other hand to strict subdivision according to age, gender, place of residence, and professional group, in order to make them distinguishable and maneuverable in subunits, and thus also manipulable. A main function of these ceremonies, of which David was the master from 1792, was to create places of national identifica-

Fig. 3: Fédération générale des Français au Champ de Mars, le 14 juillet 1790. Dessiné par C. Monet, gravé par Isidore Stanislas Helman, de l'Académie des Arts de Lille en Flandre, eau-forte de A.J. Duclos, 1790. Public domain.

---

7 De Baecque 1993.

tion, places of the constitution of an ancient Roman republican community. Public communication spaces accessible to everybody were to be created, in which patriotic sentiment could be formed in the new post-revolutionary man, the *homme régénéré*.[8]

The new ideal of *fraternité*, the community of equal brothers, was expressed in the final manifestation of the Fête de la Fédération, which was organized for the first time on July 14, 1790, with the greatest personnel and staging effort (Fig. 3). As the first year anniversary of the storming of the Bastille, this festival marked the zero hour from which new, eternally valid memories were to be created. The 'poetic idea' here was the bringing together and centering of all French people in a unifying act on the Champ de Mars. The highlight of the staging was the actual act of *fédération*, with the oath of the General of the National Guard, Lafayette, at the altar of the Fatherland. This ceremonial act of military unification turned into a demonstrative unification of the entire nation. The ritualized act – a community building repetition of the civic oath – was intended to swear the masses to the new revolutionary ideals for all future, to unite them into a community of faith, and at the same time to renew the *contrat social* every year. Accordingly, the people experienced themselves as a constitutive part of the new body of the state and celebrated themselves as a nation in the newly constructed national arena.

The participants of the festival were part of the aesthetic self-representation of the new political constitution, in that they contributed as individuals to the creation of the ornament of the mass. At the same time, however, each participant was also a beholder of this new type of artwork and, to that extent, a spectator in this theatrical staging of politics. In the simultaneous act of watching and participating, he was supposed to recognize himself as an indispensable part of the new republican order, ranking equal with all others. In fact, the revolutionary period was characterized by constantly repeated acts of swearing in a still crisis-prone young republic to its new ideals. The oath as a community-building act of pure presence with the character of a commitment for the future is best handled as a mass staging, because it is witnessed by as many fellow citizens as possible and can be called in later. In the crisis-ridden early phase of the republic, it represents a ritual before any writing down of laws and civic duties and thus guarantees the political functioning of the new state even before the enactment of the constitution, which first secures the new political institutions and standardizes their functioning.

---

8 On this and the following, with numerous further references: Tauber 2010, 208–219.

Fig. 4: Jacques-Louis David, Le Serment du Jeu de Paume à Versailles le 20 juin 1789, 1791. Versailles, Musée national des Châteaux de Versailles et de Trianon. Public domain.

In the early days of the Revolution, David tackled a single large history painting that would depict such an oath scene. His famous *Serment du Jeu de Paume* (Fig. 4) is also the first painting that found a contemporary, daily political mass event worthy of depiction in a monumental format.[9] Around 600 persons are shown here, who are only individualized by portraits in the front, relief-like action zone (e. g. later committed Jacobins like Robespierre – his pathetic pose modeled on a Roman soldier in David's sketchbook from Rome;[10] Fig. 5 –, the Abbé Grégoire or the Abbé Sieyès as the theoretician of the Third Estate). This zone of the painting recalls David's drawing of an antique-style frieze depicting the *Funeral of a Hero* from 1778, executed during his stay at the Académie de France à Rome from 1775 to 1780.[11] Behind this frieze-like relief, however, the representation of the Tennis Court Oath merges into a crowd of people homogenized in the act of swearing. The action shown thus contains contradictory elements: on the one hand, the community is immobilized in the moment of the oath, especially in the center of the action around the mayor of Paris and president of the Assemblée nationale. On the other

---

9 Bordes 1983; Kemp 1986; Tauber 2010; Kernbauer 2011.
10 Stein 2022, 25.
11 Stein 2022, cat.no. 18, 106–109.

hand, there are moments of enthusiastic actionism on the fringes: here, flaming speeches are brandished, among others by Mirabeau and Antoine Barnave as the most important orators of the Revolution, whereby speech gesture and oath gesture are hardly to distinguish.

Fig. 5: Jacques-Louis David, Un groupe de soldats from a sketchbook with studies for The Oath of the Tennis Court, 1790/91. Versailles, Musée national des Châteaux de Versailles et de Trianon.

The object of the oath of June 20, 1789 was the constitution of a new social contract. Its core passage was "de ne jamais se séparer, et de se rassembler partout où les circonstances l'exigeront, jusqu'à ce que la Constitution du royaume soit établie et affermie sur des fondements solides." It was thus a matter of giving up individuality in favor of an inseparable community that corresponded to the ideal of a united social body. In his completely unrealistic depiction of a political idea, David abandons the unity of time and place – the Aristotelian *unité* – in favor of the depiction of a choreographically enacted *unité de doctrine*. He shows the motoric conditioning of bodies, which, according to Robespierre, was to culminate in a total synchronization of every day movements and time sequences.[12] The bodies subordinate themselves to an idea of unity, which manifests itself in a stereotype of formal design. Here, this idea of a fusion in the unifying act of a patriotic republican oath has found its artistic realization. In formal terms, regulated uniformity, *uniformité*, results from the prescribed *unité*, as found in the uniforms designed by David for the citizens, representatives of the people, and administrative officials of the new republic of 1794 (Fig. 6).[13]

Fig. 6: Jacques-Louis David, Le Représentant du peuple en fonction, 1794. Paris, Musée Carnavalet.

---

12 On this and the following: Tauber 2009, 236–243.
13 Stein 2022, cat.no. 56, 197–199.

2 Resurgence Attempts: Virtuous Heroes of the Early Roman Republic in the Paris Salon

This pictorial idea is not entirely new – nor was it born directly out of the revolutionary process. David had already established himself as a specialist in uniformizing body conditioning with his famous *Serment des Horaces*, created in 1781–84 and exhibited in the Salon of 1785 (Fig. 7).[14] Here, too – with obvious reference to Füssli's *Rütli oath* – it was a matter of unbreakable *unité*, indissoluble solidarity, but also inseparability until the definite execution of a historical-political mission: The tragedy of the situation lies in the fact that those chosen by lot for the proxy fight between Rome and Alba Longa are, of all things, three brothers who are bound to each other by family ties and marriages. Therefore, they must be particularly strongly sworn in beforehand in their fighting morals. David forges the three brothers Horatii, who look completely identical (which is not surprising, since they are triplets), into a triple bond of a combative body through their gesture of embracing and the parallelization of their legs and arms; he congeals them into a pictorial formula of steel-hard determination. His painting provides an emblem, then readily taken up by the *Terreur*, for uncompromisingly correct mindset, which manifests itself in the painting in the metallic lines of the swords, the muscularly tense legs spread at right angles,[15] and in the spartan construction of the room in which the oath scene is 'performed' as if on a stage.[16] The straight lines symbolize rigid virtue that knows no compromise. The bodies are conditioned to steadfastly uphold the republican ideal of the early Roman Republic even unto death.[17]

The revolutionary family model of all-embracing *fraternité*, newly established after the *patricide* of the French king on January 21, 1793, which was to replace the patriarchal monarchy as a leadership collective,[18] is also already present in the *Oath of the Horatii*: The father in the center of the picture shields the sons from the group on the right, forming an impenetrable barrier to the women and children, to whom he turns his back, and who, both in their coloring and in their soft, hunched forms, represent the complete opposite of the battle-ready male ma-

---

14 Cf. Crow 1978.

15 Körner 1988, 156, speaks appropriately of the "Utopie des rechten Winkels".

16 Cf. Ledbury 2005.

17 On the representation of the so-called "foundation rape" in two of David's late drawings cf. Ledbury 2007.

18 Hunt 1992, Chap. 1: "The Family Model of Politics", 1–16, and Chap. 2: "The Rise and Fall of the Good Father", 17–52. Cf. Bordes 2005, 12, who calls David's *Brutus* "an unnatural father."

Fig. 7: Jacques-Louis David, Le Serment des Horaces, 1784. Paris, Musée du Louvre. Public domain.

chinery of destruction on the left.[19] The fanatical actionism of the "band of brothers," (as Lynn Hunt so aptly put it)[20] whose phalanx aggressively strives to the outside, pushes the women, with their fears, to the outermost periphery of the action. Family considerations, which would be oriented toward the biological perpetuation of the family, are sacrificed to the virtuous ideal of republican glory and male honor conveyed to the sons through Spartan education, which are to be placed far higher in the canon of values because they do not create a materialistic or procreative, but an ideologically idealistic future. Here a heroic age has visibly

---

19 Cf. on this and the following, the convincing analysis of the "Funktion der kompositionellen Ordnung für die intendierte Bildaussage" in the *Oath of the Horatii* and in *Brutus* by Körner 1988, esp. 131–160, here 135. Cf. Körner 1988, 137: "Die augenscheinliche Gewaltsamkeit, mit der die männlichen Figuren in dieses ordnende Gefüge eingepaßt sind, hebt die Radikalität der Gesinnung, die Gewaltsamkeit der Forderung, alles Persönliche dem überpersönlichen Gesetz zu opfern, ins Sichtbare." Cf. also the analysis of the *Horatii* by Rosenblum 1967, 67–73. Cf. Rosenblum 2006, 50: "an unforgettable icon of feminine despair in the midst of both public and private civil wars".

20 Hunt 1992, Chap. 3: "The Band of Brothers"; cf. David 1987.

dawned in which there is no longer any mediation between the former spheres: The men who only follow their own ratio of republican virtue have long since been removed from the influence of women. They are already inwardly far away from the domestic hearth, the former traditional family triad has been blown up.[21] David has juxtaposed the absolutely straightforward male willpower with two pyramidal groups of women and children in a marginalized position. These follow the pictorial scheme of the Holy Family, as prototypically found in Raphael's *Sacra famiglia Canigiani*; they try in vain to maintain the intactness of the familial triad, since the central element, the man, is missing. The latter has opted instead for the *unité* of the brotherly bond, also composed of three elements, in which absolute equality and equivalence prevailed. However, Joseph had also made a not very convincing

Fig. 8: Jacques-Louis David, Les Licteurs rapportant à Brutus les corps de ses fils, 1789. Paris, Musée du Louvre. Public domain.

---

21 Even without an explicit gender theory, David's paintings can be profitably analyzed for these representations of gender differences; cf. Bryson 1984; Bryson 1993; Solomon-Godeau 1997; Fend 2003.

father figure in the three-person constellation of the Holy Family.[22] There is no longer room in this strictly republican system for private sensitivities that attempt to circumvent a clear partisanship for the *bonum commune*.

In his 1789 painting *Les Licteurs rapportant à Brutus les corps de ses fils* (Fig. 8),[23] still commissioned by the king and shown in the Salon of 1789, David created a kind of emblem for the severity and ruthlessness of the republican and patriotic ideals that must be adhered to at all costs for the purpose of preserving the new form of government. The painting shows Lucius Junius Brutus, the founder of the Roman Republic, in his house, at the moment when the bodies of his two sons, Titus and Tiberius, are brought to him for burial. He himself ordered their execution without the slightest hesitation on the mere suspicion of an anti-republican conspiracy and an attempt to reinstate the monarchy he had just overcome. David has depicted neither the deed itself nor Brutus' decision-making difficulties in the forefront of this action suspending paternal love in favor of patriotism, but the fertile and at the same time dreadful moment of reflection in which Brutus gains profound psychological dimension as he ponders the consequences of his action.[24]

Yet he seems to have no doubts about the correctness of his decision. Grim determination and the highest tension (down to the muscles of his toes) show the inevitability of his judgment in the interests of republican ideals. The sacrifice of the individual future – of his own male offspring – for the preservation of the republic is presented as completely justified. At the same time, the inhumanity of this decision, made by him on his own but unavoidably for the sake of the reason of state, marginalizes him in the picture as well as in the family circle. He is isolated on the left, secluded and shadowed, an internally split personality, while the empty center of the picture seems to be filled with the emotional numbness that his decision evokes in the other members of his family. Above Brutus lurks the rigid, black and threatening statue of Dea Roma, given only in silhouette, representing merciless law as an abstract, rational principle and thus the basis of the later republican terror of virtue and Robespierre's Rousseauist-supported *vertu* ideology of the so-called "Incorruptible," which chose Brutus as one of their exempla. This systematic

---

22 Cf. Koschorke 2000. In the women's and children's group of his *Horatii*, David incorporates further elements from Christian iconography, such as Anna Selbdritt, the Virgin of the Protective Mantle, and the Holy Family, which has been expanded to a constellation of five by St. Elisabeth and the boy John, and which has once again lost Joseph.

23 Herbert 1972; Puttfarken 1981; Bordes 1996a; Bordes 1998.

24 Germer and Kohle 1986; cf. Ledbury 2007, 172: "[. . .] the very interiority of the peripety points to an issue with which David would struggle in many of the ideas for his compositions: his desire to convey pictorially scenes which are resistant to visual representation but which carry the great weight of the insoluble tragic dilemma."

terror of virtue was based on Rousseau's premise that man only comes to himself completely when he either expresses the natural man in himself or internalizes the *raison d'état* in such a way that he becomes the property of the state as a perfect citizen.[25] The law, in which impartial justice manifests itself, and the *bonum commune* are to be placed above any personal interest – of course, only a man is capable of such an act. The tears and screams of his wife and his daughters, who are close to fainting and who, like bacchantes, indulge in hysterical lamentations and thus give free rein to their expression of passion (to quote Thomas Kirchner's famous *expression des passions*), disturb Brutus (according to David in his own description of his painting) in his stoic and composed manly grief, as shown in the drawing after the painting (Fig. 9).[26]

In this painting, too, a rift that can never be mended runs through the family constellation; here, too, it runs along gender lines, and here, too, the chair that separates the two spheres turns its back on the main protagonists; unlike the father of the Horatii, however, it shields and closes off the female sphere. The public space, dominated by men, invades with the corpses the private one, feminine in its architectural design as well as in its decoration,[27] and destroys it and its protective function. Significantly, the scene takes place in the atrium of a Roman domus or villa, which was a semi-public space of transition from outside to inside. Only allegedly are the women protected from the intrusion of the public sphere into domestic intimacy by the space within the room draped with white cloths, and marked in the center of the picture as feminine by the still life of the needlework basket on the table.[28] The baseless Doric columns – connoting "mas-

---

25 Cf. Körner 1988, 150.

26 Cf. David in his letter to his student Jean-Baptiste Wicar on June 14, 1789, i.e. one month before the storming of the Bastille: "Donc je voulais vous dire que je fais un tableau de ma pure invention. C'est Brutus, homme et père, qui s'est privé de ses enfants, et qui, rentré dans ses foyers, on lui rapporte ses deux fils pour leur donner la sépulture. Il est distrait de son chagrin, au pied de la statue de Rome, par les cris de sa femme, la peur et l'évanouissement de la plus grande fille"; Wildenstein 1973, no. 207, 28. According to Rosenblum, David transforms "the women of the family into a group of hysterical bacchantes" (Rosenblum 1967, 77). In the same letter, David asks Wicar, who still has direct access to the ancient models in Rome, to draw bacchante heads from antique sarcophagi to serve as models for the female heads in *Brutus*: "Vous me feriez un plaisir de me croquer sur ce. . . tête pour la coiffure et dans la position que je vais vous marquer. Il me semble que vous trouveriez plutôt cela dans les Bacchanales. On y voit souvent de ces Bacchantes avec ces espèces d'attitudes." Cf. Ledbury 2007, 184, who speaks of "the affective power of the *Brutus*."

27 Cf. Bätschmann 1986, 160: "Wie im Bürgerhaus des 18. Jahrhunderts geht in Davids römischem Privathaus die Trennungslinie zwischen öffentlich und privat mitten durch das Gebäude."

28 Cf. Bryson 1990, 156–157; Stein 2022, 168, on the preparatory drawing of 1787, cat.no. 42: "[Brutus's wife] raises her shawl in a Niobe-like pose, a gesture emphasizing the futility of her maternel protectiveness. [. . .] Reinforcing this sense of intrusion into the feminine sphere is the detail of the discarded sewing basket on the floor, a single ball of yarn rolling into the foreground."

Fig. 9: Jacques-Louis David, Brutus, 1790. Private collection. Public domain.

culinity" even in the ancient order of columns – signal outwardly, as in the *Serment des Horaces*, defensive austerity and strict adherence to the law, and are only poorly concealed on the inside. The mother, however, refuses to swear to the right republican cause; her arm has lowered into a lamentory and at the same time accusatory gesture. In fact, in David's depiction, the totally politicized outside world has long since penetrated into the innermost parts of the family structures, as demonstrated by the Republican, tricolor color scheme throughout the right half of the picture.[29] Here it does not help anything, as in the case of the nurse on the far right, to conceal the expression of the passions by covering one's face. Withdrawal into the privacy of the family has become impossible here: In the Roman Republic, everything is public, everything is *res publica*, and subject to its goals; consequently, every transgression must be punished publicly. The new

---

[29] This is not meant to support the methodologically absurd research opinion, widespread in the older David literature, that the painter anticipated the revolution seismographically in the *Horatii* and *Brutus* (i.e. in this picture with a royal commission, the content of which was quite compatible with a monarchical ideology); cf. Duncan 1981, 194; Hunt 1992, 21–26; Carrier 2006.

political system in Paris, which was then to radicalize into a surveillance state during the *Terreur*, demands total and merciless submission to its inhuman ideals.

3 Socrates as the precursor of the Roman republican hero of virtue?

In an autobiographical sketch from the spring of 1793, David referred to his *Socrate buvant la ciguë* of 1787 as his artistic testament (Fig. 10).[30] The Praeceptor of the Attic school of philosophy is depicted at the moment when he takes the cup of hemlock; perhaps he was the heroic role model for David in 1794 in his generous offer to Robespierre: the very day before the latter's arrest, 8. Thermidor, David is reported to have declared to both the Welfare Committee and the Jacobin Club that, if it came to the worst, he would share the cup of hemlock with Robespierre in solidarity: "Si tu bois la ciguë, je la boirai avec toi."[31] There was no longer any talk of this after the execution of Robespierre and his closest partisans;[32] David obviously rather preferred the chalice to pass him by. In contrast to the painter, the philosopher draws the last consequence from his thoughts and actions. Even in this final crisis he is entirely a teacher, he lectures until the very last moment.[33] In the salon criticism of 1787 by Count Stanisław Kostka Potocki,[34] the Polish translator of Winckelmann por-

---

30 Bordes 1983, 175; Schneemann 1994, 170–179; cf. Einecke 2001; cf. also some stimulating observations on the role of Plato and Xantippe in the picture in Satish Padiyar's (otherwise, however, overly sexualized) interpretation: Padiyar 2008.

31 *Réimpression de l'Ancien Moniteur* 1841, 367–368: "Ce n'était pas pour venir faire l'accueil à Robespierre", David tries to relieve himself on the 13th thermidor, "que je descendis de son côté, c'était pour monter à la tribune et demander que l'heure de la fête du 10 fût avancée. Je n'ai pas embrassé Robespierre, je ne l'ai même pas touché, car il repoussait tout le monde. Il est vrai que, lorsque Couthon lui parla de l'envoi de son discours aux communes, je dis qu'il pourrait semer le trouble dans toute la République. Robespierre s'écria alors qu'il ne lui restait plus qu'à boire la ciguë; je lui dis: Je la boirais avec toi." Wildenstein 1973, no. 1117, 1118, 1119, 114.

32 Only in the closest private circle David is said to have expressed himself positively about Robespierre in front of his sons after the 9th Thermidor. Wildenstein 1973, no. 1124, 113: "On vous dira que Robespierre était un scélérat; on vous le peindra sous les couleurs les plus odieuses, n'en croyez rien. Il viendra un jour où l'histoire lui rendra une éclatante justice." Cf. Padiyar 2011, 6–14.

33 Cf. Padiyar 2008, 27: "Socrates continues to teach, his philosophical integrity remaining undiminished even at the moment of self-annihilation."

34 In his anonymously published *Lettre d'un étranger sur le Salon de 1787.* Cf. Zóltowska 1974; 1980; Polanowska 2000.

trayed by David in a brilliant equestrian portrait, Socrates is stylized as the ultimate *exemplum virtutis*: "Socrate [. . .] lui seul [est] calme et tranquille, occupé d'une plus grande idée [. . .]. Voyez ce groupe d'amis, de disciples désolés, placés au chevet de son lit; ce que la nature, ce que le choix de l'antique nous offre de plus beau est réuni sur leurs figures; leur expression est vraie, variée et touchante. Par quel contraste puissant, par quel charme, Socrate, le difforme Socrate, écrase tant de beauté, de grace et de sentiment réunis! C'est le triomphe de la vertu, qu'un courage héroïque, qu'une âme divine élèvent au-dessus de tout."

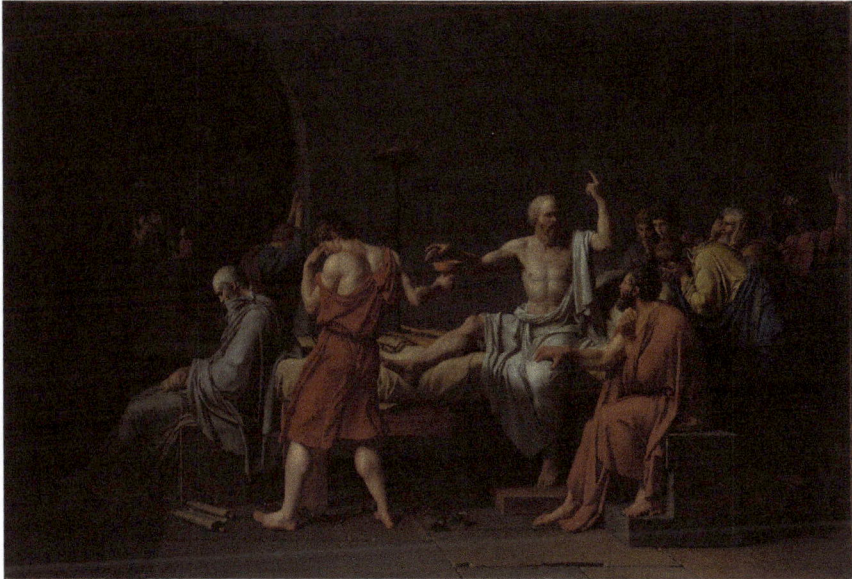

Fig. 10: Jacques-Louis David, La mort de Socrate, 1787. New York, Metropolitan Museum of Art. Public domain.

David's Socrates is the ancient virtue hero par excellence, because he stoically carries out a fate recognized as inevitable and the sentence of a political authority he unquestioningly recognizes, that is democracy, but at the same time he upholds the highest autonomy in this act of self-chosen submission to the only correct form of state: suicide becomes the ultimate proof of a noble, high-minded, and self-determined life until the end. Socrates thus advances to a role model for the autonomous artist. Attic democracy becomes a mirror image for David's radical conception of the Republic. But the aspirational state of stoic equanimity depicted here can only be achieved in the knowledge that one's own ideas and aesthetic ideals will surely survive oneself. The genealogical model of a harmonious teacher-student relationship designed by David in the picture is one primarily focused on safeguarding the future: it is intended above all to serve the preservation of the teacher's aesthetic legacy – which, after all, was and is always also a political legacy. Formally, the group of students, depicted as a homosocial association,[35] forms the dramatic-emotional contrasting foil that allows the stoicism of "father" Socrates to emerge even more authentically. The teacher can comfort his students by referring to a power beyond this earthly life. By pointing out that his kingdom is not of this world, he assumes a role similar to that of Christ at the Last Supper; the philosopher's students refer typologically to the flock of disciples.

At the same time, the group of students is not only homogeneously structured and characterized as a community of solidarity by the fact that they are exclusively men, but also by the fact that their diversely modeled affects balance each other out so that the overall state of mind of the group ultimately reflects the heroic stoicism of their father/teacher. The female element (especially the unrationalizable female emotionality) takes its leave in the form of Xantippe waving her ultimate farewell in the background and departing up the stairs, thus finally disappearing from David's male cosmos. The extremes of expression among the students balance each other out in a kind of averaging of the emotional values down to a zero state of all passions.[36] In this way, they become both the ideal model of a perfectly functioning republican state and the chief witnesses of the genealogical model propagated by David, in which the inheritance of the teacher is taken up by the students: "Jeunesse intéressante et sensible, [je] te dirai souvent, garantis-toi de l'influence des froides passions, de la haine, de la jalousie, de l'envie [. . .]. Le génie ne respire que par les plus nobles sentimens, et les passions viles le tuent. Unissant ainsi les maximes de la morale aux leçons des beaux arts et aux préceptes de l'exemple, je guiderai tes pas dans le sentier difficile de la gloire, heureux de pouvoir bientôt les suivre sans distraction, et de laisser au bout de la carrière, des artistes plus dignes que moi de ses couronnes immortelles."[37]

Socrates ensured his post-mortem memoria in time by enlisting disciples who would surely carry on his philosophical ideals – the belief in a world of ideas, in the immortality of the soul, or, applied to David, in an art that transcends time. Here, as in many of David's paintings, an authority documenting the painting's message for posterity is integrated into the picture: Plato, Socrates' favorite stu-

---

35 Cf. Crow 1995.
36 Cf. Goethe's reassuring description, balancing extremes, of the character and affective equivalents in the arrangement of the disciples in Leonardo's Last Supper, a subject matter also related to the Socrates theme in content: Christ announces at the Last Supper that there is a traitor among them who will bring about his, that is Christ's, death by betrayal; Goethe 1994, 408–409.
37 Wildenstein 1973, no. 1198, 132.

dent, assumes the role of future historiographer. Sitting at the foot of the bed, momentarily overcome by his despair but nevertheless upright, he will soon fulfill his documentary duties by writing down the dialogues that will conserve Socrates' wisdom for all time. The whiteness of his robe and the antique drapery make him a sort of double of his teacher, to whom he seems to have made a silent vow to act as his perpetual memory that will outlast all future political upheavals. The figure of Plato represents a hinge in the temporal structure of the picture that is appropriate to his historiographical task: he sits with his back to Socrates, turned to the left, and thus – in accordance with the conventions of European reading direction – facing the past in the temporal structure of the picture, to which, however, he closes his eyes. His ears, though, are open, he is listening to the message for the future that Socrates is pronouncing in his back and that he will pass on – just as David was to immortalize the republican ideals and his hopes for the future in the picture. David's signature on the stone cubus on which Plato sits makes the historian and philosopher in his turn the double of the painter.

4 Leonidas as a Hero in a Lost Position: the Demise of the Roman Republican Ideals under Napoleonic Imperialism

The message of the last example to be analyzed here, *Léonidas aux Thermopyles* (Fig. 11),[38] seems to be that the republican *unité de doctrine*, which had been so conspicuously represented in David's festive stagings of the revolutionary period, was irretrievably broken after the 18th Brumaire of the year VIII (1799), but at the latest after Napoleon Bonaparte's self-empowerment as Emperor of the French in 1804 and his increasingly disastrous military expansion efforts, and that it makes the one who wants to continue to cling to it a hero in a lost cause.[39] This most curious picture, begun in 1799, completed in 1814, probably also wants to point out that the

---

38 Padiyar 2007, Chap. 1: "Heroism After the French Revolution: David's Leonidas at Thermopylae", 9–50 and Chap. 5: "Sade/David, in Chains", 142–174; Bordes 2005, 196–204. Rohlmann 2014, 269, interprets *Bonaparte at the Great Saint Bernard* as a deliberate counter-image to *Leonidas*, begun in 1798/99. Cf. Levin 1981; Gaehtgens 1984; Jonker 1990; Janzing 2007. An important source for understanding the picture is David's twelve-page self-description of the *Léonidas: Explication du tableau des Thermopyles, de M. David*, Paris 1814. This ego-document must, of course, be treated with due critical distance from any artists' self-statement.
39 Wilson-Smith 1996; Telesko 1998. Towards a Differentiated Evaluation of David's Relationship to Napoleon cf. Bordes 2005, Chap. "In the Service of Napoleon", 19–123.

revolutionary ideal of Spartan self-restraint and autonomous self-determination is no longer sustainable in the new post-revolutionary political context of the imperialist regime, especially since the Russian campaign of 1812 with its body count of more than 500,000 victims: One can only reflect melancholically that it is a bygone one.[40] David writes in the *ekphrasis* of his painting, "Léonidas, roi de Sparte, assis sur une roche au milieu de ses trois cents braves, médite, avec une sorte d'attendrissement, sur la mort prochaine et inévitable de ses amis."[41] It is the correspondence of the situations in terms of content that prompted David to choose an ancient gem depicting Ajax (after Winckelmann's *Monumenti antichi inediti* of 1767) as a model for the posture of Leonidas:[42] Here Ajax is on the verge of suicide because he cannot bear the opprobrium of being defeated by Odysseus in the contest for Achilles' weapons and then, in his frenzy, blinded by Athena, having slaughtered a herd of rams instead of his hated opponent.

As Werner Busch has noted for what he calls the third stage of the diagnosed crisis of the history painting around 1800, the hero himself also falls into the crisis, he becomes incapable of action, the moment of reflection suspends all activity.[43] The representation of his heroic action is replaced by meditation on the decision lying in the past (as already shown in the case of *Brutus*). Occasionally, unmotivated, blind actionism replaces action – in *Léonidas*, for example, the warriors on the left with their rosy buttocks, prancing in front of the altar and raising wreaths of flowers, turn away from Leonidas and toward an oath of ultimate collective readiness for death, which does not fit at all with their frivolous behavior. They turn the physical union of the brothers Horatii into its opposite and thus invert, even pervert it.[44] The homoerotic component of effeminate men resonates at various points in

---

40 On the equation of the Spartans at Thermopylae with Jacobin ideals in the second half of the 1790s, cf. Rubin 1976, 567: "The sacrifice of Leonidas exemplified a kind of patriotism that now seemed outdated – a completely conscious, perhaps fanatic willingness to face or even to seek a martyrdom in the name of a greater cause"; cf. Rawson 1969, esp. 230–291 (on Rousseau and Robespierre). Cf. Stemmrich 1990, 64–65: "Unter politisch repressiven Bedingungen wollte David das republikanisch-patriotische Ideal der Revolution 'zumindest' ästhetisch gewahrt sehen; Kunstautonomie gilt ihm als Minimalbestimmung eines politisch-patriotischen Ideals."
41 David 1814, 5.
42 Nash 1979.
43 Busch 1993, 137–180.
44 Cf. Michel 2000, 122–123: "Léonidas lui-même, qui se tient de face, au centre de la scène, dans une frontalité rigoureuse, laquelle est, en bonne rhétorique, le registre attitré de la première personne – le registre du sujet. Léonidas dit *je*. Aussi n'est-il plus dans l'action, mais dans une *parenthèse*, qui est digressive, sinon suspensive. À la ferveur de la troupe s'oppose la hauteur du chef: à la suractivité des figurants, la discursivité du héros. [. . .] [un] *remake* des *Horaces* en version *soft*, trente ans après."

Fig. 11: Jacques-Louis David, Léonidas aux Thermopyles, 1799–1814. Paris, Musée du Louvre. Public domain.

the painting: The farewell scene between father and son[45] is clearly marked by male-male desire in the graphic alternative of 1817. The female component seems to be absorbed and thus covered here by the exclusively male personelle.[46]

The young men on the right jumping after their weapons suspended in the tree are equally disqualified by their formal model, Giambologna's Mercury, as overdone mannerism in the eyes of the arch-classicist David. All the figures in the painting exhibit mannered elongations and compressions that are contrary to the classical figural ideals of the eighteenth century. Their postures are *recherché*, they

---

45 David 1814, 6–7: "*Deux jeunes gens de dix-sept à dix-huit ans,* que, par intérêt pour leur âge, et à cause des liens de sang, Léonidas avait voulu éloigner du combat, sous le prétexte d'une commission secrète pour les magistrats de Lacédémone, ont pénétré l'intention de leur général; ils lui font cette réponse énergique: *Nous ne sommes pas ici pour porter des ordres, mais pour combattre;* et, sans attendre sa réponse, impatiens de se placer dans les rangs, l'un se hâte de rattacher son cothurne, l'autre court embrasser son vieux père qui lui fait ses derniers adieux."

46 Alex Potts, referring to the *Léonidas*, has spoken of the image's "representation of an exclusively male imaginary world" and of its "quasi-totalitarian monism [. . .] in its repressive projection of an exclusive masculinity." Potts 1994, 237; cf. Potts 1990.

assume meaningless poses and turn empty pirouettes. While the *expression des passions* in Socrates was still balanced among the philosopher students and thus normatively and aesthetically correct, which is why David himself called this image "peut-être son chef-d'œuvre d'expression,"[47] here everything runs out of control. A more unheroic and unspartan appearance than the lascivious male dance on the left, a more effeminate one than that of the sandal-binder in the foreground or the libidinal homoerotic scene in the background is hardly conceivable: In this environment there is no more place for the hero of Sparta and thus for the revolutionary ideals of David. Wild jumping around counteracts the described dynamics of the *Serment du Jeu de Paume*, but also the static stance of the Horatii. These bodies are no longer republican and virtuously conditioned, but seem to perform the persiflage of an ancient Roman oath scene. The flower-wreathed band of brothers on the left makes a senseless sacrifice, for neither Hercules, the warrior, nor Aphrodite, the goddess of love and procreation, can do anything in the future for the doomed, who unite for the last time in barren *fraternité*.[48] But the emblem of futility of the actions depicted here is the blind old man on the left, who, despite his invalidity rendering him unfit for battle (iconically condensed in his unprofessional holding of the spear), insists on going into battle in blind zeal – after all, he cannot see the overwhelming power of the Persian army, which obscures the entire horizon. In contrast to the strong primary colors used in the *Horatii* and *Socrates*, which have masculine connotations and signal potency in the eyes of contemporary art critics, David uses the pink of Rococo boudoir painting, which has been criticized as effeminate, in a defamatory manner.[49]

Leonidas as the personification of the doomed ideal of the revolution can no longer fulfill the compositional function of binding the other figures to himself, of being a leader and figure of identification in this context – he is completely alone, he does not interact with those around him, he is in 'exile' (like David himself after 1816 in Brussels, where he took the Leonidas canvas). The rest of the painting's personelle, wildly animated and driven by their unrestrained passions, writhes away from him to the margins of the painting. The *unité* of the composition dissolves,[50] the solidary community of unbreakable *fraternité* no longer exists

---

47 Bordes 1983, 174.
48 Johnson 1993, 140–145.
49 "Son coloris est mâle et vigoureux, sa touche ferme et hardie, sa manière large, son pinceau facile, bien que d'une exécution qui ne laisse rien à désirer [. . .]." Quoted from Schnapper 1980, 83; cf. Bordes 2016. On David's rococo criticism cf. Padiyar 2015.
50 Jean-Baptiste-Bon Boutard already criticized this "défaut de clarté, et celui de précision et d'unité d'action" in his critique of the painting in the *Journal des Débats* of December 11th, 1814, 1–2; cf. Gaehtgens 1984, 243.

as *unité de doctrine*. The position of Leonidas marks the empty center, which, since the *régicide*, cannot be filled by any brotherhood, which is depicted here as perverted.[51] No one can spare an eye for the main figure. The gaze of the one sitting below him, his brother-in-law Agis, is blocked by the shield; only the blind man paradoxically stares in his direction – and the dark-skinned slave who leads him and who, as an outsider, holds a position just as marginalized as the failed hero in the center of the scene. In the excessive male ballet of the doomed, the *beau idéal* of the republican David is depicted as having failed. The *Léonidas* appears immediately as a resigned image that was no longer politically "functional" in the post-revolutionary period, but could only maintain patriotism on the canvas.[52]

But the moral victory is nevertheless carried away by this martyr for the right republican cause:[53] Leonidas preserves his autonomy in the picture by the fact that he – like Brutus – has made a lonely decision, which he realizes with deadly consequence – like Socrates – and which thus becomes his last. It is no coincidence that he is the only figure who has an unshaded place in the picture; he remains, completely isolated, in stoic calm and separated from the tumult in his strictly frontal position.[54] Dorothy Johnson has rightly pointed to the differentiation of *expressions des passions* in the years after 1800,[55] naming the facial expression of Leonidas, admiringly described by contemporaries as "sublime,"[56] as an example of these more subtle modes of depicting interiority, of feelings of disruption and alienation in the post-revolutionary, 'modern' hero.[57] Leonidas, in his passionless

---

51 On the genesis of this psychotic father image cf. Hunt 1992; Duncan 1981. James H. Rubin (1973) has pointed to the conjuncture of Oedipus imagery in post-Revolutionary French painting.

52 Stemmrich 1990, 80; cf. Levin 1980. In a similar way, Heather McPherson has interpreted the late portrait of Alexandre Lenoir, calling both the sitter and the painter "troubling anachronisms, battered gladiators from another era"; McPherson 2007, 229.

53 Cf. Kemp 1969, 183: "The message is one of moral beauty before physical power. Though Leonidas was to be defeated militarily, David wished to make it clear that the moral and spiritual victory after death was to belong to him, the virtuous martyr, not to Xerxes, the violent aggressor."

54 Cf. Ubl 2009, 150: In the *Sabines*, David has in a comparable way "die laterale Ausrichtung auf die Betrachter geöffnet und als Reflexionsraum bestimmt."

55 Johnson 1993, 151–162. Cf. Regius 1815, 23–24: "Comment bien exprimer cette vertu héroïque, cette fermeté invincible de Léonidas, ce caractère moral si difficile à peindre, puisque l'action en est toute intérieure. [. . .] la difficulté de ce tableau étoit sur-tout de rendre d'une manière animée des sentiments calmes; comme la vertu, et la mort pour la patrie et pour la loi?".

56 Cf. Regius 1815, 27–28: "Dans cette tête sublime, toutes les expressions sont réunies, c'est le *justum et tenacem*, l'homme viril et plein de courage; toute la grandeur de la patrie est présente à son *âme profonde*; l'invocation fixe ses yeux vers le ciel dans une immobilité qui exprime toute l'étendue de son dévouement."

57 Cf. Bordes 2005, 270–271.

diagnosis of the present, becomes a role model for radical modern subjectivity, focused solely on itself. He no longer takes part in the actual pictorial narrative; his gaze, which as in Brutus opens up the space of reflection for the beholder, is directed upwards out of the pictorial space and into the future, in which alone hope still exists.

The letter at his feet, with which Leonidas wanted to send two of his young comrades-in-arms to Sparta under the pretext of a secret mission and thus save them from their certain death, is wastepaper, since it belongs to the past. The only thing that will outlast the scene given in the painting is the historical documentation of the event as a future past, its memoria carved into the mossy rock by the Spartan on the left with the sword pommel. Here – as already in the *Tennis Court Oath*,[58] in *Socrates* and in the early *Death of Seneca* from 1773 –,[59] the historiographer is the actual hero in the picture, and he becomes the double of the painter, who transmits him in his painting to a future generation, which will perhaps someday be able to translate the lessons of history into political reality in a genuinely revolutionary sense.[60]

David's *Léonidas*, like all his paintings, reflects the political context of its time. It is an attempt to depict, through formal means, the post-revolutionary crisis and the transition to a restorative constitutional monarchy, which for David was impossible to accomplish.[61] The *Léonidas* is an image "that is all about the fragility of a legacy, the problem of an inheritance, and the prospects of its persistence."[62] David here historicizes his own revolutionary past, which, by being told as history in the mirror of historicity, appears in retrospect to be legitimized as worthy of representation and narrative.

---

58 Kernbauer 2011, 206.

59 In *Bonaparte on the Great Saint Bernard*, we find in the foreground the inscriptions, anonymous in this case, of the names of famous conquerors of the Alps (including Napoleon). Here, history has inscribed itself on the rock. Cf. Rohlmann 2014.

60 David 1814, 7–8, depicts this moment of time-transcending future foundation as sublime: "Un autre guerrier veut, avant le combat, transmettre à la postérité le souvenir de cette terrible et glorieuse journée: il s'élance, et grave avec le pommeau de son épée, sur la roche couverte de mousses, ces mots à jamais mémorables: [. . .] *Étranger, va dire aux Lacédémoniens que nous sommes morts ici, en obéissant à leurs ordres.* Non moins passionnés pour la gloire de leur pays, quatre jeunes Spartiates, quatre amis se tenant étroitement serrés, s'embrassent pour la dernière fois, et jurent, en offrant leurs couronnes, de réaliser par une mort glorieuse l'obligation que ces mots leur imposent."

61 Cf. Athanassoglou 1981.

62 Padiyar 2007, 16; 48: "The paradox of the image is that even within its conditions of postrevolutionary fragmentation of the political subject, Leonidas as such asserts the continuing possibility of a politically engaged radical art practice. In the same way, it articulates both the possibility of community-to-come, and, in its very 'incoherence', the historic conditions of its fragmentation."

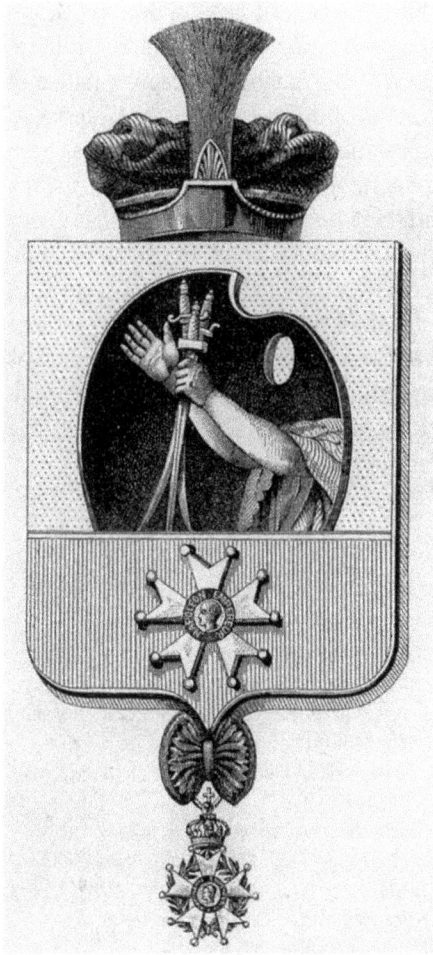

Fig. 12: Les armes de David, peintes par lui-même. Collection particulière.

The fact that David's unswerving loyalty (in German, untranslatable: "Nibelungen-treue") remained the highest good in his political and artistic inheritance even as *premier peintre* of the parvenu Napoleon Bonaparte (a title he was awarded in 1804) is documented not only by the *Léonidas*, but also by his self-designed coat of arms from 1808, four years after the former *Jacobin* had been appointed *chevalier de l'Empire*.[63] On this fantasy coat of arms (Fig. 12), his most successful early work, *The Oath of the Horatii*, is recalled once again. The painter's palette is now trans-formed into a shield that ostentatiously recites the artistic as well as political credo

---

63 Cf. Bordes 2005, 53.

of David the Republican. In the lower third, the coat of arms shows the Grand Cross of the Légion d'honneur and the "Empereur Napoleon" present on it in inscription as well as in a portrait bust all'antica. The emblematic representation of David's extremely productive phase as court artist to the emperor thus intervenes in and partially covers and conceals the revolutionary prehistory. The upper part, however, contains the painter's legacy to the future, which refers to the founding phase of his art: Just as the father of the brothers Horatii had passed on the swords to his sons, so he passes on his palette to the next generation of artists. But a significant deviation from the *Serment des Horaces* is to be noted: The hands of the sons have been eliminated from the picture – the one who is holding up the ideals here is apparently no longer supported by anyone from the next generation, which is split into factions. The question of who might still take up the swords to fight relentlessly for the Republic remains unanswered in the years after 1812. The incorrigible republican David paints it on his palette only as a defiant self-confession.

Bibliography

Athanassoglou, Nina. "Under the Sign of Leonidas: The Political and Ideological Fortune of David's *Leonidas at Thermopylae* under the Restauration." *Art Bulletin* 63.4 (1981): 633–649.

Bätschmann, Oskar. "Das Historienbild als 'Tableau' des Konflikts. Jacques-Louis Davids 'Brutus' von 1789." *Wiener Jahrbuch für Kunstgeschichte* 39 (1986): 145–162.

Bordes, Philippe. *Le Serment du Jeu de Paume de J.-L. David*. Paris: Éditions de la Réunion des Musées Nationaux, 1983.

Bordes, Philippe. "'Brissotin enragé, ennemi de Robespierre': David, conventionnel et terroriste." *David contre David. Actes du colloque au musée du Louvre*. Ed. Régis Michel. Vol 1. Paris: Éditions de la Réunion des Musées Nationaux, 1993. 319–347.

Bordes, Philippe. Ed. *La mort de Brutus de Pierre-Narcisse Guérin*. (Exh. Cat. Vizille, Musée de la Révolution Française). Vizille: Musée de la Révolution Française, 1996a.

Bordes, Philippe. "Le Robespierrisme de Jacques-Louis David." *Yearbook of European Studies*. Special Issue: *Robespierre – Figure-Réputation*. Ed. Annie Jourdan. 9 (1996b): 121–141.

Bordes, Philippe. "Les mânes de Brutus: Le roman noir de la vertu républicaine." *Histoire, images, imaginaires (fin XVe siècle–début XXe siècle). Actes du colloque international des 21–22–23 mars 1996 tenu à l'Université du Maine*. Eds. Michèle Ménard and Annie Duprat. Le Mans: Université du Maine, 1998. 365–379.

Bordes, Philippe. *Jacques-Louis David. Empire to Exile*. (Exh. Cat. Los Angeles, J. Paul Getty Museum and Williamstown, Mass. Sterling and Francine Clark Art Institute). New Haven and London: Yale University Press, 2005.

Bordes, Philippe. "The Rococo in France: The Politics of a Decorative Style." *Politikstile und die Sichtbarkeit des Politischen in der Frühen Neuzeit*. Eds. Dietrich Erben and Christine Tauber. Passau: Klinger, 2016, 177–199.

Bryson, Norman. *Tradition and Desire. From David to Delacroix*. Cambridge: Cambridge University Press, 1984.

Bryson, Norman. *Looking at the Overlooked. Four Essays on Still Life Painting*. London: Reaktion Books, 1990.

Bryson, Norman. "David et le *gender*." *David contre David. Actes du colloque au musée du Louvre*. Ed. Régis Michel. Vol. 1. Paris: Musée du Louvre, 1993. 703–724.

Busch, Werner. *Das sentimentalische Bild. Die Krise der Kunst im 18. Jahrhundert und die Geburt der Moderne*. München: C.H. Beck, 1993.

Carrier, David. "Was David a Revolutionary Before the Revolution? Recent Political Readings of 'The Oath of the Horatii' and 'The Lictors Returning to Brutus the Bodies of his Sons'." *Jacques-Louis David: New Perspectives*. Ed. Dorothy Johnson. Newark, DE: University of Delaware Press, 2006. 108–118.

Clark, T. J. "Painting in the Year Two." *Representations*. Special Issue: *National Cultures before Nationalism* 47 (1994): 13–63.

Clarke, Joseph. *Commemoration of the Death in Revolutionary France. Revolution and Remembrance, 1789–1799*. Cambridge: Cambridge University Press, 2007, ²2011.

Crow, Thomas E. "*The Oath of the Horatii* in 1785: Painting and Pre-Revolutionary Radicalism in France." *Art History* 1 (1978): 424–471.

Crow, Thomas E. *Painters and Public Life in Eighteenth-Century Paris*. New Haven and London: Yale University Press, 1985.

Crow, Thomas E. *Emulation. Making artists for revolutionary France*. New Haven and London: Yale University Press, 1995.

David, Jacques-Louis. *Léonidas: Explication du tableau des Thermopyles*. Paris: Imprimerie d'Hacquart, 1814.

David, Marcel. *Fraternité et Révolution française, 1789–1799*. Paris: Aubier, 1987.

De Baecque, Antoine. "Le corps meurtri de la Révolution. Le discours politique et les blessures des martyrs (1792–1794)." *Annales historiques de la Révolution française* 287 (1987): 17–41.

De Baecque, Antoine. *Le corps de l'histoire. Métaphore et politique (1770–1800)*. Paris: Calmann-Lévy, 1993.

Dowd, David L. *Pageant-Master of the Republic. J.-L. David and the French Revolution*. Lincoln, NE: University of Nebraska Press, 1948.

Duncan, Carol. "Fallen Fathers: Images of Authority in Pre-Revolutionary French Art." *Art History* 4 (1981): 186–202.

Ehrard, Jean, and Paul Viallaneix. Eds. *Les fêtes de la Révolution. Actes du colloque à Clermont-Ferrand (juin 1974)*. Paris: Éditions Garnier Frères, 1977.

Einecke, Claudia. Ed. *Final Moments. Peyron, David, and "The Death of Socrates."* Ohama, NE: Joslyn Art Museum, 2001.

Fend, Mechthild. *Grenzen der Männlichkeit. Der Androgyn in der französischen Kunst und Kunsttheorie 1750–1830*. Berlin: Reimer, 2003.

Gaehtgens, Thomas W. "Jacques-Louis David: Leonidas bei den Thermopylen." *Ideal und Wirklichkeit der bildenden Kunst im späten 18. Jahrhundert*. Eds. Herbert Beck, Peter C. Bol, and Eva Maeck-Gérard. Berlin: Gebr. Mann, 1984. 211–251.

Germer, Stefan and Hubertus Kohle. "From the Theatrical to the Aesthetic Hero: On the Privatization of the Idea of Virtue in David's *Brutus* and *Sabines*." *Art History* 9 (1986): 168–184.

Goethe, Johann Wolfgang von. "Joseph Bossi über Leonard da Vinci Abendmahl zu Mayland." *Sämtliche Werke nach Epochen seines Schaffens. Münchner Ausgabe*. Vol. 11.2. Eds. Johannes John, Hans J. Becker, Gerhard H. Müller, John, Neubauer, and Irmtraut Schmid. Munich: Hanser, 1994. 403–437.

Herbert, Robert L. *David, Voltaire, Brutus and the French Revolution: An Essay in Art and Politics*. New Haven and London: Yale University Press, 1972.

Hunt, Lynn. *The Family Romance of the French Revolution*. London: Routledge, 1992.

Janzing, Godehard. "'Leonidas' at the Crossroads: The Crux of the Composition." *David after David. Essays on the Later Work*. Ed. Mark Ledbury. New Haven and London: Yale University Press, 2007. 72–89.

Johnson, Dorothy. *Jacques-Louis David. Art in Metamorphosis*. Princeton, NJ: Princeton University Press, 1993.

Jonker, Marijke. "David's 'Leonidas aux Thermopyles' in the art-criticism of the Restauration." *Frankreich 1800. Gesellschaft, Kultur, Mentalitäten*. Eds. Gudrun Gersmann and Hubertus Kohle. Stuttgart: Steiner, 1990. 49–63.

Kemp, Martin. "J.-L. David and the Prelude to a Moral Victory for Sparta." *Art Bulletin* 51.2 (1969): 178–183.

Kemp, Wolfgang. "Das Revolutionstheater des Jacques-Louis David. Eine neue Interpretation des 'Schwurs im Ballhaus'." *Marburger Jahrbuch für Kunstwissenschaft* 21 (1986): 165–184.

Kernbauer, Eva. "Die Repräsentation der Menge. Jacques-Louis Davids Schwur im Ballhaus." *Bilder und Gemeinschaften. Studien zur Konvergenz von Politik und Ästhetik in Kunst, Literatur und Theorie*. Eds. Beate Fricke, Markus Klammer, and Stefan Neuner. München: Fink, 2011. 205–234.

Körner, Hans. *Auf der Suche nach der "wahren Einheit". Ganzheitsvorstellungen in der französischen Malerei und Kunstliteratur vom mittleren 17. bis zum mittleren 19. Jahrhundert*. Munich: Fink, 1988.

Koschorke, Albrecht. *Die Heilige Familie und ihre Folgen. Ein Versuch*. Francfort/M.: Fischer, 2000.

Ledbury, Mark. "Stages of creation. History, epic and theatre in David's early history painting projects." *Studiolo* 3 (2005): 169–190.

Ledbury, Mark. "Roman dreams. Two late drawings." *David after David. Essays on the Later Work*. Ed. Mark Ledbury. New Haven and London: Yale University Press, 2007. 170–187.

Lenoir, Alexandre. "David. Souvenirs historiques." *Journal de l'Institut historique* 2 (1835): 1–13.

Levin, Miriam R. "David, De Staël, and Fontanes: The Leonidas at Thermopylae and some Intellectual Controversies of the Napoleonic Era." *Gazette des Beaux-Arts* 95 (1980): 5–12.

Levin, Miriam R. "La définition du caractère républicain dans l'art français après la Révolution. Le *Léonidas aux Thermopyles* de David." *Revue de l'Institut Napoléon* 137 (1981): 40–67.

McPherson, Heather. "Endgame and Afterimage: David's *Portrait of Alexandre Lenoir*." *David after David. Essays on the Later Work*. Ed. Mark Ledbury. New Haven and London: Yale University Press, 2007. 218–231.

Michel, Régis. "La solitude de Léonidas." *Posséder et détruire. Stratégies sexuelles dans l'art d'Occident*. (Exh. Cat. Paris, Musée du Louvre). Ed. Régis Michel. Paris: Éditions de la Réunion des Musées Nationaux, 2000. 121–123.

Michel, Régis, and Marie-Catherine Sahut. *David, l'art et le politique*. Paris: Hazan, 1988.

Nash, Steven A. "The Compositional Evolution of David's Leonidas at Thermopylae." *Metropolitan Museum Journal* 13 (1979): 101–112.

Ozouf, Mona. *La fête révolutionnaire 1789–1799*. Paris: Gallimard, 1987.

Padiyar, Satish. *Chains. David, Canova, and the Fall of the Public Hero in Postrevolutionary France*. University Park: Penn State University Press, 2007.

Padiyar, Satish. "Who is Socrates? Desire and Subversion in David's *Death of Socrates* (1787)." *Representations* 102 (2008): 27–52.

Padiyar, Satish. "Last Words: David's *Mars Disarmed by Venus and the Graces* (1824)." *RIHA Journal* 0023 (June 1, 2011): URL: https://journals.ub.uni-heidelberg.de/index.php/rihajournal/article/view/69103, 1–45 [02.09.2022].

Padiyar, Satish. "Out of Time: Fragonard, with David." *Rococo Echo. Art, Theory and Historiography from Cochin to Coppola*. Eds. Melissa Lee Hyde and Katie Scott. Oxford: Oxford University Press, 2015. 213–231.

Polanowska, Jolanta. "Lettre d'un étranger sur le salon de 1787 Stanisława Kostki Potockiego: tekst z pogranicza sztuki i polityki." *Ikonotheka: prace Instytutu Historii Sztuki Uniwersytetu Warszawskiego* 14 (2000): 237–246.

Potts, Alex. "Beautiful Bodies and Dying Heroes: Images of Ideal Manhood in the French Revolution." *History Workshop Journal* 30.1 (1990): 1–21, URL: http://hwj.oxfordjournals.org/content/30/1/1.full.pdf [02.09.2022].

Potts, Alex. *Flesh and the Ideal. Winckelmann and the Origins of Art History*. New Haven and London: Yale University Press, 1994.

Puttfarken, Thomas. "David's Brutus and Theories of Pictorial Unity in France." *Art History* 4 (1981): 291–304.

Rawson, Elizabeth. *The Spartan Tradition in European Thought*. Oxford: Oxford University Press, 1969.

Regius, Claire, Comtesse Lenoir-Laroche. "Analyse du tableau de Léonidas aux Thermopyles." Claire Regius. *La France, ou réflexions sur le tableau de Léonidas de M. David, adressées aux défenseurs de la patrie, par une française*. Paris: Chez l'auteur 1815. 13–42.

Réimpression de l'Ancien Moniteur (Mai 1789–Novembre 1799). Vol. 21. Paris 1841.

Rohlmann, Michael. "Bonaparte versus Leonidas. Zur Psychomachie der Bilder bei Jacques-Louis David." *Wallraf-Richartz-Jahrbuch* 75 (2014): 267–284.

Rosenblum, Robert. *Transformations in Late Eighteenth Century Art*. Princeton: Princeton University Press, 1967.

Rosenblum, Robert. "David and Vien: Master/Pupil, Father/Son." *Jacques-Louis David: New Perspectives*. Ed. Dorothy Johnson. Newark, DE: University of Delaware Press, 2006. 45–57.

Rubin, James Henry. "Oedipus, Antigone and Exiles in Post-Revolutionary French Painting." *Art Quarterly* 36 (1973): 141–171.

Rubin, James Henry. "Painting and Politics, II: J.-L. David's Patriotism, or the Conspiracy of Gracchus Babeuf and the Legacy of Topino-Lebrun." *Art Bulletin* 58 (1976): 547–568.

Schnapper, Antoine. *David. Témoin de son temps*. Paris: Flammarion, 1980.

Schnapper, Antoine. "A propos de David et des martyrs de la Révolution." *Les Images de la Révolution Française. Actes du colloque*. Ed. Michel Vovelle. Paris: Publications de la Sorbonne, 1988. 109–117.

Schnapper, Antoine. Ed. *Jacques-Louis David, 1748–1825*. (Exh. Cat. Paris, Musée du Louvre). Paris: Éditions de la Réunion des Musées Nationaux, 1989.

Schneemann, Peter J. *Geschichte als Vorbild. Die Modelle der französischen Historienmalerei 1747–1789*. Berlin: Gebr. Mann, 1994.

Solomon-Godeau, Abigail. *Male Trouble. A Crisis in Representation*. London: Thames and Hudson, 1997.

Stein, Perrin. Ed. *Jacques Louis David. Radical Draftsman*. (Exh. Cat. New York, Metropolitan Museum of Art). New York: Metropolitan Museum of Art, 2022.

Stemmrich, Gregor. "Davids 'Leonidas bei den Thermopylen'. Klassizistisch vollzogene Kunstautonomie als 'Patriotisme sur la toile'." *Frankreich 1800. Gesellschaft, Kultur, Mentalitäten*. Eds. Gudrun Gersmann and Hubertus Kohle. Stuttgart: Steiner, 1990. 64–80.

Tauber, Christine. *Bilderstürme der Französischen Revolution. Die Vandalismusberichte des Abbé Grégoire*. Freiburg im Breisgau: Rombach, 2009.

Tauber, Christine. "Nachwort: Bauen auf der *tabula rasa*." Kersaint, Armand-Guy. *Abhandlung über die öffentlichen Baudenkmäler. Paris 1791/92*. Ed. Christine Tauber. Heidelberg: Manutius, 2010. 175–284.

Tauber, Christine. "Neue Identitäten – neue Genealogien. Jacques-Louis Davids künstlerische Selbstdarstellung nach dem 9. Thermidor 1794." *Zeitschrift für Kunstgeschichte* 79.3 (2016): 331–364.

Telesko, Werner. *Napoleon Bonaparte: der "moderne Held" und die bildende Kunst 1799–1815*. Wien: Böhlau, 1998.

Ubl, Ralph. "Eugène Delacroix' Figuration der Freiheit." *Ästhetische Regime um 1800*. Eds. Friedrich Balke, Harun Maye, and Leander Scholz. München: Fink, 2009. 139–164.

Wildenstein, Daniel, and Guy Wildenstein. *Documents complémentaires au catalogue complet de Louis David*. Paris: Les Éditions de la Bibliothèque des Arts, 1973.

Wilson-Smith, Timothy. *Napoleon and his Artists*. London: Thames and Hudson, 1996.

Zóltowska, Maria-Évelina. "La première critique d'art écrite par un Polonais: la *Lettre d'un étranger sur le salon de 1787*, par Stanislas Kostka Potocki." *Dixhuitième siècle* 6 (1974): 325–341.

Zóltowska, Maria-Évelina. "Stanislas Kostka Potocki, David, Denon et le Salon de 1787, ou la première critique d'art écrite par un polonaise." *Antemurale* 24 (1980): 9–65.

IV Romanticism and Realism

Barbara Vinken
Heinrich von Kleist's Napoleanic Romans in the Teutonic Woods

Some texts get caught. Red-handed. History played a cruel joke on Kleist's *Herrmannsschlacht*. The years from 1933 to 1945 came to be seen as a hideously accurate translation of the play into reality. Kleist's Herrmann was understood as having given the sign for National Socialism's call to total war and the ruthless extermination of Germany's enemies within and without. Against the nationalist ideology, Kleist stages the so-called wars of liberation from Napoleonic imperialism as a re-run of the Roman civil wars. The difference between friend and enemy dissolves: imperialistic Romans, i.e. French, and authentic Germanics are just the same. Kleist's play refuses to tell the birth of the German nation as a story of Arminius' wholesome, just national war against Roman or, for that matter, Neo-Roman (Napoleonic) imperialism.

Rarely has a text been read so brutally against the grain of what is clearly written in its pages. Rarely have whole generations of readers done such unseeing violence to a work of literature. What Kleist's drama actually does has been grotesquely distorted by a catastrophic history of reception, mired in the depths of a barbaric nationalism. This horizon of reception in which *Herrmannsschlacht* found itself – and which, far from reinforcing, it in fact radically opposes – nevertheless proved so powerful that Kleist's attempt at subverting the nationalist ideology of his time and, even more, that of the coming generation, died away nearly unheard. If Kleist's contemporaries were unable to understand the "farce" that *Herrmannsschlacht*, in their opinion, was, later audiences did not exactly share in their perplexity. They thought they understood perfectly what Kleist had wanted to communicate with his play: in their view, Kleist's *Herrmannsschlacht* is a call to total war against the occupying Napoleonic army – an exhortation to victory at any price. The end of liberating German lands from the French usurper justified, indeed sanctified, any means. Herrmann was understood without hesitation as Kleist's mouthpiece, and the drama as a clear call to political action.

The notion that *Herrmannsschlacht* was not only compatible with National Socialist ideology, but indeed in many ways even formed its basis, remained the general consensus even after the general condemnation of Nazi principles. The teleological reading of the play – a reading for which the play's reception under National Socialism only provided empirical confirmation – continued unabated. Kleist was seen as one of the prime originator of a geo- and biopolitical "blood and soil" agenda, inventor of ethnification, creator of the myth of a German na-

https://doi.org/10.1515/9783111334776-008

tion united by blood and marked by a common territory. In such a reading, Kleist speaks with the same voice as Fichte in the latter's *Address to the German Nation*: the German earth directly calls on the German people to wage total war against the enemy.[1]

As far as a more historically circumscribed reception is concerned, Carl Schmitt's apodictically pronounced thesis that *Herrmannsschlacht* is the "greatest partisan poem of all time" has been fatal.[2] Countless readers have willingly remained stuck to the flypaper of his claim for the play as a lesson in unconditional self-defense.

What this enthusiasm for the partisan and "all the horrors of unfettered war [alle Gräul des fessellosen Krieges!]" (IV, 3, 1484)[3] has allowed readers to overlook, however, is the fact that Schmitt never once refers to the issues of gender and generation that are so central to Kleist's total deregulation of war – that is, the dehumanizing utilization, as cynical as it is systematic, of wife, sons, and subjects by husband, father, and sovereign. Schmitt never asks the question of just how far the strategic sexual instrumentalization of women, girls, and children by their husbands, fathers, and sovereigns is permitted to be taken; indeed, such a concern lies wholly outside the scope of his imagination. In Schmitt's vision of partisan warfare, there *are* no parents or children, no women or men, only one gender and one generation. Kleist, however, sees things quite differently. No play stages as emphatically as *Herrmannsschlacht* the destruction of the "holiest bonds of nature" – to speak with Schiller – by the very one who should guarantee them, the *pater familias* and *pater patriae*.

Herrmann denies any warlike ambition, claiming he was never raised to be a hero, but rather that "a gentler goal was given to me: / It is my lot to be a husband to my wife, / A father to my dear children, / And a good ruler to my people [das sanftre Ziel sich steckte:/ Dem Weib, das mir vermählt, der Gatte,/ Ein Vater meinen süßen Kindern/ Und meinem Volk ein guter Fürst zu sein.]" (II, 1, 435–438). Appropriately enough, then, Herrmann indeed does not step heroically out onto the field of battle, but wages total war *precisely as* spouse, father, and sovereign on the patriarchal terrain of the family. It is to this war against his own family – against his wife, his children, and his subjects – that Herrmann owes his success. Instead of the heroic battle in which man struggles against man, in *Herrmannsschlacht* we watch scenes from a bestial war of the sexes that has as little virtue

---

1 Cf. Werber 2008.
2 Schmitt 1963, 15.
3 Kleist 2008. Translations slightly modified where necessary.

as it does heroics. Family ties – between father and children, husband and wife, sovereign and subjects – are *Herrmannsschlacht*'s real subject matter.

With this displacement of war onto the terrain of family, Kleist, in almost di-dactic fashion, utterly undermines the foundation myth of the Germanic nation current at his time. The German man, ideally incarnated in the character of Herr-mann, is doubly defined. In public he is heroic, warlike, striving for freedom against the – male and armed – foreign enemy. In the home, in contrast, he is a tender husband, a loving son, a caring father. Herrmann already inverts the norm of the heroic warrior by deliberately turning war into a hunt and men into beasts. But still more striking is his betrayal of that which should be most intimate, most private. Herrmann perverts the *patria potestas* with a vengeance. This husband uses his own wife as a decoy and thus dehumanizes her into an animal. This father plays the gambler and entrusts his own children to fickle *Fortuna*, making them hostages without their or their mother's knowledge or consent and nonchalantly putting their lives at risk. For this sovereign, nothing could be more opportune than the rape, slaughter, and dismemberment of one of his subjects.

The terrain of the family, the space of the *patria potestas*, is crucial for the legitimation of war, for the *bellum iustum*. The husband and father's obligation to protect and defend home and family is what makes a war just. For the ancient Romans, precisely this need to protect the family, to not leave women and chil-dren to the mercy of the enemy, was what justified the waging of wars. Livy, in one scene of his *History of Rome*, has Verginia's father define war, first, as the protecting of property, home, and livestock, but, second and more important, as the safeguarding of women and children from sexual enslavement, that is, from their violation, their penetration, but also, from their animalization.

Baudelaire would later also make use of this metaphor of animalization, de-scribing Andromache, made into sexual slave of the victorious Greeks, as a "vil bétail." The intactness of the secure state, on the other hand, is what guarantees that women will not be penetrated by foreign violence. This at least is one thing that the partisan war shares with traditional warfare: both derive their legiti-macy from the need to protect that which is most intimate, most private. Both are meant to safeguard "proper" family relations, the "proper" relation of parents to children, husbands to wives. A society, a nation, a people may not be cultivated at the expense of a deliberate and systematic animalization of the most intimate human relationships. Insofar as Kleist lets his Herrmann wage war in the very space that war is meant to protect, the very space for which war is taboo – the interior space of the family – he inverts with breathtaking accuracy the classic *topos* of war at each of its decisive points. Such marksmanship on Kleist's part can be no mere coincidence.

Against those readings that simply merge Herrmann's point of view with that of Kleist, other voices have lately been raised that read *Herrmannsschlacht* not as a work *of* propaganda, but as a work *on* propaganda.[4] To be both at the same time is not possible, as Joseph Goebbels, who was no stranger to such questions, well knew: "The moment one becomes conscious of propaganda, it is no longer effective."[5] Given this, Kleist's play can only do one of two things: it can either *call* for total war, or it can demonstrate *how* a call for total war is made. In the case of the latter, the play is indeed not effective, but instead explains how effectiveness is produced. If this is so, then Herrmannsschlacht would not be a play designed to instigate the people to action; rather, it would be a play *about* a populist instigator. Recent scholarship on *Herrmannsschlacht* has accordingly focused on the issue of Herrmann's rhetoric in Kleist's play. In so doing, it has revealed certain unsettling parallels. Herrmann, partisan fighter, unifier and liberator of Germany, is exposed as a Machiavellian politician, who with lies and deception artfully seeks to secure the power that he has usurped: an even more devious version of Fiesco, the tyrant of Schiller's eponymous drama. Herrmann, the quintessential German hero, is depicted in Kleist's play as wholly un-German in his use of cunning, perfidy, deception, and sensationalist propaganda: he appears in fact as an allegory of rhetoric, which Jesuitically sanctifies every means in light of its ends. Herrmann, the upright German, turns out in Kleist's play to be a con man, the very personification of the dissembling courtly flatterer and artist of equivocation. Herrmann is, in short, the epitome of everything that smacks of Frenchness. Indeed, could Kleist's Herrmann actually be – Napoleon?

But if this is the case, what is the play actually doing? Is Kleist trying to tell the politicians of his era that, to defeat Napoleon, one has to be even more Napoleonic than Napoleon himself? This, however, would logically mean that there is no reason and no possible moral justification for this war. We can agree right away that this war is fought in the most extreme manner possible: war against one's own family, the animalization of everything human into hunting spoils, animals for the slaughter, or raging beasts. But to what end? What purpose does such brutality serve, if at the same time the play not only fails to cement the opposition between the Germans and the Romans/French, but indeed simply discards it? What is the point of such a war, if friend and enemy are identical, if the play is no longer about the liberation of the freedom-loving, upright Germans from a Romano-French tyrannical-manipulative enslavement and usurpation, if

---

4 Angress 1977; and later under the name of Klüger 1994. See also: Greiner 2000, 104–106; Fischer, 2001, 166–168.
5 Joesph Goebbels in a speech to the first annual conference of the *Reichsfilmkammer*, Berlin 1937.

there is in fact nothing authentically German to defend or save? Would not such a war lack all legitimacy? What kind of political action could *Herrmannsschlacht* actually be a call *to*, if the play, using every artistic means at its disposal *against* the expected presentation of the Herrmann myth, demonstrates that Herrmann and Augustus/Napoleon are, in fact, interchangeable? How could a reader of the play "hate Rome and love the Germans," if the Germans are more Roman than the worst anti-Roman cliché? In this case, wouldn't Herrmann's success be just another catastrophe in a *series calamitatum*?

With the exception of minor characters such as the chambermaid Gertrud, the play – and here is of course one of the major difficulties it presents to interpretation – lacks any figure who might serve as stand-in for the reader and offer a perspective other than that of Herrmann's unvarying fomentation. The play is thereby, I would suggest, less a call to action than the mirror that Kleist defiantly holds up to what for him was an age without solace. I read Kleist's *Herrmannsschlacht* less as a piece of agitprop than as an analysis and interpretation of the historical situation. In fact, the image with which the Germans are presented in Kleist's mirror of the times can be determined with historical and political accuracy. *Herrmannsschlacht* offers much more than just a general suspicion of language or a declaration of the bankruptcy of Enlightenment humanism. For the reader's missing stand-in – or simply a different perspective from that of Herrmann – is in fact there after all; it is written into the play through the play's Roman intertexts and their reception in Kleist's time.

With *Herrmannsschlacht*, Kleist dismantles the nascent national consciousness of a German Nation, reversing and reverting Herrmann's process of Germanification. The Roman-German opposition, which Herrmann, originally the Roman Arminius, embodies, now falls to pieces. At the same time, this opposition between the Germans, supposed defenders of the intimacy of hearth and home, protectors of their freedom, their women and children – and the Roman servants of despots – who, themselves enslaved, wish to enslave all others – is precisely the condition for just war that in *Herrmannsschlacht* is *not* given.

Instead of this, Kleist resolutely rewrites German history as *translatio Romae*. The "farce" that *Herrmannsschlacht* was for Kleist's bewildered contemporaries offers no autochthonous beginnings of the German nation – as those forgetful of Rome and ignorant in matters of *translatio* would latter assume – but instead stages the impossibility of escaping the *translatio Romae*'s curse. Not the glorious founding of a freedom-loving nation of free men through their self-liberation from foreign domination, but just one more civil war is the tale Kleist tells.

Herrmannsschlacht is a palimpsest of its ancient Roman intertexts and their contemporary reception. In Kleist's time, Roman history lay under historical reflection in general as a kind of *basso continuo*. *Herrmannschlacht* contradicts the form of *translatio Romae* proposed previously by Schiller and Klopstock. Kleist evokes the commonplaces of their idea of *translatio Romae*, but only to invert, shift, and eventually reappropriate them. Already in Klopstock, however, the figure of Herrmann – despite all gestures to Germanic bard mythology – is inscribed into a *translatio Romae*. The democratic Germans strike back at the tyrannical Roman, thus becoming the heirs of the good part of Rome's legacy, i.e., Republicanism. Such a division of the *translatio Romae* between its two heirs apparent – the republican, freedom-loving Germans, full of warlike virtues, and the Romans, predisposed toward tyranny – is in fact already established in Tacitus. His Germans, as is well known, are primarily a projection screen for all the virtues – *libertas, gloria, virtus* – that the decadent and effeminate aristocracy of the Roman Republic in his opinion no longer embodies.[6] Since Romans have already lost the quintessential Roman virtues, the Rome of the early imperial phase comes entirely under the sway of a corrupt, tyrannical leadership whose victory the civil wars had already prefigured.

Hence in Klopstock the Hermannschlacht is presented less as a clash of two distinct peoples than a conflict between two different principles of governance, tyranny and republicanism. In his *Herrmanns Schlacht*, Klopstock embodies these two forms of governance in two separate nations: everything Roman ends up on the side of tyranny, everything German on the side of the Republic. The beginning of *Herrmanns Schlacht* makes this equation between Germans and Republicans explicit: the German's dagger piercing the heart of the Roman enemy is compared to Brutus's dagger in the "heart of the dictator [das Herz des Diktators]" Caesar (17). This is as much as to say that in the contemporary German reception of this Roman episode, republican principles and the rule of despots are set in opposition to one another. In contrast to the Germans, the Romans wage war not for reasons of justice but simply out of a tyrannical lust for power.

In Kleist's era, this crucial division of the *translatio Romae* already present in Klopstock takes on even greater political import. For Rousseau, the French Revolution was to bring about the reestablishment of the Roman Republic. After the Terror, however, the Revolution effectively became, for contemporary witnesses, a reprise of the Roman civil wars. Thus Napoleon could style himself as a new Augustus and peacemaker after the long, bloody conflicts of the civil war/the Revolution.[7] Now the *translatio* of the Roman Republic, having proved a failure in France, would be realized through the resolve of the German Storm and Stressers within the German lands. Schiller, in several of his plays, emerged as the most influential advocate of

---

6 Cf. Fuhrmanns Afterword 1972.
7 Cf. Morrissey 2013.

this *translatio* to Germany, even if he remained pessimistic about its chances for success: "The public did not understand *Fiesco*. In this country republican freedom is only a sound without meaning, an empty name – in Palatine veins flows no Roman blood. [Den Fiesko verstand das Publikum nicht. Republikanische Freiheit ist hier zu Lande ein Schall ohne Bedeutung, ein leerer Name – in Adern der Pfälzer fließt kein römisches Blut.]"[8]

With his *Herrmannsschlacht*, Kleist demonstrates that, to the contrary, in German veins flows *nothing but* Roman blood– albeit a very different kind than that which Schiller had hoped for. This Kleistian Roman blood does not bind all men together as brothers in republicanism; instead, just as Marius and Sulla waged the first of the Roman civil wars for the purpose of establishing tyrannical rule, Germans and Romans fall upon one another not as two different nations, but as factions of the same nation. In *Herrmannsschlacht*, Kleist inscribes the German war of liberation in the tradition, not of the Roman Republic, but of Rome devastated by civil war, where all republican spirit founders in the self-destroying struggle for tyrannical power at any price. Kleist shows that not only the founding of the German nation, but also the founding of a French empire by the new Augustus and bastard scion of the French Revolution, follows the ruinous logic of the Roman civil wars. No bleaker or more pessimistic perspective on European history is imaginable. Neither the Roman Republic promised by both German Idealism and the French Revolution, nor the pacified, eternal and global Augustan empire of which Napoleon dreamt – to put an end to civil strife, such as the French Revolution was then interpreted, once and for all – would become reality. In Kleist's vision, European history was at the moment of Napoleon's ascent the effective return of Rome torn apart by civil war, in which everyone, French and Germans alike, is engaged in the selfsame struggle for imperial, tyrannical dominance. In other words, the self-destruction staged in *Herrmannsschlacht*, its scorched-earth politics, is inspired not by considerations of partisan warfare but rather by the Roman civil wars' disastrous mutual, fratricidal annihilation.

Herrmann positions himself from the play's beginning explicitly within a *translatio* of the Roman civil wars. He cites Marius and Sulla, the protagonists of the first of the civil wars, expressing the wish to triumph "As Marius and Sulla never did [Wie nimmer Marius und Sylla triumphierten]" (I, 3, 356). Thus, not the liberation of Germania, but Rome as it was for those embroiled in the civil wars is his goal from the very outset: "Not very far, you claim? I wouldn't exactly say that. / To Rome – My fine gentlemen [. . .]! / If luck is even slightly on my side [Nicht weit? Hm! – Seht, das mögt' ich just nicht sagen./ Nach Rom – ihr Herren [. . .]/ Wenn mir

---

8 Schiller to Reinwald, May 5, 1784. Schiller 1983, 277.

das Glück ein wenig günstig ist]" (I, 3, 365–368). *Herrmannsschlacht* ends, meanwhile, with an image of Rome in ruins. This war is not about the liberation of "Germania's sacred soil [der Gemania heil'gem Grund]"; its goal is "to boldly set out [*aufzubrechen*] for Rome [nach Rom selbst mutig aufzubrechen]," to transform it into "a heap of desolate ruins [öden Trummerhaufen]" over which "nothing [. . .] but a black flag [nichts als eine schwarze Fahne]" waves (V, Final Scene 2629–2637). In a pointed reversal of the *pax augusta*'s limitless empire of eternal peace, Herrmann dreams of a both temporally and spatially limitless eternal *war* that will continue through to the generation of his grandsons. After the end of the first Roman civil war, to which Marius and Sulla gave their names, comes that sentence known to every schoolchild from Latin class. *Alia iacta est,* "the die is cast": this pithy phrase marks the January 10th, 49 BC crossing of the Rubicon, the river designating Rome's border, by Caesar and his armed legions, thus precipitating the second civil war. Marbod, in *Herrmannsschlacht*, likewise asks, "Where [. . .] / are the dice to fall? [Wo ist [. . .]/ Der Ort, an dem die Würfel fallen sollten?]" a few lines later repeating, "And which day has been fixed, / Finally and irrevocably, for the casting of the dice? [Und welchen Tag unfehlbar und bestimmt/ Hat er zum Fall der Würfel festgesetzt?]" (IV, 2, 1450–1455). With his Rubicon crossing, Caesar is following in the footsteps of Remus, who was the only one before him to have crossed the borders of the rising wall of the nascent city, with well-known consequences. Thus, in Caesar's actions, which mark a new beginning of the civil wars, Roman history also reveals itself as a repetition of the fratricide that lies at its origins. This is precisely what Marbod says – indeed not once but twice, in case anyone missed it the first time – allowing Kleist, with singular disambiguation, to identify the "German war of liberation" as civil war.

What Kleist stages is in fact the precise opposite of what his Herrmann says; namely, that, nationalist stereotypes of the time notwithstanding, Romans and Teutons, Germans and French do not represent fundamentally different forms of violence, but are fraternally united/divided within the very same violence. This helps to explain a fact about the play that has always been troubling, even disturbing, for its readers. Kleist keeps the question of who did what to whom artfully open. Is it the Germans or the Romans who rape Hally? Is it the Romans who kill the Germans in revenge for the deed, the other way around, or the Romans who kill other Romans? Is it Ventidius or Herrmann who writes the letter in which a lock of Thusnelda's golden hair is enclosed as a sample for the Roman Empress? With the greatest virtuosity, Kleist constructs a text that makes it impossible to determine just who commits these atrocities. Indeed, the question *cannot* be decided – this is what the text demonstrates and stages for the spectator – because in the end it doesn't matter. Romans and Germans are, *quid pro quo*, mutually interchangeable; they are, in fact, one and the same.

Using metaphors of sexual animalization, Kleist describes this civil war specifically as a hunt. The privileged terrain of this hunt is that terrain which falls under the jurisdiction of the *patria potestas*, the *pater patriae*. For this reason, the protagonists of two scenes crucial to the action of *Herrmannsschlact* are, respectively, a girl, a child, a daughter of the people ruled over by the sovereign Herrmann, and Thusnelda, Herrmann's own wife and sovereign consort.

Hally's rape is the turning point of the play. It is the gang rape of a young girl that finally succeeds in unifying the German tribes. Her own dismembered body, cut into fifteen pieces and sent to the fifteen separate clans, transforms the Germans into a single body united in the struggle against Roman foreign domination. This is in any case what the "noble sons of Teut [wackern Söhne Teuts]" emphasize as they finally stand "in the silent oak grove [im Hain der stillen Eichen]" on "Germania's sacred soil [der Germania heil'gem Grund]" (V, Final Scene, 2625–2629), now, thanks to Teut, without women:

> Hally, the despoiled virgin,
> Whom you sent, dismembered, to all the tribes
> As a symbol of our fatherland,
> Shook the torpor from our people.

> [Hally, die Jungfrau, die geschändete,
> Die Du, des Vaterlandes Sinnbild,
> Zerstückt in alle Stämme hast geschickt,
> Hat unsrer Völker Langmuth aufgezehrt.]
> (V, 23, 2548–2551)

Whether Hally's rape has been carried out by Romans, or by Germans disguised as Romans and incited by Herrmann to "scorch, burn, and plunder [sengen, brennen, plündern]" (III, 2, 953) is a question that cannot be answered. It is certain, however, that Hally, chased down by a pack of lustful hounds, is in the end turned fully into a hunting trophy through her kinsmen's expert "gutting [Aufbrechen]" (see IV, 5, 1570) of her violated body and Herrmann's subsequent administration of its dismemberment. The girl's butchered body is deployed as lure, granting a literal truth to the metaphor that underlies Kleist's description of the Roman/German conflict, the metaphor of the sexualized hunt. It is thus the transformation of human being into animal – hunting spoils, lure, or raging beast – that founds the German nation.

The monstrous brutality of the Hally scene, of a kind rarely equaled in literature, derives its themes from two foundational texts of the European tradition.
On the narrative level, Kleist is alluding both to a story in the Old Testament and
the Verginia episode of Livy's *Ab urbe condita*. The scene's imagery, on the other
hand, is indebted to a text no less central to the European tradition: namely,
Ovid's *Metamorphoses*. The metamorphosis of Ovid's Echo, in particular, is decisive for both the Hally and the Thusnelda narratives and ties these two hunting
scenes of Kleist's play together.

The scene of the dismemberment of Hally's body is modeled on Judges 19–29.
Rousseau mentions the story in his *Essay on the Origin of Languages*, a text with
which Kleist was familiar. Rousseau cites the story as an example of the power of
the symbol – here, Hally's dismembered body – a power that words can never
have. Indeed, the biblical dismemberment made such an impression on Rousseau
that he rewrote the story in his *The Levite of Ephraim*. For our considerations,
however, two factors in particular are relevant: first, Kleist alters the biblical act
of dismemberment insofar as he translates it from an act of despair, born of powerlessness, into an act of cunning and high rhetoric in which the body is turned
into decoy and lure. Also significant is the war of brothers that underlies both the
Old Testament narrative and Rousseau's retelling. A man, not wishing to sleep
among strangers, spends the night among one of the tribes of Israel, the tribe of
Benjamin. It is his own kinsmen who first desire to rape him and finally content
themselves with the substitute of his wife. His wife dies at dawn on his threshold,
where she has dragged herself with the last bit of her strength. The man carves
up the violated corpse of his wife and sends a piece to each of the twelve tribes of
Israel. The war that is thereby set off is described throughout as a war against a
tribe of one's own people, as a war of brother against brother, as civil war.

Still more crucial is the Hally episode's reversal of the Verginia narrative in
Livy.[9] In Livy, the narration of the intended rape and eventual murder of the
maiden Verginia heralds the banishment of the Decemviri in 449 BC and the rein-
statement of the Republic. In its linking of political upheaval to the question of
patria potestas, the story establishes politics as gender politics and defines tyranny as an encroachment upon *patria potestas*.

Hally's rape and death by stabbing is a mutilated echo, a reverberation of the
Verginia story. Echo – nonsensically garbled, mechanical repetition – is the figure
that not only regulates the plot of the scene in mimetic violence, but also deter-
mines the scene's interrupted, staccato, mechanically repeating speech. Thus,
Hally names *Herrmannsschlacht*'s poetics, in the same way that the wretched

---

9 Livius, Titus. *Ab urbe condita* III, Ed. Ludwig Fladerer. Stuttgart: Reclam, 1988.

girl's name holds her fate: for Hally is also a mutilated reverberation, an echo of the hunting call *halali.*

In Livy, the beautiful Verginia, daughter of the plebian Verginius and bride-to-be of the former plebian tribune Icilius, is desired the Roman Decemvir Claudius Appius. Verginia, however, will not be seduced by money and sweet talk; therefore Appius, blinded by animal lust, abuses his status as judge in a "measureless act of violence" and turns from lawgiver to lawbreaker. He declares Verginia to be the daughter of the slave of one of his clients. With the enforcement of this judgment, Verginia no longer comes under Verginius's *patria potestas*; now as the child of a slave she comes under a proxy *patria potestas* and, effectively, under Appius's power of disposition.

Verginia's father, in the field, once alerted to the situation by the men of his family is able to reach the city before Appius, who will stop at nothing, can post a dispatch to arrest him. Arriving just in time for the trial, Verginius appears before the assembled crowd and appeals for protection from his countrymen. To this end, he, a heroic guardian of the city, expounds to the Romans upon the nature of war, stating that his protection of the city's safety on the field of battle is for naught if within the secure city's own walls its women and children "must suffer that which in a conquered city one fears as the worst" (III, 47) – violation, rape. But on this particular morning the announced trial never happens: force takes over from words. In a grotesque distortion of legal procedure, Claudius Appius awards Verginia to his proxy as slave. This judgment dispossesses Verginius of his daughter, stripping him of his *patria potestas* and delivering her over to her rapist. The judgment is enforced by the authorities, the lictors called up for the occasion, against which the unarmed crowd is powerless. Thereupon Verginius uses a subterfuge and leads his daughter away to the shrine of Venus Cloacina, the goddess of purity. The weaponless man swipes a knife from a butcher and pierces his daughter's breast: "With the only means at my disposal, I release you, my daughter, to freedom. [. . .] You, Appius, and your head, with this blood I curse" (III, 48).

Thus, Verginia does not become sexual chattel and remains an unsullied virgin. She is stabbed by her father so as not to be penetrated by the Decemvir. The knife wielded by the father's hand preserves her purity and her freedom. This sacrifice effects a regime change: Claudius Appius, the ruler who rules himself so poorly that he comports himself towards his subjects' wives and children like a victorious enemy, is deposed, and Rome liberated from despotism. The state of war introduced into the city by the brutal caprice of Appius's tyranny is brought to an end. As Marie Theres Fögen has put it, "Father's hand saves fatherland."[10]

---

10 Fögen 2002, 105–108; Lüdemann 2013; Joshel 2002.

Kleist's vision of the founding of the German nation, in contrast, subverts Livy's opposition of inside and outside, enemy and friend, tyrant and *res publica*. In so doing, *Herrmannsschlact* not only alters its Roman intertext, it also distorts the founding trope of the French Revolution, as prefigured in Livy's Verginia story and later adapted and refined by Schiller in his *William Tell*. As in Livy's account and Schiller's drama, the point in the Herrmann narrative is the forging of alliance, the making of a social body for the purposes of throwing off tyranny and securing freedom. The case of *William Tell* is especially revealing for Kleist's *Herrmannsschlacht*, since both stories deal with the founding of a social body in struggle against foreign domination. If Schiller plays it straight, however, Kleist – so to speak – butchers the founding figure of the republic completely.

After Livy – and of course also after Schiller – the necessity of forming such fraternal alliances arises from the tyrant's perversion of the relation between inside and outside, friend and enemy. The revolutionary rhetoric of Schiller's play speaks precisely to this ancient problematic. The need to end such perversion is what legitimizes revolution and necessitates an insurrectionist change to the political order, or more precisely, a restoration of the republic, of the *res publica*. The tyrant is the one who interferes in the *patria potestas*, who encroaches upon families, women, and children. Already in Jean Bodin,[11] the sixteenth century theorist of monarchial legitimacy, it is this encroachment upon the home, this triumphal assaulting of women that turns the ruler from a lawful king into a lawless tyrant. The tyrant behaves like the worst of victorious enemies, exercising his power of sexual disposal on the girls and women of the city. In this way, the ruler, the tyrant, becomes himself the enemy, and as such must be disposed of by the band of fathers. So it is in Livy, as well as in Schiller. Indeed, not once but twice for Livy, at the beginning of insurrection, at the beginning of the restoration of the republic, lies the ruler's lawless interference in the *patria potestas*, the taking of other men's women, the wives and daughters of the ruler's subjects. The married Lucretia is raped in her own home, the house of her husband. Verginia, daughter and bride-to-be, is unlawfully, ruthlessly removed her father's rule before his very eyes, before the eyes of her betrothed and the horrified public, and brought under the rule of the ruler who cannot rule himself. In *William Tell*, it is the assaults on Stauffacher's wife Gertrud and on Tell's own son, at whose head Gessler forces Tell to aim his bow, that founds the revolutionary coalition. The band of brothers rebels against tyrannical rule. Not only the concerns of every husband and father, but also all those who come under the protection of husbands and fathers, must be protected against this infringement, this intrusion of

---

11 On Wilhelm Tell and the fraternity: Koschorke 2003.

that which is most hostile into that which is most intimate; the *res publica* must be defended against tyranny. The tyranny of Fiesco, in Schiller's "republican tragedy," is illustrated by the fact that he does not deem it necessary to revenge the rape of Verrina's daughter, but is instead erotically attracted to the victim. This is staged most blatantly in Fiesco's – unintentional – stabbing of his own wife. After that, his death by drowning at the end of the play is merely a formality. The restitution of the patriarchy, the protection of the domestic sphere, the rehabilitation of the inviolability of women and children – and thereby, *a fortiori* since German Idealism, the protection of the only space in which humanity can develop untainted – is what makes men into legitimate revolutionary subjects.

> Our dearest treasures call to us for aid,
> Against the oppressor's violence; we stand
> For our country, for our wives, for our children!
>
> [Der Güter höchstes dürfen wir vertheid'gen
> Gegen Gewalt – Wir stehn vor unser Land,
> Wir stehn vor unsre Weiber, unsre Kinder]
> (II, 2 V. 1275–1277)[12]

This sentence, spoken by *William Tell*'s Stauffacher, could just as easily have been spoken by Livy's Verginius. Indeed, in Livy, the "stand for our wives, for our children" takes the most extreme form possible, that of the murder of a daughter by her own father, who has in all other respects been reduced by the tyrant to powerlessness.

What, then, is Kleist's take on this motif – which in his era provided such a crucial legitimizing force for the revolution and the republic – in his *Herrmannsschlacht*? In every way imaginable, Kleist alters and distorts this heroic story into a story of abjection. He scrambles the opposition between inside and outside, between friend and enemy, between tyrant, *patria potestas*, and *res publica*. In terms of rhetoric, we descend from Livy's and Schiller's noble pathos down into the vertiginous abyss. In terms of technique, the victim upon whose sacrifice a community is founded is replaced by a *homo sacer*, the one too unclean to be sacrificed. And in terms of ideology, a story of two *fundamentally different forms* of force – a lawful force that strikes back at an intolerable, tyrannical, illegitimate force in order to save nothing less than humanity itself – is substituted by a *single, identical,* ruinous and animalizing violence.

---

12 Schiller, *William Tell*. Trans. Theodore Martin.

A helpless, nameless person, transformed by bestial violence into something abject, not even recognizable as human, is brought onto the stage. This non-person does not even appear in the play's list of characters, for, deprived of both shape and consciousness, she is in fact no longer a person at all. She is raped by at least "three of those ruttish Apennine dogs [Drei'n dieser geilen appeninschen Hunden]" (IV, 4, 1540). The sight of her is unbearable: "O the poor, shame-covered creature! / Trampled, filth-wallowed, / Head and chest smashed to pieces [O des elenden, schmachbedeckten Wesens!/ Der fußzertretnen, kotgewälzten,/ An Brust und Haupt zertrümmerten Gestalt]" (IV, 4, 1545–1547). Her gender can no longer be determined: "Who is it? A man? A woman? [Wer ist's? Ein Mann? Ein Weib?]" (IV, 4, 1548). In contrast to Verginia, who is aware of what is happening to her, she is all but unconscious and can bear no witness. This "person," at whose very sight, as at the death of Christ, the sun goes dark, must be hidden from all eyes and covered at once with a sheet. No torch may light up this nameless misery.

Kleist thus stages the question of what can and may be represented, what is permitted to be visible to the public eye, *coram publico*. That which is in the truest sense of the word *obscene* enters the scene: what the scene offers to be seen is unbearable to sight. In the bluntest words and without any rhetorical flourish the worst thing of which one can speak is spoken. The sheer magnitude of the destruction, the total eradication of human being that here takes place is further underscored by the fact that the father does not even recognize his daughter by her face by her feet.

Upon this rape and disfigurement by the "three [. . .] ruttish Apennine dogs [Drei'n dieser geilen appeninschen Hunden]" follows a second penetration of the insensible body *coram publico*, before the assembled peoples, once again by three men. Following the logic of the hunting motif, this second stabbing is also a "gutting [Aufbrechen]": "Rudolf, you take the right, Ralf, you the left! / – Are you ready, tell me? / THE KINSMEN [*unsheathing their daggers*]: We're ready, let's go! [‚Rudolf, Du nimmst die Rechte, Ralf, die Linke!/ – Seid Ihr bereit, sagt an?' DIE VETTER [indem sie die Dolche ziehen] 'Wir sind's! Brich' auf!'] (IV, 5, 1572–1573). *Aufbrechen*, "gutting," is a hunting term, referring to the act of removing the slain animal's innards so that they will not poison the meat. Through the pulling apart of her limbs – "you take the right, Ralf, you the left [Rudolf, Du nimmst die Rechte, Ralf, die Linke!]" – Hally's body is laid out for gutting. In this gesture of opening up and laying bare, the act of rape is repeated. The already destroyed person is destroyed a second time; undone anew she "collapses [. . .] in a heap [übern Haufen]" (IV, 5, stage directions).

Thus, the men of the family, in grotesque mimesis, repeat the hostile penetration of sexual violence; it is almost as if they visit this destructive violence on the "person" a second time to turn her yet again into what she already is: an abject nothing. In a pointed reversal of the hope of Lessing's Emilia Galotti, who, invoking Livy, states "There was once a father, who, in order to save his daughter from disgrace, stabbed her through the heart with the first dagger he could find – and thus gave her life for the second time,"[13] this father grants his daughter no second life, but only a second and final death. He does not just stab her but gives her over to *damnatio memoriae*. Her blood will not wash over the tyrants in vengeance like the blood of Verginia; instead, she is to be namelessly consigned to oblivion: "Die! Return to dust! And may your tomb / Be sealed by ever-lasting oblivion [Stirb! Werde Staub! Und über Deiner Gruft/ Schlag' ewige Vergessenheit zusammen]" (IV, 5, 1573–1574).

With Hally, Kleist radically undermines the paradigm of the founding and fundamental sacrificial victim staged by Livy in his tale of Verginia. In its place emerges the paradigm of hunting spoils. Hally is the precise antithesis of Verginia: instead of being "pure," she is infinitely soiled; instead of her body remaining "intacta," it is multiply penetrated, "trampled [fußzertreten]," "smashed [zertrümmert]" (IV, 4, 1546–1547); instead of voluntarily offering herself as sacrifice, her insensate flesh – which, reduced to the status of prey, no longer has anything human about it – is "gutted." No noble blood flows from this body; its form is "filth-wallowed [kothgewältzt]" (IV, 4, 1546). Hally's execution does not avenge the enemy's defilement of her body; rather, the defilement is simply repeated and consummated by her own kinsmen: first hunted down by hounds, the victim is then "gutted" by father and brothers, the leaders of the pack.

The speech given by Herrmann, himself the possible author of the rape, completes this hunting scene: as a last step, the girl turned prey is carved up into fifteen pieces. The double entendre of Herrmann's echoically repeated "Brich auf!" evokes once again the disembowelment of hunted animals and makes clear just exactly what is going on in this scene. In contrast to the good father Verginius and the sacrifice of his Verginia that founds the *res publica* stands the unnatural father Herrmann, who animalizes the child Hally into quarry. The sovereign is but the double of this unnatural father: with both, not only every *patria potestas*, but also every *res publica* founded on its basis is ruined from the very beginning.

Go, unnatural father [*Brich', Rabenvater, auf*] and, with your kinsman
Carry this despoiled virgin
To a remote corner of your house!
The German tribes number fifteen;
With the sharp edge of your sword,

13 Gotthold Ephraim Lessing, *Emila Galotti: A Tragedy in Five Acts.* rans. Edward Dvoretzky (New York: Frederick Ungar Publishing Co., 1962).

Divide her body accordingly, and by fifteen messengers,
I'll give you fifteen horses for this, send the parts
To each of the fifteen tribes of Germany.
Helping you to your revenge, the corpse will rouse
Across Germany even the deadest elements.
The storm winds howling through the woods
Will shriek Rebellion! And the sea beating
The ribs of the shore will shout Freedom!

[Brich', Rabenvater, auf, und trage, mit den Vettern,
die Jungfrau, die geschändete,
In einen Winkel Deines Hauses hin!
Wir zählen funfzehn Stämme der Germaner;
In funfzehn Stücke, mit des Schwerdtes Schärfe,
Theil' ihren Leib, und schick' mit funfzehn Boten
Ich will Dir funfzehn Pferde dazu geben,
Den funfzehn Stämmen ihn Germaniens zu.
Der wird in Deutschland, Dir zur Rache,
Bis auf die todten Elemente werben:
Der Sturmwind wird, die Waldungen durchsausend,
Empörung! rufen, und die See,
Des Landes Ribben schlagend, Freiheit! brüllen.]
(IV, 6, 1608–1620)

The people echo what Herrmann prompts them to say: "Rebellion! Revenge! Freedom! [Empörung! Rache! Freiheit!]" (IV, 6, 1621). True to his aims, with this dismembered corpse Herrmann turns Germania's member tribes into one unified body, burning with hatred. His mission accomplished, Herrmann can now turn to other tasks: "Come Eginhardt! There remains nothing for me / To do here! Germany is aflame [Komm Eginhardt! Jetzt hab' ich nichts mehr/ An diesem Ort zu thun! Germanien lodert]" (IV, 6, 1623–1624).

In this scene there is no tyrant, no enemy to whose expropriatory violence a legitimate force might be opposed. There is no band of fathers protecting "Our dearest treasures [der Güter höchstes]" from seizure or standing up "for our wives, for our children. [unsre Weiber, unsre Kinder]" For, again, it is always possible that not the enemy usurpers, but Herrmann himself, is the one who has presided over the rape. Whatever the case may be: for this sovereign, Hally's rape is a godsend. "Our wives, our children" are not the dearest treasures; they are nothing but coldly appraised and strategically deployed means to an end, namely, the end of unifying the German lands. In Kleist, father and tyrant act identically, joined together in one and the same history of violence. Fathers, kinsmen, and sovereigns only complete what the rapacious enemy – themselves? – has already begun: the brutal animalization of just these "dearest treasures." For Kleist, Germanness means that husbands turn their wives, fathers and sovereigns their daughters, into mere beasts. This is the total perversion of what the Roman principle of the just war and the legitimate revolution alike were meant to protect: through the *patria potestas*, the inviolability of the *res publica*.

Herrmann is not Kleist's mouthpiece. *Herrmannsschlacht* is neither a call to total war nor an instruction manual for partisan warfare, and Kleist does not demonstrate that any means are sanctified by the end of the German lands' liberation from their French usurpers. The aim of the drama is not to incite to political action; it is on the contrary an analysis of the historical situation that seals the end of all hopes for the French Revolution, particularly in its Schillerian-republican version. There will be no *translatio Rei publicae* to Germany. Kleist conveys this through the deliberate breakdown of Livy's iconic scene of republicanism, which – obviously – as the foundation myths of the Roman Republic, was intended to mark the end of tyrannical domination. Herrmann is a depraved Verginius, a distorted Brutus, a perverted Collanus. As sovereign, father, and husband, he transforms the very space whose protection constituted the republic's legitimacy into the space of a despotic rapaciousness. The *patria potestas* is no longer safeguarded from tyranny by a fraternal covenant of fathers; the fathers themselves tyrannize.

European history is *translatio Romae*. In Kleist, however, this phrase no longer expresses a promise, as it once had for Klopstock and Schiller, but a curse. Kleist understands the wars of liberation not as a *translation Rei publicae* but as a *translatio Tyrranidis*. The so-called wars of liberation only continue what the Roman civil wars had begun. Germans and Frenchmen are identical, fraternally divided under one reign of violence. History is destined to remain a mutilated echo, the repetition of itself in the battle of like with like. With *Herrmannsschlacht*'s Hally, echo of the hunting cry *halali*, Kleist, invoking Ovid's *Metamorphoses*, gives this European history its Roman name.

Bibliography

Angress, Ruth K. "Kleist's Treatment of Imperialism. 'Die Herrmannsschlacht' and 'Die Verlobung in St. Domingo'." *Monatshefte* 69 I (1977): 17–33.
Fischer, Bernd. "Fremdbestimmung und Identitätspolitik in *Die Hermannsschlacht.*" *Kleists Erzählungen und Dramen. Neue Studien.* Eds. Paul Michael Lützeler and David Pan. Würzburg: Königshausen & Neumann, 2001. 165–178.
Fögen, Marie Theres. *Römische Rechtsgeschichten. Über Ursprung und Evolution eines sozialen Systems.* Göttingen: Vandenhoeck & Ruprecht, 2002. 105–108.

Fuhrmann, Manfred. "Afterword." Tacitus. *Germania*. Stuttgart: Reclam, 1972. 98–111.

Greiner, Bernhard. *Kleists Dramen und Erzählungen*. Tübingen and Basel: A. Francke, 2000. 104–106.

Klüger, Ruth. "Freiheit, die ich meine. Fremdherrschaft in Kleists 'Hermannschlacht' und der 'Verlobung in St. Domingo'." Klüger, Ruth. *Katastrophen. Über deutsche Literatur*. Göttingen: Wallstein, 1994.

Lessing, Gotthold Ephraim. *Emila Galotti: A Tragedy in Five Acts*. Trans. Edward Dvoretzky. New York: Frederick Ungar Publishing Co., 1962.

Lüdemann, Susanne. "Weibliche Gründungsopfer und männliche Institutionen Verginia-Variationen bei Lessing, Schiller und Kleist." *Deutsche Vierteljahrsschrift für Literaturwissenschaft und Geistesgeschichte* 87 (2013): 588–599.

Joshel, Sandra. "The Body Female and the Body Politic: Livy's Lucretia and Verginia." *Sexuality and Gender in the Classical World: Readings and Sources*. Ed. Laura McClure. Oxford: Wiley-Blackwell, 2002. 163–190.

von Kleist, Heinrich. *The Battle of Herrmann*. Trans. Rachel MagShamhráin. Würzburg: Königshausen & Neumann, 2008.

Morrissey, Robert. *The Economy of Glory: From Ancien Régime to the Fall of Napoleon*. Chicago: University of Chicago Press, 2013.

Schiller, Friedrich. *Die Verschwörung des Fiesko zu Genua*. Schiller, Friedrich. *Schillers Werke*. Nationalausgabe, Eds. Norbert Oellers and Siegfried Seidel, Weimar: Hermann Böhlhaus Nachfolger, 1983.

Livius, Titus. *Ab urbe condita III*. Ed. Ludwig Fladerer. Stuttgart: Reclam, 1988.

Schiller, Friedrich. *William Tell*. Trans. Theodore Martin. http://www.gutenberg.org/cache/epub/2782/pg2782.html. 2001 Translation slightly altered. Schiller, Friedrich. *Wilhelm Tell*. https://www.projekt-gutenberg.org/schiller/tell/tell22a.html. (Accessed Date: June 13, 2023)

Schmitt, Carl. *Theorie des Partisanen*. Berlin: Duncker & Humblot, 1963.

Werber, Niels. "Die geopolitische Erfindung von Volk und Reich. Heinrich von Kleists 'Hermannsschlacht' als Gründungsmythos." *Deutsche Gründungsmythen. Jahrbuch Literatur und Politik*. Eds. Matteo Galli and Heinz-Peter Preusser. Vol. 2. Heidelberg: Universitätsverlag Heidelberg, 2008. 91–104.

Stephan Leopold
Empire – Typologie – Apocalypse
La double temporalité romaine dans le roman de Stendhal
à Proust

À la mémoire de Rainer Warning

I Le Temps en Occident : saint Jean, Virgile, saint Augustin

L'Occident, selon la diction de François Hartog, est aux prises avec le temps. Dans son livre récent, *Chronos*, l'historien français retrace cette notion issue de la pensée grecque jusqu'à notre âge, mais, bien évidemment, ce qui est décisif dans ce parcours-là c'est la temporalité judéo-chrétienne (Hartog 2020, 33–85). Depuis la canonisation des Saintes Écritures au quatrième siècle de notre ère, le temps en Occident suit une portée typologique : dès lors, il se compose de deux phases complémentaires dont la relation est celle d'une préannonce et d'un accomplissement, ou bien, en latin, l'interaction de *figura* et *implementum*. L'Ancienne Alliance est régie par la temporisation dans ce sens que le Messie, préannoncé à plusieurs reprises par les prophètes, se fait attendre, tandis que la Nouvelle Alliance se fonde précisément sur l'arrivée du Messie et sa mission salvatrice. Ces deux temps, on le sait, entretiennent des rapports, car les Évangiles répondent, pour ainsi dire, d'une façon intertextuelle aux prédictions des prophètes. Mais ce n'est pas tout. Quoique la vie, la mort et la résurrection du Sauveur mettent fin à l'attente messianique de l'Ancienne Alliance, le temps au sens propre ne s'épuise que plus tard. À peu près contemporaine des Évangiles, le Livre de la Révélation de saint Jean annonce l'abrogation du temps dans l'éternité et la descente de la Jérusalem céleste après le Jugement final. Écrite après l'an 70 à la suite de la destruction du temple de Jérusalem par Tite, la Révélation de saint Jean est un livre apocalyptique dans notre sens moderne mais, au même titre, un livre romain ou bien anti-romain. Sous le numéro 666 de la bête apocalyptique (Ap, 13, 18) se cache le César[1], et la grande prostituée de Babylone (Ap, 17s.) n'est autre que la

---

[1] « En grec comme en hébreu, chaque lettre avait une valeur numérique selon sa place dans l'alphabet. Le chiffre d'un nom est le total de ses lettres. Ici "666" serait César-Néron (lettres hébraïques) ; "616" (Var.) César-Dieu (lettres grecques). » Cf. *La nouvelle Bible de Jérusalem*, 1116, note 17a.

https://doi.org/10.1515/9783111334776-009

cité qui domine à ce moment-là toute la Méditerranée, la Germanie et la Bretagne. L'Apocalypse est donc un livre sur la fin de Rome et sa substitution par la Jérusalem céleste.

La problématique de cette conception est bien connue : la parousie du Christ, laquelle doit initier le temps proprement apocalyptique, ne s'est pas réalisé, et Rome, quoique détruite, se présente sous la forme d'un spectre hantant la temporalité en Occident. Cela est lié à plusieurs raisons, entre autres, au fait que le pouvoir temporel récupéré par les Carolingiens ne peut pas laisser de côté le mythe romain qui est à la base de son récit de légitimation. Dans cette optique, le Saint-Empire est le successeur légitime de Rome, ou bien, pour revenir à la double temporalité mentionnée plus haut, son accomplissement typologique. Ce qui était l'empire païen devient désormais un empire sacré : de l'*imperum* au *Sacrum imperium*. Le prix de cette transposition n'est pas mince, on le sait, car il en résulte les frictions continuelles entre le pouvoir temporel et le pouvoir spirituel, donc entre la royauté et l'église (cf. Dempf 1929 ; surtout le chapitre « Christ und Antichrist », 285–334).

Néanmoins, ce qui m'intéresse avant tout ici est autre chose, par ailleurs non moins importante, qui nous renvoie encore une fois à l'Antiquité. Je me réfère à l'épopée fondatrice de l'empire augustéen, *L'Énéide* de Virgile, qui se construit, elle aussi, à partir d'une double temporalité. La première phase du parcours du héros se déroule comme une errance. En quête d'une nouvelle Troie, Énée arrive chez Didon à Carthage.[2] Cependant, le possible mariage entre la reine punique et Énée ne serait qu'un faux apogée : le héros serait subordonné à Didon et sa mission fondatrice, par conséquent, à jamais inaccomplie. Il faut donc que cette prise de pouvoir à demi fasse place à une véritable conquête du pouvoir, cette fois-ci en Italie, qui fera d'Énée ce qu'il doit être : le fondateur d'une Rome provisoire à Alba Longa. Quelle Rome en résultera est mis en évidence par le bouclier d'Énée (VIII, vv. 626ss), dont le programme pictographique renvoie au propre empereur Auguste, qui, au cours de la guerre civile et fratricide, avait conquis le mandat suprême.

Or, la structure de *L'Énéide* est typologique dans la mesure où un premier parcours incomplet est remplacé par un second qui l'accomplit. Ce qui est crucial dans cette double temporalité c'est la volonté de Jupiter qui est au-dessus, à savoir une nécessité téléologique qui la régit en lui fournissant une légitimation divine. Cependant, celle-ci ne s'arrête pas là. Dans sa finalité ultime, le temps typologique de la conquête est modelé sur la garantie d'une temporalité hors temps : c'est la promesse d'un « imperium sine fine » (I, vv. 278s) et donc d'un empire qui ne

---

2 Pour la double temporalité de *L'Énéide* voir Quint 1990, 50–97. L'association avec la typologie est de moi.

connaît ni fin ni confins. Voilà le récit de légitimation romain qui, dès le début, était propagé dans toutes les écoles de l'empire. Il était répandu, même parmi les classes populaires, à tel point qu'on a trouvé sur les murs de Pompéi des jeux intertextuels se référant à lui.

Cela me ramène à ma première réflexion sur la double temporalité chrétienne qui, comme j'ai essayé de montrer, se caractérise à cause de son élément apocalyptique par une temporalité anti-romaine et cela d'autant plus parce qu'elle vise justement à l'abrogation de l' « imperium sine fine ». Je voudrais donc soutenir l'hypothèse qu'il y a un rapport causal entre ce qu'on pourrait appeler, avec Homi Bhabha, le récit pédagogique du pouvoir impérial centralisé à Rome et le récit performatif et subversif d'un écrivain périphérique comme saint Jean.[3] En d'autres mots, saint Jean s'approprie ce récit pédagogique en le présentant comme une fausse promesse qui doit être annulée par la temporalité chrétienne.

Trois siècles plus tard, un autre écrivain périphérique approfondira cette dialectique. Au début des *Confessiones*, saint Augustin se réfère à sa lecture juvénile de *L'Énéide* pendant laquelle les erreurs/l'errance d'Énée le firent oublier ses propres erreurs/sa propre errance (I.20)[4] : s'identifier avec *L'Énéide* équivaut donc à oublier Dieu. Dans son œuvre majeure, *De civitate Dei*, l'évêque d'Hipone reformule ce postulat dans une vaste construction historico-typologique : Rome, la nouvelle Babylone, n'est que le successeur de la première *civitas terrena* construite par Caïn ; mais celle-ci a toujours eu son contrepoids dans la *civitas Dei*, qui, en pèlerinage pendant des siècles, se réalisera finalement dans la Jérusalem céleste. En ce qui concerne l' « imperium sine fine » de la temporalité romaine, saint Augustin nous dit assez clairement qu'il a été illégitime dès le début, car ce n'est que le vrai Dieu qui peut le donner : « sed deus unus et uerus nec metas rerum nec tempora ponit, imperium sine fine dabit. » (II.29)[5]

Parmi les théologiens, la version augustinienne a été dominante pendant les siècles à venir (cf. Rehm 1969). Elle constitue par ailleurs ce millénarisme apocalyptique qui est au cœur des monarchies en Occident. Toutefois, cela n'empêche pas que ces mêmes monarchies avaient besoin de la *Roma eterna* – notamment pour se constituer et pour se légitimer. De là résulte une rivalité profonde et peut-être inextricable entre ces deux modèles temporels : à savoir la lutte entre une conception apocalyptique du temps d'une part et la répétition et le resurgissement de Rome dans ces presque innombrables *renovationes Romae* qui ont vu le jour depuis le temps des Carolingiens de l'autre. Cet antagonisme s'accentue

---

3 J'emprunte la terminologie du pédagogique et du performatif à Bhabha 1996, 139–146. L'association avec saint Jean est de moi.
4 Pour faciliter la localisation, je cite Saint Augustin selon le livre et le chapitre.
5 Dombart/Kalb 1981 I, S. 96.

considérablement à la suite de la Révolution française de 1789. C'est à ce moment-là que la plus ancienne monarchie chrétienne trouve sa fin tandis qu'une temporalité toute autre s'ouvre à un avenir incertain : ce qui serait le temps d'un salut républicain pour les uns, devient désormais un temps apocalyptique pour les autres, et lorsque Hegel accueille l'empereur Napoléon en tant qu'agent du *Weltgeist*, les adhérents de l'Ancién Régime le considèrent comme l'incarnation de l'Antéchrist.[6] Il n'est donc pas surprenant que le dix-neuvième siècle français se caractérise par une oscillation entre des moments révolutionnaires et restauratifs qui ont en commun une forte tension eschatologique, dont le sens dépend du point de vue et de la couleur politique de ceux qui l'interprètent.

II *Imperium sine fine* ? Variations typologiques et d'autres apocalypses

1 Zola

Je vous prie de m'excuser pour cette exposition un peu longue. Mais elle est nécessaire. Sans la concurrence des deux temporalités du discours impérial et du discours apocalyptique, je ne pourrais pas mettre en lumière ce que je souhaite ébaucher maintenant par rapport au soi-disant roman réaliste français. Car, à mon avis, c'est justement la juxtaposition de ces deux temporalités qui est au fond d'une écriture puisant – de Stendhal à Proust – dans un trajet historique marqué par des guerres civiles et le resurgissement de diverses formes de la monarchie, y inclue l'Empire. En ce qui concerne la dimension eschatologique souvent négligée par la recherche, elle s'avère sous-jacente, parfois même dominante chez les auteurs que je veux présenter par la suite. Je commence mon panorama par Émile Zola, dont l'œuvre nous offre à première vue la réflexion la plus complète sur cette question. Typologiquement parlant, cette œuvre est régie par une double temporalité qui se réalise respectivement dans le premier et le dernier cycle de l'auteur : à savoir dans les vingt romans des *Rougon-Macquart* et *Les Quatre Évangiles*.

On le sait, Zola commence à concevoir *Les Rougon-Maquart* à la fin du Second Empire qu'il considère « une étrange époque de folie et de honte » (I, 3)[7]. La nar-

---

6 Cf. dans ce sens Faber 1815. Par rapport à Napoléon voir aussi Newman 1995.
7 Afin d'éviter des redondances inutiles, je citerai désormais toutes les éditions d'un auteur en plusieurs volumes par volume et par page.

ration commence à Plassans, dont on lit tout au début de *La Fortune des Rougon*, que l'on en sort, « par la porte de Rome » (I, 5). Inutile de dire qu'on y entre aussi par cette voie, et nous voilà à Rome. Or, ce n'est pas la ville que le narrateur nous présente aussitôt, mais un étrange cimetière délaissé : l'« Aire Saint-Mittre », qui est, pour ainsi dire, le berceau des deux familles, les Rougon et les Macquart, dont la mère fondatrice est Adélaïde Rougon, dite la tante Dide. Née en 1768, elle se marie avec Rougon en 1786. Avec celui-ci, elle a un fils en 1787. Rougon meurt en 1788 « d'un coup de soleil » (I, 41). Un an plus tard, Adélaïde prend comme amant Macquart, un déséquilibré, ivrogne et contrebandier, qui sera le père de ses deux enfants illégitimes : un fils né en 1789 et une fille qui vient au monde en 1791. Vingt ans plus tard, Macquart, « la terreur des bonnes femmes du faubourg » (I, 43), est tué par un gendarme quand il veut entrer en France avec une cargaison de montres de Genève. Adélaïde en devient folle. Elle ne récupère jamais sa lucidité et meurt, centenaire, en 1871.

Voici un cadre temporel assez suggestif. Rougon, le mari légitime, meurt à la veille de la Révolution ; Macquart, l'amant illégitime et violent, sera tué sous la Restauration. Adelaïde, perturbée mentalement pendant les années où se succèdent trois différentes formes de la monarchie, décède juste après la proclamation de la IIIe République. Entre-temps, les deux branches de la famille ont une destinée antagonique : les Rougon font fortune, tandis que les Macquart représentent, à quelques exceptions près, la classe prolétaire exclue de tout progrès social. Les deux branches ont, à mon avis, une fonction allégorique : la première est au service du système monarchique dominant, la dernière symbolise la république trois fois vaincue. Ce n'est donc pas anodin que le premier roman du cycle commence sous le signe de la « porte de Rome » qui s'ouvre à mesure que la narration avance. *La Fortune des Rougon* est un roman romain dans ce sens qu'il nous raconte le coup d'État de Napoléon III comme une reprise de la guerre civile romaine. L'Aire de Saint-Mittre, quant à elle, est, pour ainsi dire, le lieu des lieux, ou bien l'archi-lieu du cycle. En tant que cimetière délaissé, c'est un endroit de la mort, mais en même temps, elle se caractérise par une végétation excessive et inquiétante. C'est là encore que Silvère, petit-fils de la tante Dide et militant de la IIe République, sera tué de la main d'un soldat par un coup de fusil, de la même façon que son grand-père Macquart a été tué une trentaine d'années auparavant. Ce côté « mortaliste » trouve son contrepoids dans la végétation excessive qui constitue l'Aire Saint-Mittre et doit se lire comme le vitalisme d'une République qui sortira vainqueur en 1871.[8] Nonobstant, ce vitalisme débordant n'est pas sans

---

8 Voir à cet égard Leopold 2014, 87–90 et 2018, 168s. J'emprunte le terme à Foucault 1963, 147s, qui l'utilise en opposition au vitalisme dominant dans les sciences humaines.

danger. Associé à des forces irrationnelles et ataviques, il témoigne avant tout du scepticisme bourgeois du propre Zola vis-à-vis de la prise de pouvoir du prolétariat. Mais ce scepticisme n'empêche pas qu'il y a une dialectique entre les forces populaires et la classe dominante. Celle-ci arrive à son comble dans l'avant-dernier roman du cycle. Dans la plus grande part de *La Débâcle*, Zola se dédie à la Guerre franco-prussienne qui provoque la chute du Second Empire. Mais le roman se clôt sur la suite : à savoir les horreurs apocalyptiques de la semaine sanglante qui mettra fin à la Commune en 1871. La IIIe République naît donc d'un sacrifice sanglant du peuple.

Les parallèles entre *La Fortune des Rougon* et *La Débâcle* sautent aux yeux. Là, le Second Empire se constitue à la suite d'une première guerre civile ; ici, la IIIe République surgit d'une autre guerre civile. Et bien que l'idée d'un « imperium sine fine », inhérente au Second Empire, soit annulée par la IIIe République, rien n'a changé en réalité. Sont abattus ceux qui veulent une vraie république dans laquelle tous les Français participent aux processus politique. Néanmoins, dans *La Débâcle*, Zola se sert des images propres à la Révélation de saint Jean, notamment de la Grande « Babylone en flammes » (V, 888 ; cf. Anfray 2012, 109–114), et cela fait émerger, bien évidemment, un horizon d'expectatives : la IIIe République serait-elle l'équivalent politique de la Jérusalem céleste ? Il ne faut pas oublier que Zola écrit longtemps après cet événement. *La Débâcle* date de 1892. Vingt ans se sont donc écoulés depuis les faits racontés dans ce roman, et la IIIe République s'est avérée tout sauf un état idyllique. Voici la réalité politique et peut-être aussi la déception de ce fervent républicain qu'était Zola. Certes, *Le Docteur Pascal* (1893), le dernier roman des *Rougon-Macquart*, se termine sur le motif d'un « messie attendu » (V, 1218). Mais pour réaliser pleinement son programme typologique, Zola aura besoin d'un nouveau parcours, et ce parcours se réalisera (presque) dans sa dernière tétralogie qui porte le titre suggestif des *Quatre Evangiles*. Dans cette succession de romans, Zola dessine le développement d'un monde utopique qui aura son apogée dans une Jérusalem où se réunissent toutes les races du monde au sein d'un paradis socialiste. Ce serait donc la vision augustinienne selon Zola. Cependant, le dernier roman, *Justice*, n'a jamais paru, il en existe à peine des esquisses, car Zola fut assassiné avant de pouvoir l'écrire (cf. Leopold 2014, 102).

2 Stendhal

Dans l'œuvre de Zola se cristallise un messianisme laïque qui caractérise la fin du siècle et qui se retrouve sous une forme plus au moins nuancée dans les mouvements socialistes et anarchistes. Mais, comme je disais au début, le double temps du roman réaliste commence bien avant. Dans *Le Rouge et le Noir* de Stendhal, écrit sous la Restauration et paru en 1830, peu avant la Révolution de Juillet, nous avons déjà un parcours double et par surcroit un cadre explicitement apocalyptique. Commençons par ce dernier. C'est la première et moins célèbre des deux scènes de miroir. Nous sommes dans le chapitre XVIII, « Un roi à Verrières », dans la première partie du roman. Julien Sorel se trouve dans une abbaye restaurée sous la Restauration et regarde un jeune homme qui fait à plusieurs reprises le geste de la bénédiction en se regardant en même temps dans une glace. L'appartement où se déroule l'étrange scène est décoré, comme nous dit le narrateur, avec « tous les mystères de l'Apocalypse » (314) qui sont y figurés en bois. Un peu plus tard, le jeune homme devant la glace se révèle être le jeune évêque d'Agde qui doit accompagner le roi dans un service commémoratif dans la chapelle de Saint-Clément. Qu'est-ce qui se passe donc dans ce mystérieux appartement ? Le jeune évêque d'Agde manque d'assurance. Il répète le geste de la bénédiction devant la glace, parce qu'il est incertain d'être à la hauteur de sa tâche. Pensant qu'à cause de son âge, il ne dispose pas de la gravité nécessaire de son office, il recourt à une espèce de répétition : il se comporte donc comme un acteur qui prépare son rôle. Voici le rapport avec Julien Sorel. N'oublions pas que celui-ci aussi joue un rôle car, quoique sachant la Bible par cœur, il ne reste pas moins admirateur de Napoléon. Cependant, la différence entre les deux jeunes hommes est que le jeune homme devant la glace est le vrai évêque tandis que Julien Sorel est un hypocrite qui joue seulement le religieux. Or, il faut que nous nous demandions pourquoi tout cela se déroule dans un appartement décoré par toutes les scènes de l'Apocalypse. Le mimétisme latent de la scène nous fournit la clé. Nous avons affaire à une relation pareille à celle qu'il y a entre le Christ revenu et son double mimétique qu'est l'Antéchrist : ici, le vrai évêque, représentant d'un catholicisme restauré en France ; là, le bonapartiste déguisé en religieux. Beaucoup plus tard dans le roman, cette sémantique sera fortifiée : quand Julien essaye de séduire une pieuse Marquise par des lettres recopiées et tout à fait dépourvues de vrais sentiments. Néanmoins, la dame, qui malgré elle commence à s'éprendre de Julien, trouve ces lettres d'une « profondeur sublime et presque apocalyptique » (610). La sémantique de l'Antéchrist se solidifie donc autour de Julien.

Regardons maintenant le double temps du roman. On le sait, Julien a deux maitresses : Mme de Rênal, qui est dans sa trentaine, et Mlle de la Mole, qui a le même âge que le jeune homme. Mme de Rênal appartient à Verrières, le village qui domine la première moitié du roman ; Mlle de la Mole, à Paris où se déroule la seconde moitié. Ce double parcours est, en outre, marqué par la typologie. À deux reprises, notre héros séduit une femme mais ce qui reste incomplet à Verrières semble s'accomplir à Paris : à savoir l'ascension sociale de Julien. Mlle de la Mole tombe enceinte de lui et le père de la jeune femme se dispose à cacher le scandale en faisant anoblir Julien. Ivre de joie, celui-ci commente son succès de la manière suivante : « Après tout, [. . .] mon roman est fini et à moi seul le mérite » (639). Mais malheureusement, cet accomplissement du premier parcours dans le second fait défaut, car Mme de Rênal, contrainte par son confesseur, écrit cette lettre fatale dans laquelle elle qualifie Julien d'hypocrite et d'irréligieux. En conséquence, Julien tire sur elle deux coups de pistolet. Mme de Rênal n'en meurt pas et pardonne son ancien amant. Néanmoins, Julien est condamné à mort. Mais le roman n'est pas encore arrivé à sa fin. À la prison, Mme de Rênal se joint à Julien, ce qui équivaut, structuralement parlant, à un retour au premier parcours. D'un point de vue sémantique, ce retour entraîne un changement encore plus considérable. Petit à petit, Julien, qui auparavant était associé avec l'Antéchrist, devient le double de Louis XVI attendant son exécution au Temple (cf. Xuan 2011, 253–261). Mais il y a encore plus : après l'exécution, Mlle de la Mole s'approprie la tête tranchée de son amant dont elle fait enterrer les restes mortels dans une cérémonie digne d'un roi. L'imposteur et l'hypocrite a finalement trouvé sa place.

Le Rouge et le Noir est un roman plutôt bizarre. Modelé sur le double temps de la préannonce et de l'accomplissement, le vrai accomplissement se réalise avec un retour inespéré qui entraîne en même temps une reprogrammation du personnage principal : cette dernière devient encore plus remarquable quand nous prenons en considération que la condamnation à mort de Julien a lieu un vendredi, donc ce jour de la semaine où nous commémorons la mort du Seigneur. Mais à quoi aboutit tout cela ? Certes, le roman ne nous conduit pas directement à Rome. Cependant, le Paris de Stendhal est un endroit de bien curieuses répétitions : c'est la cité d'une monarchie restaurée, d'un roi qui est le double de son frère guillotiné et c'est là qu'un imposteur est mis à mort comme le roi avant lui. N'oublions pas non plus qu'il y a deux grandes scènes de miroir dans ce roman où le mimétisme joue un rôle majeur. Sans aucun doute, on peut lire tout cela comme le symptôme de la Restauration : d'une monarchie à l'ancienne hantée par un passé qui autrefois, sous Napoléon, visait à l'avenir. On sait bien que Stendhal, qui avait fait carrière sous l'Empire, s'opposait au retour des Bourbons. Tenant compte du fait que *Le Rouge et le Noir* a paru à la veille de la Révolution de Juillet, il serait séduisant d'interpréter ce roman comme la préannonce d'une nouvelle ère où le plébéien peut devenir roi. Ceci nous fournirait par ailleurs l'explication de l'association de Julien avec l'Antéchrist et Napoléon : ce qui est apocalyptique sous la Restauration sera salvateur dans la nouvelle ère bourgeoise.

Néanmoins, à mon avis, cette lecture ne ferait pas tout à fait justice au roman. Je disais plus haut que, dans l'ère postrévolutionnaire, les deux temporalités, l'impériale et l'apocalyptique, coexistent d'une telle façon que leur interprétation dépend en grande mesure du point de vue de ceux qui en parlent. C'est dans ce sens-là que *Le Rouge et le Noir* est un texte symptomatique, car il résiste justement à une interprétation univoque. C'est un roman portant sur la répétition spéculaire et donc sur un mimétisme fondamental où ce qui est du côté du Christ et ce qui est du côté de l'Antéchrist ne se laisse plus distinguer avec netteté. Et c'est précisément là, dirais-je, que *Le Rouge et le Noir* est un roman romain : un roman qui s'insère dans une série d'interminables *renovationes Romae*, qui définit notamment le panorama politique du XIXe siècle en France.

3 Flaubert

Stendhal crée le modèle narratif de ce qui sera le roman réaliste. De Balzac à Proust, il n'y a aucun grand roman qui ne serait pas stendhalien. Le chef d'œuvre de ce courant est certainement *L'Éducation sentimentale* : une réécriture du *Rouge et le Noir* qui termine par ailleurs sur le signifiant de Rome. À l'instar de Stendhal, Flaubert se sert d'un double parcours et d'un double temps ; mais ce dernier est encore plus nuancé, car une partie du roman se déroule sous la monarchie de Juillet, tandis que l'autre est encadrée par la révolution de 1848 et le coup d'état de Louis Napoléon en 1851. Ce qui est, à proprement parler, pervers dans cette structure c'est la typologie : en 48, la jolie Mme Arnoux, tant désirée par Frédéric Moreau, sera remplacée par la prostituée Rosanette dont Frédéric devient l'amant. Au niveau symbolique, cela implique – surtout chez un grand connaisseur de la littérature chrétienne comme Flaubert – que la grande prostituée de Babylone serait l'accomplissement de la bonne bourgeoise qui la préannonce. Aucun doute que cela mène directement au Second Empire, si discrètement omis par Flaubert dans son fameux blanc, mais également évoqué par le portrait de Rosanette qui se trouve encore dans le cabinet de Frédéric en 1867, lors de la visite de Mme Arnoux à la fin du roman. C'est pour cela qu'à la différence de Julien Sorel qui retrouve le bonheur avec Mme de Rênal à la prison, Frédéric et Mme Arnoux se séparent sans que rien ne se passe. Dans cette optique, il ne nous surprend pas que le dernier séjour de Mme Arnoux soit à Rome (IV, 551).

Mais ce n'est pas tout. La typologie de l'*Éducation* est encore plus perverse, puisque tout à la fin du roman, nous apprenons avec stupéfaction que l'expérience la plus importante que Fréderic et son ami Deslauriers ont fait dans leur vie a été la visite d'une maison de passe tenue par une certaine Zoraïde Turc à Nogent. Cette visite, d'ailleurs ratée, s'est passée en 1837, trois ans avant que Fréderic ne rencontre Mme Arnoux pour la première fois. Voilà un retour digne de Stendhal, mais beaucoup plus étonnant que la fin du *Rouge et le Noir*. Là c'était le retour au premier parcours, mais ici, nous sommes devant un évènement qui change totalement la valeur du premier parcours. Et c'est en relisant le roman que nous nous rendons compte que, dès sa première « apparition » (IV, 154), Mme Arnoux est associée avec l'Orient : aux yeux de Frédéric, elle semble être une « andadalouse » (IV, 155), elle est accompagnée d'une « négresse » (ibid.) et écoute avec grande émotion, semble-t-il, « une romance orientale » (ibid.) qu'un harpiste payé par Frédéric joue devant elle. À la première lecture, tout cela semble plutôt grotesque, mais désormais, nous pouvons reconstruire une véritable isotopie de l'Orient qui parcourt le roman du début jusqu'à la fin. Est-ce donc Zoraïde Turc dont l'établissement « projetait dans tout l'arrondissement un éclat fantastique » (IV, 553) qui est le vrai degré zéro du roman ?

Je veux bien le croire, car, de la même manière que le dernier séjour de Mme Arnoux à Rome, cette mise à l'orientale n'est pas sans signification historique. L'année 1837 est décisive dans la conquête de l'Algérie et marque le début du colonialisme français qui sera renforcé sous Napoléon III. Vu de la fin du roman, Zoraïde Turc s'avère donc la vraie préannonce de Rosanette. En outre, cette cocotte porte le surnom de la Maréchale dont la signification se révèle pendant les évènements de 48 : c'est lors du pillage du château des Tuileries que Frédéric, en passant par la salle des maréchaux, remarque le portrait du Maréchal Bugeaud, alors commandant de l'armée, connu pour avoir gagné la guerre en Algérie en 1837. Le fait que Frédéric, en sortant, voit dans l'antichambre de la salle du trône « une fille publique, en statue de la Liberté » (IV, 425) complète la référence. Rosanette, dite la Maréchale, est donc une espèce de noyau sémantique où le projet colonial en Afrique, la guerre civile et le resurgissement de l'Émpire s'entrecroisent. Zoraïde Turc, avec son « éclat fantastique », serait ainsi un bien curieux butin de guerre. Elle personnifie un Orient soumis qui néanmoins s'approprie la France ; et c'est pourquoi cette France, en redevenant Empire, ne sera pas seulement une autre Rome mais aussi une nouvelle Babylone.[9]

Mais quel est le rôle de Mme Arnoux là-dedans ? On serait tenté de la lire comme la personnification de la monarchie bourgeoise, donc comme une option historique ratée. Cependant, au niveau symbolique, elle remplit une fonction double parce qu'elle s'appelle Marie et sa ville d'origine est Chartres, dont la cathédrale est consacrée à la Mère de Dieu. C'est donc bien curieux que Frédéric ne puisse la désirer qu'en tant qu'orientale. D'un point de vue typologique, c'est encore plus curieux, car la Mère de Dieu est au début de la Nouvelle Alliance qui doit accomplir l'Ancienne. Cela est, en outre, justement le programme iconographique de la cathédrale de Chartres.[10] Ici c'est l'envers : la Marie de Chartres sera substituée par Rosanette, la Babylonienne, et ce qui est pire encore : Frédéric n'aimait que l'« éclat fantastique » que Zoraïde Turc projetait sur elle. Quant au mo-

---

9 Voir à cet égard Leopold 2020.

10 Le déchiffrement des cathédrales est à la mode dans la deuxième moitié du dix-neuvième siècle. Voir dans ce contexte surtout l'étude exhaustive de Mâle 2021.

ment central de la typologie, la mort et la résurrection du Sauveur, celui-ci semble faire défaut. Néanmoins, peu avant le fameux blanc avec lequel Flaubert omet discrètement le règne de Napoléon III, il y a une allusion assez claire : c'est le moment où se produit le coup d'État qui fait initier le Second Empire. Dans la foule, Frédéric remarque son ami Dussardier, lequel, tout au long du roman, représente l'amour du prochain. Celui-ci se dirige vers un agent bonapartiste en criant : « Vive la république ! » (IV, 545) Il est abattu d'un coup d'épée et « tomb[e] sur le dos, les bras en croix » (ibid).

4 Balzac

L'Éducation sentimentale termine (presque) sur le signe de la croix, mais cette croix, comme l'a démontré Barbara Vinken dans son merveilleux ouvrage dédié à Flaubert, est devenue un signe vide et sans aucune puissance salvatrice.[11] Une génération plus tôt, chez Balzac, la situation n'était pas mieux. Il nous suffit de penser au Père Goriot qui meurt comme un « Christ de la paternité » (III, 231), abandonné par ses deux filles égoïstes et gaspilleuses. Le roman éponyme raconte l'histoire du jeune Rastignac qui veut faire fortune à tout prix et, pour toucher à cette fin, il entretient une relation adultère avec une des filles de Goriot, Delphine, qui est mariée au banquier Nucingen. Avant que cela ne se passe, Rastignac essaie une autre voie qui le mène vers une figure paternelle alternative, à savoir son « petit papa Vautrin » (III, 137). Vautrin est peut-être le personnage le plus fabuleux de *La Comédie humaine* : c'est le premier héros ouvertement homosexuel dans la littérature du dix-neuvième siècle, il est plébéien et le chef d'un mouvement anti-gouvernemental qui vise à la subversion de la monarchie restaurée des Bourbons. Déguisé en bon bourgeois, il aborde le jeune Rastignac dans la pension Vauquer, où les deux hommes sont voisins. La première rencontre entre eux, dans le jardin de cet établissement, est devenue si fameuse – notamment grâce à Proust qui la reconfigure dans sa *Recherche* – que je me limite à ce qui est essentiel pour mon argument. C'est un pacte que Vautrin propose à ce jeune homme dont il voudrait être l'amant, un pacte d'ailleurs amoral qui implique un meurtre mais fournirait à Rastignac une fortune considérable. Ce dernier comprend tout de suite ce qu'il devrait faire en retour, mais il accepte de collaborer. Voilà ce qu'il en pense : « Il avait vu passer au-dessus de sa tête ce démon qu'il est si facile de prendre pour un ange, ce Satan aux ailes diaprées qui [. . .] revêt d'un sot éclat les trônes (III, 149) ».

11 *Flaubert Postsecular. Modernity Crossed Out*, Stanford : Stanford U. P.

Si Goriot est le « Christ de la paternité », Vautrin en est certainement l'Anté-christ. Cette sémantique sera par ailleurs renforcée lors de la détention du crimi-nel qui met fin au pacte proposé à Rastignac. Voici la description de Vautrin alias Jacques Collin :

> En un moment Collin devint un poème infernal où se peignirent tous les sentiments hu-mains, moins un seul, celui du repentir. Son regard était celui de l'archange déchu qui veut toujours la guerre. (III, 219)

Dans cette perspective, il n'est peut-être pas surprenant que Vautrin, qui est le banquier de tous les criminels en France, soit considéré par eux « leur drapeau, leur soutien, leur Bonaparte enfin » (III, 208).

Vautrin ne restera pas longtemps au bagne. En été 1822, nous le rencontrons à nouveau, sur une grande route, dans une calèche. C'est la fin des *Illusions per-dues* et plus précisément le moment où il sauve le jeune Lucien de Rubempré du suicide. Cette fois-ci, il a pris l'identité d'un certain Abbé Herrera et il gardera ce déguisement digne de son rôle d'Antéchrist tout au long de *Splendeurs et misères des courtisanes*, le troisième roman du cycle Vautrin. Or, il y a plusieurs structu-res typologiques dans ce parcours. En premier lieu, c'est la relation entre Rasti-gnac et Lucien qui saute aux yeux. Ce dernier accomplit le pacte proposé au premier, quoiqu'à la fin, Lucien soit mort, tandis que Rastignac deviendra minis-tre. Le parcours de Lucien a aussi une portée typologique. Dans les *Illusions per-dues*, le jeune écrivain gravit les échelons de la hiérarchie sociale à Paris, mais finit par faire faillite. Une fois sauvé et financé par Vautrin, il rentre avec son protecteur à Paris et y mène, pendant la plus grande partie de *Splendeurs et misè-res des courtisanes*, une vie extrêmement luxueuse. Mais de la même manière que dans *Le Rouge et le Noir*, le dytique de Lucien manque de l'apogée social et termine à la prison. C'est dans cet endroit-là que Lucien, qui se voit accusé d'être le complice de Vautrin, réalisera le suicide différé à la fin des *Illusions perdues*. Quant à la relation entre Rastignac et Lucien, on pourrait l'interpréter naïvement comme la bonne et la mauvaise voie. Mais Rastignac et Lucien ne se distinguent pas par une différence étique, mais par une différence intellectuelle. En outre, Rastignac a beaucoup moins de scrupules que Lucien et il reste aussi toujours un peu associé à Vautrin.

Celui-ci est le vrai personnage principal de *Splendeurs et misères*. Tandis que Lucien a un caractère faible et passif, le faux abbé se sert de mille déguisements pour tuer qui et quand et il veut. Dans ce contexte, le narrateur parle très souvent de la toute-puissance de Vautrin, ce qui approche ce Napoléon des criminels considérablement du souverain de l'Ancien Régime et cela dans un moment histo-rique où le vrai roi, Charles X, se contente d'aspirer au mandat suprême. A la différence de son protégé, Vautrin n'échoue pas, car grâce à la connaissance de tous les secrets de la classe politique, il restera intouchable. Il a même « le secret de deux rois » (VI, 905), ce qui lui donne une « suprême puissance » (VI, 934) devant laquelle tous doivent se plier. Mais ce n'est pas tout : à la fin du roman, il devient le chef de la Sûreté et obtient alors un pouvoir légitime qu'il exercera presque tout au long de la monarchie de Juillet.[12] Honni soit qui mal y pense. Dans la logique du cycle Vautrin, cela équivaut au règne de l'Antéchrist.

5 Proust

On sait bien à quel degré Proust était influencé par Balzac, dont il se sert à plusieurs reprises. Le baron de Charlus, par exemple, est clairement modelé sur le personnage de Vautrin. Quant à la structure de la *Recherche du temps perdu*, Proust y perfectionne le modèle du double parcours en utilisant une typologie qui, à la fin, se révèle d'être tout à fait apocalyptique. Je veux donc terminer mon propre parcours par quelques remarques sur ce qui me semble le plus important de la vaste structure temporelle que nous présente Proust. Celle-ci a son degré zéro à Combray où, pendant son enfance, Marcel arrive régulièrement à la semaine de Pâques pour y passer les vacances. C'est avec la même régularité qu'il y reçoit, le dimanche de Pâques avant la messe, une madeleine de sa tante Léonie. Le rituel se répétera tous les dimanches de son séjour. Dans ce contexte, on ne parle pas peu du « pain béni » (I, 70, 112), mais très souvent en métaphore. Même l'église, aux yeux de Marcel, ressemble à une immense « brioche bénie » (I, 64). Curieusement, au niveau de la narration, la messe et l'eucharistie sont omises ; elles font un blanc absolu. Cela semble encore plus étonnant quand on prend en considération que les repas dominicaux de la famille, quant à eux, font l'objet des descriptions d'un accent carnavalesque. Dans la logique du récit, on est donc face à une substitution de la nourriture spirituelle, qui est l'hostie, par une (sur-)alimentation au sens littéral du terme. Ce processus est initié par la madeleine, laquelle, en tant que double de l'hostie, annonce déjà une gloutonnerie qui sera dominante chez les parents de Marcel. La gloutonnerie, il ne faut pas l'oublier, est un des sept péchés cardinaux et donc tout à fait anti-eucharistique.[13]

C'est pour cette raison que Combray n'est pas le paradis de l'enfance que de nombreux chercheurs veulent encore voir. Derrière l'apparence idyllique se cachent des choses bien sinistres. Il y a des soldats qui éveillent chez la cuisinière

---

12 En ce qui concerne le personnage de Vautrin voir aussi Leopold 2011.
13 Voir à cet égard Leopold 2022, 47–70.

Françoise le souvenir de la Guerre franco-prussienne, donc la fin de la monarchie en France. Cette même Françoise – nomen est omen – coupe la tête à un poulet en lui fendant « le cou sous l'oreille » (I, 120) et cela peu après que Marcel a admiré des « légères couronnes d'azur » (ibid) sur les pointes des asperges. La sémantique monarchique voire révolutionnaire est ici de mise puisque toute Combray semble être un lieu de mémoire de la monarchie française. La crypte de l'église est remplie de tombeaux merovingiens, les vitres montrent des rois, dont un, Gilbert le mauvais, fut décapité. Les rues, qui portent toutes des noms de saints – même du Saint Esprit –, éveillent chez Marcel des rêveries du passé médiévaux. Pour couronner le tout, la tante Léonie, en se comportant comme Louis XIV, est considérée par sa cuisinière comme « sa souveraine, son mystérieux et tout-puissant monarque » (I, 151). Tante Léonie est la grande exception de la famille. Toujours au bord de la mort, elle n'est pas seulement profondément religieuse, mais elle est aussi le seul personnage qui ne participe pas à la gloutonnerie dominicale.

Voici le panorama. Nous sommes en pleine IIIᵉ République et la tante Léonie représente une monarchie pas encore tout à fait défunte et ainsi l'« attente monarchique » propre aux cercles conservateurs. C'est pour cette raison, à mon avis, que les éléments un peu gênants sont poussés en dehors de la ville, et notamment du « côté de chez Swann » : là séjournent parfois Odette, jadis une courtisane et maintenant l'épouse de Swann, et la jeune Gilberte, sa fille, dont Marcel tombera amoureux à cause d'un geste obscène. Mais de là on arrive aussi à Montjouvain où habite le compositeur Vinteuil avec sa fille « qui avait l'air d'un garçon » (I, 112) et qui, justement à cause de cet air, plaît aussi à Marcel. Celui-ci aime surtout les « taches de rousseur » (I, 112) dont est « semé » (ibid.) le visage de cette jeune fille androgyne ; une fois, dans l'église, pendant le mois de Marie, quand elle est assise de son côté, il s'imagine qu'il se dégage de ces taches une odeur amère. D'après certains chercheurs, cette odeur rappelle celle du sperme (cf. Lagercrantz 1997, 51). Quoi qu'il en soit, le mot « tache » n'est pas innocent chez Proust et fonctionne toujours comme indicateur d'homosexualité (cf. Leopold 2022, 73, 108–111). Cette homosexualité se fait jour précisément après la mort de tante Léonie. Entre-temps, M. Vinteuil est mort aussi, et, envahi d'une curiosité morbide, Marcel se rend à Montjouvain pour épier sa fille qui y vit avec son amante. Ce qu'il voit à travers une fenêtre ouverte est la scène la plus choquante du premier volume de la *Recherche* : comme ouverture du jeu érotique, les deux jeunes femmes profanent une photographie du père récemment disparu.

À l'époque, la scène de Montjouvain déplaisait aux lecteurs. Elle semblait être mal à propos. Pourtant, elle est d'une extrême importance au niveau typologique, car elle annonce ce qui se passera dans la *Recherche* à partir de *Sodome et Gomorrhe*. Ce qui, à Combray, ne semblait être que le cas isolé d'une perversion particulière, s'avère désormais la norme d'une société où l'homosexualité se trouve partout. Le titre du quatrième volume de la *Recherche* indique un retour en Orient et notamment en un Orient associé aux cités maudites de l'Ancienne Alliance. Certains ont voulu y voir une déviation de Proust par rapport à son projet initial qui, selon eux, consisterait en une récupération joyeuse du passé. Je ne suis pas de cet avis et j'oserais même dire que la structure typologique de la *Recherche* est d'une netteté quasiment augustinienne. Chez l'évêque d'Hippone, Rome, le successeur de la première *civitas terrena* construite par Caïn, avait toujours eu son contrepoids dans la *civitas Dei*, qui, en pèlerinage pendant des siècles, se réaliserait finalement dans la Jérusalem céleste. Chez Proust, c'est exactement l'envers. Ce qui d'abord n'était qu'un petit noyau exclu de la ville de Combray – Montjouvain –, fait en réalité partie d'une vaste population homosexuelle des deux sexes qui, dès les temps bibliques, font leurs pérégrinations à travers la terre.

> Ces descendants des Sodomistes [Gomorrhe y compris ; S. L.], si nombreux qu'on peut leur appliquer l'autre verset de la Genèse : « Si quelqu'un peut compter la poussière de la terre, il pourra aussi compter cette postérité », ce sont fixés sur toute la terre, ils ont eu accès à toutes les professions et entrent [. . .] dans les clubs les plus fermés [. . .]. Certes ils forment dans tous les pays une colonie orientale [. . .] qui a des qualités charmantes et d'insupportables défauts. (III, 32)

Or, cela entraine une revalorisation de ce qui est du côté de la *civitas terrena* et de ce qui est du côté de la *civitas Dei*. Contrairement à Flaubert, qui d'ailleurs aimait bien les prostituées, Proust ne condamne pas la nouvelle Babylone qu'est devenu Paris. Chez lui, et cela est un changement important, Babylone n'est pas non plus le symptôme d'un resurgissement de l'Empire, mais quelque chose de bien républicain. Souvenons-nous : la scène de Montjouvain est directement précédée par la mort de tante Léonie, la représentante du roi et de l'attente monarchique. Or, cette relation entre l'homosexualité et la forme républicaine de l'État devient encore plus claire dans « Un amour de Swann ». Swann entretient « des relations avec le Président de la République » (I, 213) et la sonate de Vinteuil est « l'air national » (I, 215) de son amour pour Odette, qu'il soupçonne par ailleurs d'être lesbienne. Toute à la fin de *Du côté de chez Swann*, Marcel, qui vient de voir passer Odette au Bois de Boulogne, entend un homme se vantant qu'il avait couché avec elle « le jour de la démission de Mac-Mahon » (I, 413). Mac-Mahon était le dernier président républicain qui soutenait encore l'option monarchique.

Mais quel sera l'accomplissement de cette typologie à l'envers ? Chez Saint Augustin, c'est l'Apocalypse qui sera suivie de la descente de la Jérusalem céleste. Chez Proust, la typologie s'accomplit dans la Grande Guerre. Un soir, en 1916, à peine rentré d'un séjour prolongé au sanatorium, Marcel se promène dans une Paris menacée par les bombardements aériennes. Quelques jours plus tôt, il a pu admirer le piqué des avions-bombardiers en ce « moment où ils *font apocalypse* » (IV, 338). Maintenant, toujours en pensant à « l'apocalypse dans le ciel » (ibid.), il se rend compte que Paris est devenu une ville d'« Orient », qui se ressemble « à une Jérusalem ou une Constantinople » (IV, 338) peinte par Carpaccio. C'est à ce moment-là qu'il tombe sur son vieil ami, le baron de Charlus. Celui-ci commence aussitôt une harangue un peu confuse, en parlant de la guerre, de Nietzsche et bien d'autres choses, avant d'aborder la question de la vie festive des Parisiens : « Les fêtes remplissent ce qui sera peut-être [. . .] les derniers jours de notre Pompéi. » (IV, 385) Charlus semble s'égayer de cet avenir possible, et, en racontant qu'on a trouvé sur un de murs à Pompéi l'inscription « *Sodoma, Gomorra* » (IV, 386), il fait allusion aux « villes maudites de la Bible » (ibid.), dont Paris deviendrait la dernière. Ce serait un scénario apocalyptique parfait si Charlus n'était pas le grand prêtre de l'homosexualité dans la *Recherche*. Mais laissons de côté, pour l'instant, les implications qui en découlent. Charlus disparait dans la nuit, et Marcel se promène à nouveau seul dans les rues de plus en plus désertes. Toutefois, peu après, il arrive à la seule maison encore éclairée, et, la prenant pour un hôtel, il y entre. Le prétendu hôtel s'avère vite une maison close pour hommes et, ce qui est encore plus étonnant pour Marcel, c'est que l'établissement est tenu par Jupien, le grand ami de Charlus. En réalité, il appartient secrètement à ce dernier. C'est par hasard que Marcel apprendra un peu plus tard de quoi la maison sert au baron : à travers un œil-de-bœuf dont on a oublié de tirer le rideau, il voit, enchainé à un lit de fer, Charlus en se faisant fouetter de la façon la plus atroce par un apache qui ne manque pas de l'insulter en même temps.

Cette scène nous ramène, bien évidemment, à Montjouvain, où la photographie de M. Vinteuil était insultée par l'amante de sa fille, et ici et là les insultes servent à la stimulation érotique. Mais tandis qu'à Montjouvain, on ferme les rideaux, ici Marcel peut finalement tout voir. Typologiquement parlant, Montjouvain s'accomplit dans la nuit apocalyptique que Marcel passe dans la maison close de Jupien. Mais ce n'est pas encore tout. A peine a-t-il quitté l'établissement que les attaques aériennes commencent :

> Quelques-uns même de ces Pompéiens sur qui pleuvait déjà le feu du ciel descendirent dans les couloirs du métro, noirs comme des catacombes. Ils savaient en effet de n'y être pas seuls. Or l'obscurité qui baigne toute chose comme un élément nouveau a pour effet, irrésistiblement tentateur pour certaines personnes, de supprimer le premier stade du plaisir et de nous faire entrer de plain-pied dans un domaine de caresses où l'on n'accède d'habitude qu'après quelque temps. Que l'objet convoité soit en effet une femme ou un homme, même à supposer que l'abord soit simple, et inutiles les marivaudages qui s'éterniseraient dans un salon (du moins en plein jour), le soir (même dans une rue si faiblement éclairée qu'elle soit), il y a du moins un préambule où les yeux seuls mangent le blé en herbe, où la crainte des passants, de l'être recherché lui-même, empêchent de faire plus que de regarder, de par-

ler. Dans l'obscurité, tout ce vieux jeu se trouve aboli, les mains, les lèvres, les corps peuvent entrer en jeu les premiers. Il reste l'excuse de l'obscurité même et des erreurs qu'elle engendre si l'on est mal reçu. Si on l'est bien, cette réponse immédiate du corps qui ne se retire pas, qui se rapproche, nous donne de celle (ou celui) à qui nous nous adressons silencieusement, une idée qu'elle est sans préjugés, pleine de vice, idée qui ajoute un surcroît de bonheur d'avoir pu mordre à même le fruit sans le convoiter des yeux et sans demander permission. Cependant l'obscurité persiste ; plongés dans cet élément nouveau, les habitués de Jupien [. . .] célébraient, aux grondements volcaniques des bombes, au pied d'un mauvais lieu pompéien, des rites secrets dans les ténèbres des catacombes. (IV, 413)

Ce passage-ci est, selon moi, le véritable point de culmination de la *Recherche*. Voilà pourquoi : premièrement ce ne sont pas que des hommes, qui, en tant que « Pompéiens », cherchent refuge dans les couloirs du métro ; ce sont les deux sexes s'y rencontrant dans une obscurité tellement complète que l'on ne peut absolument rien voir. On ne parle pas non plus : il n'y a que « la réponse immédiate du corps ». Deuxièmement, pour pouvoir nous raconter ce qui s'est passé dans cette obscurité, Marcel a dû participer dans le jeu muet des corps. Bien entendu, c'est une orgie qui se déroule dans cet endroit, une orgie où la différence du sexe ne joue plus aucun rôle. C'est donc, troisièmement, un petit peu scandaleux que le narrateur approche cette orgie « au pied d'un mauvais lieu pompéien [. . .] des rites secrets dans les ténèbres des catacombes ». Mais c'est ingénieux malgré tout, car, ainsi, les Pompéiens et Pompéiennes se transforment tout à coup en des premiers chrétiens pratiquant leur nouvelle religion en secret par peur d'être persécutés.

Parmi les proustiens, on ne parle pas peu de profanations. Mais ce à quoi nous avons affaire dans les couloirs du métro n'est pas une profanation, mais, pour utiliser un terme cher à Proust, une *inversion* de la typologie.[14] Dans les ténèbres, ce qui appartenait auparavant encore à Babylone se transforme désormais en ce qui, chez Augustin, appartient déjà à la *civitas Dei*. C'est un peu trop, me dira-t-on. Mais rien ne résulterait de la nuit dans les couloirs du métro si on ne l'interprétait pas de cette façon. Peu de temps après, Marcel se rend à nouveau dans une maison de santé, où il reste de nombreuses années sans que sa condition ne s'améliore. Nous ne savons pas ce qui se passe pendant ce temps ; dans le texte, il y a un blanc absolu. Néanmoins, ce blanc peut être comblé en remontant au début du roman.[15] C'est pendant des nuits d'insomnie dans un endroit vague que Marcel, dans une

---

14 C'est Roland Barthes (1989, 34–39) qui, le premier, a souligné l'importance de l' « inversion » comme paradigme structurel du roman. Toutefois, il ne fait pas attention à la typologie. Voir à cet égard Leopold 2022.

15 Cette suggestion a déjà été faite par Genette 1972, 85. Je l'approfondis dans Leopold 2022, 1–17, dans le sens de la suite.

obscurité totale, manque de tout souvenir de son passé, sauf celui du « drame de coucher » qui, selon lui, était le moment initial de sa vie malheureuse. Cette vie arrive à son point de culmination dans les couloirs du métro. La question serait donc : pourquoi ne se souvient-il pas de cet événement ? Compte tenu de la genèse du texte, la réponse serait assez facile : en 1913, Proust ne pouvait rien savoir de la Grande Guerre. Pourtant, une *lectio difficilor* est de mise. On sait que Proust a organisé son texte de manière que les événements ultérieurs puissent s'intégrer aux précédents.[16] À mon avis, c'est aussi le cas pour la nuit dans les couloirs du métro. Cette nuit serait donc responsable de cette perte de mémoire qui caractérise le narrateur au début du roman. L'expérience du décloisonnement, dirais-je, était trop forte pour Marcel, qui jusqu'à ce moment-là se croyait hétérosexuel. Mais l'opposition entre ce qui est hétérosexuel et ce qui ne l'est pas, a perdu toute son importance dans les couloirs du métro. Pour le narrateur, l'abolition de ce binarisme est le début d'une nouvelle religion à l'instar du christianisme primitif. Pour Marcel, le personnage, c'était l'enfer, une espèce de mort symbolique, l'ébranlement de tout ordre social.

C'est pour cela que la nuit dans le métro est en effet apocalyptique. Et ce n'est donc pas un hasard que le grand final du *Temps retrouvé*, appelé « L'Adoration perpétuelle », est placé sous le signe de la « résurrection » (IV, 453, 466). Le jour même de son retour à Paris, Marcel se rend à une matinée chez la Princesse de Guermantes, et là, dans la bibliothèque, il se souvient tout à coup de sa vie passée. Maintenant, il voit devant lui le grand roman qu'il veut entamer dès le lendemain et dont nous sommes en train de finir la lecture. Certes, il ne parle pas explicitement de la nuit dans le métro, mais la poétique de son roman semble néanmoins en être imprégnée. Ce qu'il pense écrire doit faire justice à tout type de lecteur : que ce soit un homme ou une femme, un prince ou un conducteur d'omnibus, un hétérosexuel ou « un inverti ». Chacun peut donner « à ses héroïnes un visage masculin » (IV, 489) et le même vaut pour les héros, car « l'inversion » (IV, 490) devient maintenant un principe herméneutique. Bien entendu : cela est bel et bien du côté de Babylone, dont le signifié est, selon Saint Augustin, « confusion » (XVI.₄)[17]. Mais comme je disais plut haut : chez Proust, Babylone n'a plus

---

16 La plus fameuse de ces « paralipses » (Genette 1972, 73) est la rencontre érotique de Jupien et Charlus dans la cour de l'hôtel de Guermantes épiée par Marcel et racontée au début de *Sodome et Gomorrhe*. Cet addendum changera tout à fait le sens de la fin du *Côté de Guermantes* où cet évènement ne figure pas. Moins connue, mais également importante : la description du sexe d'Albertine. Dans *La Prisonnière*, nous apprenons qu'il ressemble à une madeleine, ce qui change considérablement le sens de la madeleine que Marcel, âgé, reçoit de sa mère au début de *Du côté de chez Swann* (cf. Leopold 2022, 37–45).
17 Dombart/Kalb 1981, II, 129.

rien à voir avec l'Empire. Elle est désormais tout à fait républicaine voire démocratique. Ainsi, l'art envisagé par Marcel sera définitivement « le vrai Jugement dernier » (IV, 458) d'une société battue sur des binarismes.

Bibliographie

Ouvrages

Augustin, Aurélien [Saint]. *Confessiones.* Éd. et Trad. Wilhelm Thimme, Düsseldorf/Zurich : Artemis & Winkler, 2004.

Augustin, Aurélien [Saint]. *Sancti Aurelii Augustini episcopi De civitate Dei libri XXII.* 2 vol. Éd. Bernhard Dombart et Alfons Kalb. Darmstadt : WBG, ^{5}1981.

Balzac, Honoré. *La Comédie humaine.* Éd. Pierre-Georges Castex. 12 vol. Paris : Gallimard (Bibliothèque de la Pléiade) 1976–1981.

La Bible de Jérusalem. Trad. et sous la direction de l'École de Jérusalem. Nouvelle Édition revue et corrigée, Paris : Cerf, 2000.

Faber, George Stanley. *Remarks on the Effusion of the Fifth Apocalyptic Vial, and the Late Extraordinary Restoration of the Imperial Revolutionary Government of France.* Londres : F.C. and J. Rivington, 1815.

Flaubert, Gustave. *L'Éducation sentimentale. Histoire d'un jeune homme. Œuvres complètes.* vol. IV (1863–1874). Éd. Gisèle Séginger. Paris : Gallimard (Bibliothèque de la Pléiade), 2021. 149–554.

Newman, John Henry. *L'Antichrist.* Trad. Genia Català et Grégory Solari. Paris : Ad Solem, 1995.

Proust, Marcel. *À la Recherche du temps perdu.* 4 vol. Éd. Jean-Yvey Tadié. Paris : Gallimard (Bibliothèque de la Pléiade), 1987–1989.

Stendhal. *Le Rouge et le Noir. Romans et nouvelles.* vol. 1. Éd. Henri Martineau. Paris : Gallimard (Bibliothèque de la Pléiade), 1952. 195–699.

Zola, Émile. *Les Rougon-Macquart.* Éd. Armand Lanoux et Henri Mitterand. 5 vol. Paris : Gallimard (Bibliothèque de la Pléiade), 1960–1967.

Recherche

Anfray, Célia. *Zola biblique. La bible dans* Les Rougon-Macquart. Éds. Gérard Genette et Tzvetan Todorov. Paris : Cerf, 2012.

Barthes, Roland. « Une idée de recherche ». *Recherche de Proust.* Éds. Gérard Genette et Tzvetan Todorov. Paris : Seuil, 1980. 34–39.

Bhabha, Homi K. *The Location of Culture.* Londres : Routledge 1994.

Dempf, Alois. *Sacrum Imperium. Geschichts- und Staatsphilosophie des Mittelalters und der politischen Renaissance.* Munich/Berlin : Oldenberg, 1929.

Foucault, Michel. *Naissance de la clinique. Une archéologie du regard médical.* Paris : PUF, 1963.

Genette, Gérard. « Le discours du récit ». *Figures III.* Paris : Seuil, 1972. 67–273.

Hartog, François. *Chronos. L'Occident aux prises avec le Temps.* Paris : Gallimard (nrf), 2020.

Lagercrantz, Olof. *Marcel Proust oder Vom Glück des Lesens*. Trad. Angelika Gundlach. Francfort : Suhrkamp, 1997.

Leopold, Stephan. « Balzac und die Volkssouveränität. Chronotopien des Politischen im Cycle Vautrin ». *lendemains* 144 (2011) : 93–117.

Leopold, Stephan. « Anfänge vom Ende der Zeit : Zolas Idyllen und der Chronotopos der Fläche ». *Anfänge vom Ende : Schreibweisen des Naturalismus in der Romania*. Éds. Lars Schneider et Xuan Jing. Munich : Fink, 2014. 81–104.

Leopold, Stephan. « Le spectre de la régénération et les ambiguïtés de l'utopie – Michel Houellebecq, lecteur du dernier Zola ». *Lire Zola au XXIe siècle. Colloque de Cerisy 2016*. Éds. Aurélie Barjonet et Jean-Sébastien Macke. Paris : Garnier, 2018. 167–183.

Leopold, Stephan. « Série, événement, hantise. Le portrait du Maréchal Bugeaud dans la structure phantasmatique de *L'Éducation sentimentale* ». *Flaubert et les sortilèges de l'image*. Éds. Anne Herschberg Pierrot, Pierre-Marc de Biasi et Barbara Vinken. Berlin : De Gruyter, 2020. 65–74.

Leopold, Stephan. *Zusammenbruch und Erinnerung. Prousts* Recherche. Paderborn : Fink | Brill, 2022.

Mâle, Émile. *L'art religieux du XIIIᵉ siècle en France* [1898]. Paris : Klincksieck, 2021.

Quint, David. *Epic and Empire. Politics and Generic Form From Virgil to Milton*. Princeton/N.J. : Princeton University Press, 1996.

Rehm, Walter. *Der Untergang Roms im abendländischen Denken. Ein Beitrag zur Geschichte der Geschichtsschreibung und zum Dekadenzproblem* [1930]. Darmstadt : WBG, 1969.

Vinken, Barbara. *Flaubert Postsecular. Modernity Crossed Out*. Stanford : Stanford University Press, 2015.

Xuan, Jing. « Le sprectre de 93 – Der Kopf des Königs und der Realismus : Stendhal, Flaubert, Barthes ». *lendemains* 142/143 (2011) : 248–277.

___

V **Palimpsests beyond Origins**

Andrea Frisch

Calendars, Commemoration, Containment: The Saint Bartholomew's Day Massacre(s) and Roman Practices of Commemorating Defeat

In a 2008 article, the distinguished historian of the French Reformation Philip Benedict sought to draw attention to early modern historical calendars as "vectors of social memory," and in particular, of the memory of the French wars of religion (1562–1598).[1] Max Engammare had previously addressed the specific layout of the protestant calendar as it appeared in Geneva during the wars of religion and into the seventeenth century; as Engammare points out, unlike the Catholic liturgical calendar that recapitulated the same saints' names over centuries, the Reformed calendar was constantly rewritten and updated, prominently incorporating events of the civil wars.[2] For Olivier Christin, this inscription of secular history onto the calendar is a quintessentially Protestant gesture.[3]

This stimulating line of inquiry is the starting point for the present essay, which uses the case of the Saint Bartholomew's Day massacre in order further to explore the genealogy, forms, and ramifications of the practice of inscribing historical events onto the calendar in early modern France. The gesture was by no means an invention of European Reformers; rather, it has a venerable precedent in Republican Rome. Growing in part out of the reappropriation of Roman history within the broader culture of Humanist letters, the gesture of incorporating secular history onto a still essentially liturgical calendar, while mainly a Protestant practice in sixteenth- and seventeenth-century France, invites reflection on the complex nature, adaptation, and impact of this particular aspect of the Roman inheritance.

---

1 Benedict 2008, 385.
2 "Le calendrier réformé, genevois et français, est . . . constamment en évolution, en réécriture, mis à jour; la particularité est à mémoriser. L'histoire de France récente prend d'ailleurs de plus en plus de place dans les événements consignés." Engammare 2004, 32.
3 Christin characterizes the inscription of the St Bartholomew's Day massacre onto the calendar day of August 24 in terms of "l'insertion protestante dans le temps cyclique du calendrier d'événements contemporains, que l'on destine par là à une commémoration répétée chaque année." Christin 2014, 80.

https://doi.org/10.1515/9783111334776-010

Dies alliensis

The most famous Roman example of a link between a historical event and a calendar date is the Day of the Allia, the *dies Alliensis*, designated as a black day or *dies ater* due to its association with the Roman defeat at the hands of the Gauls at the River Allia, which supposedly took place on a day in mid July in the fourth century BCE, and which reportedly led to the sack of Rome by the Gauls in the days that followed. I say "supposedly" and "reportedly" because the event is one that is so ideologically laden in Roman historiography that it is really not possible to offer a straightforward account of "the facts." This problem will of course be familiar to anyone who has perused the historiography of the St. Bartholomew's Day massacre.

Much has been written about the way that the *dies Alliensis* has been constructed in Roman narrative historiography, especially in Suetonius and Livy.[4] What primarily interests me here, however, is the very practice of marking it as a historical event on the calendar. Unlike the network of *fasti* which were largely religious in character and deeply connected to seasonal temporal cycles, the *dies Alliensis* commemorates a singular moment in *historical* time. Therefore, what will be important for my discussion of the commemoration of the St Bartholomew's Day massacres in France is not the historical specifics of the Day of the Allia, but the ramifications of what should rightly be characterized as a Roman genre of secular historical memory. In renaissance France, the *dies Alliensis* functions both as a paradigm for and as an enduring artefact of this type of commemoration.

Citing the lack of physical war memorials in Roman culture, Alison Cooley characterizes the establishment of the *dies Alliensis* as a distinctively Roman way of commemorating defeat, observing that the Romans "developed a . . . culture of commemoration, whereby military disasters were incorporated into the state's religious calendar."[5] The earliest extant calendar on which the *dies Alliensis* is commemorated is from the late Republic, and classicist Mathieu Engerbeaud argues that the *dies Alliensis* had become the privileged reference for a "jour funeste" only in late Republican Rome, rather than immediately after the event itself.[6] By the age of Augustus, far from simply registering or commemorating an event, references in Republican historiography to the *dies Alliensis* as a fatal day helped to consolidate the notion of a "Gallic catastrophe" that was in turn part of the con-

---

4 See e.g. Luce 1971; Rosenberger 2003.
5 Cooley 2012, 80.
6 Engerbeaud 2018, 251–266. For a more general discussion of the phenomenon of the *jour néfaste*, see Grafton and Swerdlow 1988.

struction of a larger historical narrative about the long-term fortunes of Rome as seen from the vantage point of the Golden Age.

While I am not in a position to evaluate the particulars of the ideological function of the *dies Alliensis* in Roman historiography, its obvious status as a dramatic turning point in narratives of the Republic clearly demonstrates how calendrical commemoration inevitably produces what we might call "ideologemes": fragments that can serve any number of historiographical and political agendas, since they are constantly recycled and reinterpreted by virtue of their continual appearance on the calendar. The fact that calendar commemoration of historical events allows for relatively easy movement of historical fragments across both space and time intensifies its capacity to generate plural and potentially multivalent historical narratives. The phenomenon of calendrical return, by "preserving" a minimal record of an important historical event over time, inevitably exposes the event to continual reinterpretation. Moreover, unlike a material monument that requires physical proximity or some proxy for it, the calendar day presents itself at regular intervals, no matter where one might be located in space. The immateriality of the calendar day as a space of inscription lends it a capacity for wide diffusion – an obvious advantage in a state as vast as Rome – which affords events commemorated in this way access to a wider circle of interpreters. This is, as one might expect, both a blessing and a curse.

The significance of all of this for a discussion of St. Bartholomew's Day is economically illustrated by the 1562 calendar of Gilbert Cousin, a Catholic Humanist who had served as Erasmus's private secretary (Fig. 1).[7] In the space for July 16 we find none other than the *dies Alliensis*, listed here as having occurred in 376. The presence of this event in this context signals the affiliation between Cousin's undertaking and its Roman precedents, and gives him license to add to the stock of historical information his own calendar will convey. Thus, for the previous day, July 15, we find an entry for the capture of Jerusalem by Crusader forces in 1099. On July 11, Cousin records the relatively recent death of Erasmus, in 1536, at the age of 70. At the same time, Cousin's calendar includes events of a decidedly more religious nature: the entry for July 17, just after the *dies Alliensis*, condenses the story told in Exodus 32 and 33, thereby commemorating Moses's breaking of the stone tablets he had received from God on Mount Sinai upon discovering the Israelites worshipping the Golden Calf.

---

7 Cousin 1562, 255. According to Engammare, Cousin based his calendar on that of the Protestant Crespin 1551, which, as its pages for March reproduced in Engammare clearly show, also juxtapose secular and Biblical history. Unfortunately, not having been able to consult Crespin's calendar (housed in the Bibliothèque Mazarine), I do not know whether it also lists the *dies Alliensis*.

GILBERTI COGNATI. 255

11 Matralia Romæ celebrata.
12 Κρόνια,ideſt Saturnalia,Athenis celebrata.Demoſth.contra Timocratem.
13 Quinquatria minora,feſtum Tibicinum & Poetarum Romæ.
14
15
16 μυνοδία Athenis,in memoriam beneficij Theſei,qui ciues Atticos diſperſos per agrũ,
17 coegit in unam urbem,quam uocauit Athenas.Plutarchus in Theſeo.Thucid.uocat
18 ſυνοίκια lib.2.
19
20 Perſæ memorabili ſtrage ad Antiochiam uicti à Chriſtianis Gotfredo & Balduino
21 ducibus,50.milibus hoſtium cæſis.
22
23 Inducitur prius edictum Aſſueri Regis contrarium prioribus:quo libertas fiebat Iu-
dæis trucidandi aduerſarios.Eſth.8.
24 Natalis Ioannis Baptiſtæ.Veſpaſianus moritur anno ſuæ ætatis 69.poſt Chriſtum 81.
25
26
27 Hoc die menſis tertij ita auctæ ſunt aquæ diluuij continuis imbribus 40.dierum, ut
arca ſublata ſit undis,eoʠ die imbres ruere deſierint,nihilominus tamen creſcentib.
aquis.Gen.7.
28 Alexander Magnus moritur anno ætatis 32.imperij 12.ante Chriſtum 323.
29 Petrus & Paulus.
30
¶ IVLIVS habet dies 31.Thamus,Hebræis quartus:Atticis μετηγειτνιών.
1 Cal. Hoc die apud Romanos fiebant migrationes ex ædibus in alienas ædes,ut ex
2 Cicerone,Suet.& Martiale colligi poteſt.
3
4
5 Ludi Apollinares hoc die celebrari cœperunt ſecundo bello Punico,quum antea in-
certi fuiſſent.Liuius lib.7.decad.3.
6 Capitolium Romæ conflagrauit.Sylla ex Aſia reuerſus,in ciues ſæujt.
7 Nonæ. Caprotinæ,feſtum ancillarum.Macrob.lib.1.cap.2.Plutar.in Romulo,
8 Romulus diſcerptus à Senatoribus.Athenienſes ad Cheroneam uicti,à Philippo
Macedone.
9 Vrbs Hieroſolymorum poſt obſidionem 18.menſium à Rege Babyloniorum capta
10 eſt,& Sedechias è fuga retractus,& oculis priuatus.Ieremias uinculis leuatus ab Aſ-
ſyrijs hoſtibus.Ierem.39.& 4.Regum ultimo.
11 Iſocrates Athenieſis orator moritur anno ætatis 99,Eraſmus Roterodamus obijt an
no Chriſti 1536.ætatis ſuæ 70.
12 Natalis Iulij Cæſaris.
13
14
15 Idus. Diuiſio Apoſtolorum.Hieroſolyma recuperata eſt à Chriſtianorum exercitu, anno Chriſti 1099.
16 Dies Allienſis,à clade quam Romani acceperunt ad Alliam fluuium,cæſi à Gallis Se
nonibus,anno ante Chriſtum 376.
17 Creditur inauſpicatus à Iudæorum gente propter tres calamitates,quas hoc die eue
niſſe exiſtimant. 1.Moſes confregit Tabulas,Exod.32.33. 2.Reuerſi duodecim
exploratores populum terruerunt,commemorata potentia Chananæorũ, 3.Quòd
Nabuchodonoſor cœpit obſidere Hieroſolymam,Seruantigitur Iudæi ieiunium,et
totas tres ſequentes hebdomadas,quæ in dies caniculares cadunt,ſibi aduerſas & in
fauſtas credunt.Ideoʠ abſtinēt à carnibus & uino:& non inchoant aliquod arduum
negotium his 21.diebus,numeratis ab hoc die uſʠ ad nonum diem menſis Ab.
Yy 2 16 Cani-

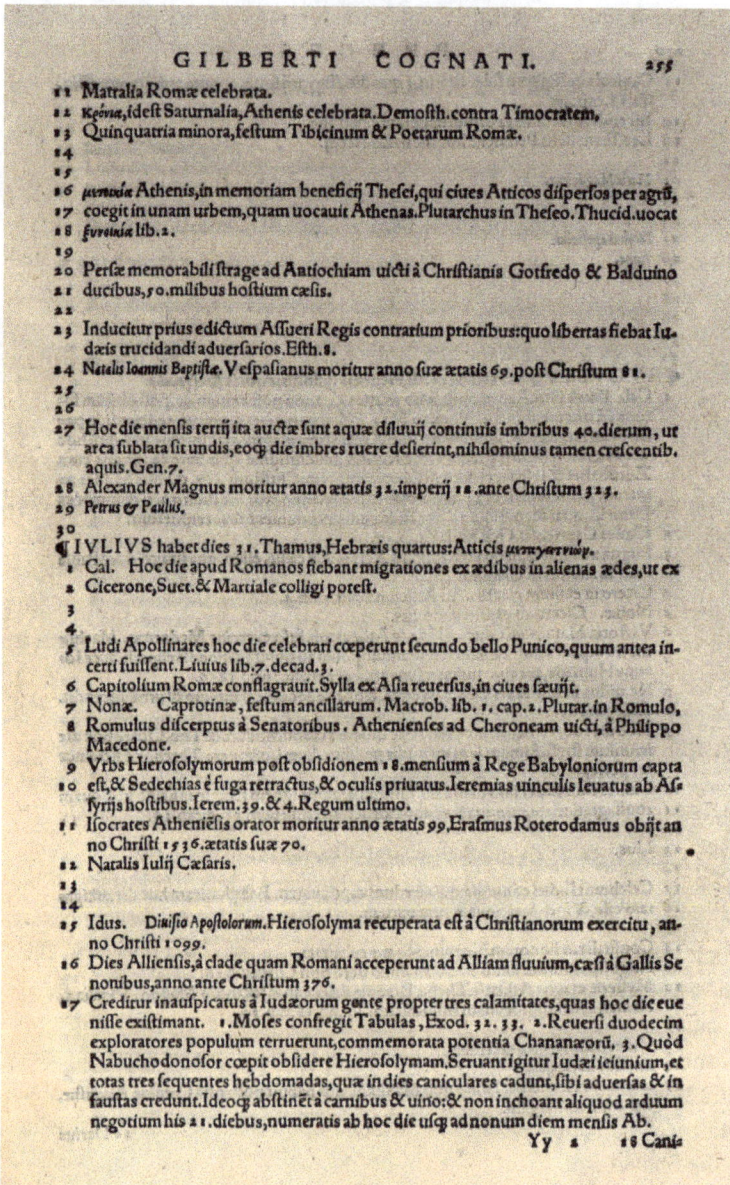

Fig. 1: The *dies Alliensis* in Gilbert Cousin's *Calendarium* (Basel, 1562). Bayerische Staatsbibliothek München.

The juxtaposition of these four entries on Cousin's calendar helps to draw attention to the fundamentally palimpsestic nature of the practice of calendar com-

memoration in the Christian Humanist circles of the European Renaissance in the very year that the French wars of religion erupted. This small sample shows that the effort to recover ancient history while retaining a Christian worldview produced a calendar on which ancient history, Old Testament material, Crusader lore, and recent secular events could be held in a state of exquisite, delicate coexistence. What I want to emphasize here when I speak of this as a palimpsest is the fact that the nature of the relation between the various events on this calendar remains profoundly opaque: in addition to serving as a locus in which history can be rewritten, the calendar functions as a place of commemoration in which several different and indeed incompatible narratives of History can abide together, their potential tensions and contradictions left unmarked. The valence of these respective events would inevitably have varied significantly according to the interests of those making and using the calendar: the historical resonance and ideological function of the *dies Alliensis* on Cousin's 1562 calendar were certainly not identical to those that it possessed on a Roman calendar in the Age of Augustus, since it is now situated next to Christian and subsequent secular history.

As Cousin's quintessentially Humanist calendar demonstrates, calendrical commemoration possesses an extraordinary capacity for containing contradiction. The potential of the calendar to bring otherwise divergent historical narratives into an apparently easy proximity, along with the other features we have evoked – mainly, periodicity and fragmentariness – will constitute a crucial dimension of the memory of the Saint Bartholomew's Day massacre in France.

August 24, 1572

What I have thus far been calling "the Saint Bartholomew's Day massacre" is characterized by contemporary historians as a whole "season" of violent attacks in French cities in the Fall of 1572, beginning in Paris but rapidly spreading to the provinces.[8] One of the first questions to consider, then, is how a single specific date was affixed to these events in the first place. Unlike the *dies Alliensis*, whose presence on extant Roman calendars postdates the time of its occurrence by centuries and whose dating was therefore bound to be somewhat imprecise,[9] the event(s) we are dealing with here are the subject of an immediate and profuse

---

[8] The historiography is considerable and ever expanding; see in particular the work of Janine Garrisson; Denis Crouzet; and Arlette Jouanna.

[9] Engerbeaud gives a good account of the different attempts at dating up through the Republican period.

historical record. While it is impossible here to give anything approaching an exhaustive account of how a single date emerged from this cacaphony, it is clear that the royal court played an important role in the process. The "vingt quatrième jour d'aoust mil cinq cent soixante-douze" is mentioned repeatedly in the peace edicts issued after 1572, first appearing in the 1573 Edict of Boulogne, and then again in the 1576 Edict of Beaulieu, where the locution appears no less than ten times. In 1577, the date appears a full thirteen times over two documents, one of which is the Edict of Poitiers, which I cite in radically abridged form here:

> auparavant *le vingt quatreiesme d'aoust mil cinq cens soixante douze* [. . .] avant *le vingt quatreiesme d'aoust mil cinq cens soixante douze* [. . .] avant *le vingt quatreiesme d'aoust mil cinq cens soixante douze* [. . .] Les desordres et excés faictz *led. vingt quatreiesme jour d'aoust et jours ensuivans en consequence dud. jour*, en nostre bonne ville de Paris et autres villes et endroictz de nostred. royaume, sont advenuz à nostre tres grand regrect et desplaisir [. . .] Deffendons de faire aucunes processions tant à cause de la mort de feu nostre cousin le prince de Condé que de ce qui advint *le jour Sainct-Barthelemy mil cinq cens soixante douze* [. . .] pour le regard desd. choses *led. vingt quatreiesme aoust mil cinq cens soixante douze* [. . .] Declarant n'estre acte d'hostilité ce qui fut faict à Paris et ailleurs *le vingt quatreiesme jour d'aoust mil cinq cens soixante douze* et es jours consecutifz en consequence d'icelluy [. . .] depuis *le vingt quatreiesme jour d'aoust mil cinq cens soixante douze* jusques à present [. . .] depuis *le vingt quatreiesme jour d'aoust mil cinq cens soixante douze* . . . . (italics mine)[10]

The 24th of August functions here as a temporal reference point with respect to which any number of monarchical policies are situated: before August 24, since August 24, on August 24, because of August 24. Even if there is a nod to events that occurred in the days that followed, the reiteration of the date of the Paris massacre privileges August 24 as a turning point, a fateful day.

One of the most famous Protestant pamphlets that appeared in the wake of these events overtly refuses the royal rhetoric of containment to a single calendar day. As the title of François Hotman's 1573 *Discours simple & veritable des rages exercées, par la France . . . et du lache et estrange carnage faict indiferemment des Chrestiens qui se sont peu recouurer en la plus-part des villes de ce royaulme* suggests, the work recounts a series of violent attacks and royal betrayals of which the St Bartholomew's Day massacre in Paris was but one spectacular episode.[11] In

---

10 The full text of the edict can be consulted at http://elec.enc.sorbonne.fr/editsdepacification/edit_08. Accessed Date: June 13, 2023.
11 The work first appeared in 1573 Latin, as *De furoribus Gallicis* . . . under the pseudonym "Ernestus Varamundus," and enjoyed immediate and widespread diffusion: in addition to the French, English and German translations were published in the same year, 1573. Despite its obvious importance, this text has not yet received a modern edition.

his detailed account of the massacre and of the pattern of treachery that preceded and followed it, Hotman approaches August 24 less as a focal point than as part of a network of longstanding practices. Attempting to embed the massacres into a much larger narrative of the royal mistreatment of the Huguenots, Hotman is not interested in singling out any particular day that would thereby assume the entire burden of monarchical misdeeds; instead, he seeks to situate the massacres as part of a political pattern, one horrific example among many of the French court's abuse of its Protestant subjects. In light of Hotman's painstaking reconstruction of the evidence of longstanding monarchical hostility to the Huguenots, we can perceive how the royal legislation's insistence on the single date, August 24, works to minimize the larger political implications that Hotman relentlessly foregrounds. Read next to Hotman, the obsessive attention to a single date clearly functions as a gesture of containment: many of the debates that had fueled over ten years of civil war were now framed in relation to a single day in 1572.

At the same time that the focus on a single day allowed the monarchy to evade larger narratives in which it found itself accused of a veritable policy of treachery with respect to the Huguenots, the memorialization of the events of Fall 1572 in terms of a single "jour" also served a more overtly dramatic strain of Protestant rhetoric that sought to frame what happened on 24 August as an unprecedented event of tragic dimensions. Adopting the characteristically Roman rhetoric of the *dies ater* or black day, the Protestant soldier-poet Agrippa d'Aubigné accords a special place to this day in his long, elaborately violent baroque poem on the French wars of religion, *Les tragiques*:

> Voici venir le jour, jour que les destinées
> Voyaient à bas sourcils glisser de deux années,
> Le jour marqué de noir, le terme des appas,
> Qui voulut estre nuit et tourner sur ses pas:
> Jour qui avec horreur parmi les jours se compte,
> Qui se marque de rouge et rougit de sa honte.[12]

The dramatic reversal of Fortune that takes place on a single fateful day is of course characteristic of Aristotelian tragedy, the discourse of which no doubt contributed to the condensation of meanings around the single day of August 24.[13] While Aubigné might be said to frame the day in terms of a tragic singularity, as we shall see, his Protestant compatriots continually repeated the date, fixing the tragic event to a recurring calendar day. Quite in spite of their decree that the

---

12 Agrippa d'Aubigné [1616] 2006 (Ed. Fanlo), Book V, v. 765–770. pp 613–614.
13 For a more sustained exploration of the interplay between tragedy and the early historiography of the wars of religion, see Frisch 2015.

events of 24 August 1572 were not to be commemorated and should indeed be entirely forgotten, then, the Edicts of Pacification themselves, by inextricably associating those events with a perpetually recurring calendar date, inadvertently provided a productive platform for what Benedict calls the "social memory" of the massacres.

La Journée de la Trahison

In contrast to Hotman's nearly 200-page tome, the platform of the calendar promotes a condensation of meanings and a simplification of message that facilitates assimilation, appropriation, and diffusion. This fact was certainly not lost on the polemicists of the period. We can clearly observe the role played by the calendar in the memory wars between French Protestants and Catholics by examining two partisan works published in the wake of the massacres, the first a well-known Protestant manifesto that was quickly translated into several European languages, and the second a direct Catholic response to it.

The *Reveille-matin des François* is a Protestant work, first published pseudo-nonymously in 1573, within less than a year of the St. Bartholomew's Day massacres (a second edition appeared in 1574).[14] Written in dialogue form, it stages a discussion among six composite figures: Aléthie (Truth), Philaléthie (Lover of forgetting), Historiographe, Politique (in this context, a moderate who rejects factional politics), the prophet Daniel, and the Church. The *Reveille-matin*, like Hotman's *Discours simple et veritable*, never uses the term Saint Bartholomew's Day: its preface refers to "les massacres de Paris"; elsewhere, the date is again emphasized ("le mois d'aoust 1572"; "le Dimanche 24. Jour d'Aoust 1572"). This work takes the paradigm of the *dies Alliensis* one step further by inscribing a moral judgment within the name of the day that it singles out as historically significant. Near the end of the first dialogue, the prophet Daniel, conveying divine judgment on the matter, issues the following decree:

> Ordonnant que dorenavant sera faite tous les vingtquatriemes jours des mois de l'an memoire solonnelle (en execration de leur abomination) du massacre fait le 24 d'Aoust & autres jours ensuyvans . . . . Que ledict jour du massacre 24. d'Aoust sera à jamais nommé, La Journee de la Trahison – *Le Réveille-matin des François et de leurs voisins*, 1574, 138

---

14 The work has recently been re-edited: Philadelphe 2016.

We can recognize here the language of the edicts of pacification, but instead of forbidding any reminders of "ce qui fut faict" on August 24, 1572, as the royal edicts did, Daniel orders that henceforth the 24th of *every month* shall serve as a memorial day. The Protestant authors of the *Réveille-matin* seek to exploit the calendar not simply to assert a right of commemoration, but also to accelerate the rhythm of commemoration; like the 13th of the month in the Roman calendar, the 24th of every month shall henceforth be a marked day. In a move that seeks to impose an ideological mark on a calendar day, it is further decreed that the 24th of August shall be forever known as "The Day of Treason."

By condensing the complex history of the massacres of Fall 1572 into a single memorable term, the *Réveille-matin's* proposal for a day of remembrance privileges one piece of Hotman's much larger narrative. This one piece is, however, considerably more flexible than Hotman's painstaking account; as an eminently portable ideologeme, "La Journée de la Trahison" allows for the economical importation of an entire political orientation into the very temporal ground of History. And indeed, like the royal edicts that preceded it, the *Réveille-matin* situates the day as a fundamental historical reference point according to which all activity shall now be measured: on its final page, it prints the announcement "Achevé d'imprimer le douzieme jour du sixieme mois d'après La Journée de la Trahison." One hears both an echo of the *dies Alliensis* and a prelude to the Revolutionary calendar here.

Saint Bartholomew's Day

Although its coinage of "La Journée de la Trahison" did not appear to catch on, the *Réveille-matin's* discussion of commemoration was a central topic in the Catholic response to the work, entitled *Le Vray Resveille-matin des Calvinistes et Publicains François*. In contrast to the royal legislation and the early Protestant works we have been discussing, the book's author, Catholic priest Arnaud Sorbin – who was by this time *prédicateur du roi*, and who is considered by some historians to have been one of the instigators of the massacre in Paris in August 1572 – makes a point of explicitly attaching, or rather reattaching, the name of Saint Bartholomew to the day in question.

It is notable that only once in the entirety of the royal legislation I refer to above – that is, in the Edicts of Boulogne, Beaulieu, and Poitiers – is the term "la Saint Barthélemy" used. In this instance, it is linked to a prohibition on processions, a specifically Catholic form of commemoration in early modern France, that would take place on the saint's day. The scrupulous repetition of the calendar date rather than the name of the saint's day suggests that the impulse of the court, however latent, was initially to *dissociate* the event from the name of the saint. Keeping references to the liturgical day out of official discourse about the massacre would help to ensure that the saint's day – an inevitably recurring feature of the Catholic liturgical calendar – would remain uncontaminated by the historical event that occurred on it in 1572. In other words, the legislative insistence on August 24 rather than on Saint Bartholomew could be seen as a way to keep the event *off* of the (liturgical) calendar.

In reclaiming the day for the Catholic calendar of saints, Sorbin assumes that he can thereby take control of the larger historical narrative on the events of that day and those around it:

> Mettez donques tant qu'il vous plaira en vos Calendriers, au lieu de la Sainct Barthelemy, le jour de la trahison: car cela vous sera bien aussi loisible, qu'il vous a esté permis par vos Pasteurs de tracer les Apostres & Martyrs de l'ancienne Eglise, pour y subroger vos confreres: Et nous ecrirons à la marge des nostres, & en nos histoires, que jamais le jour du chastiement d'Holoferne, d'Aman, & de Seba, ne furent plus memorables entre les Juifs, pour estre nommez jours de delivrance des publiques calamitez, que cestuy cy sera entre les Catholiques[15]

Sorbin downplays the potential efficacy of the Protestant recasting of August 24 as a day of Treason by asserting that this term will find no place on the Catholic calendar, where it will be annotated as a day of Deliverance. Whether his dismissal of the power of the implicit Protestant narrative to have an impact on broader social memory displays confidence or anxiety is hard to say; what is clear, however, is that his invocation of the Saint's name to designate the controversial day undoubtedly contributed to the fact that the name of Saint Bartholomew became increasingly, inexorably attached to the massacre.

Adopting Sorbin's polemical Catholic spin on the day as one of deliverance, the Jesuit military chaplain Thomas Sailly triumphantly annotates Saint Bartholomew's Day on his 1590 pocket calendar for soldiers thus: "Le 24. Charles IX. treschrestien, punissant Gaspard de Coligny & ses adherens rebelles, delivra l'Eglise

---

15 "Go ahead and write 'the day of Treason' instead of 'Saint Bartholomew's Day' in your calendars, as often as you please; since you are allowed to do so, just as your pastors allowed you to erase there the apostles and martyrs of the ancient Church and replace them with your [Protestant] colleagues. We will write in the margins of our calendars, and in our Histories, that the day of punishment of Holofernes, of Aman, and of Seba were not more memorable among the Jews as days of Deliverance than this day shall be among Catholics" (my trans.) Sorbin 1576, 88r–v.

Catholicque d'un grand dangier, l'an 1572."[16] While Sailly's take on the massacre is thoroughly anti-Protestant, it becomes clear here that the historical event had by then been established as a phenomenon that merited or even demanded inclusion on the *Catholic* calendar. The Saint's name alone did not suffice. Works like Sorbin's and Sailly's, which linked the saint's day to the historical event, surely contributed to the consolidation of the Catholic saint's day name, St Bartholomew's Day, as the site of a memory of the massacre. The calendar was thereby a means by which secular history encroached upon liturgical time, opening up the recurring calendar day to new meanings.

Certainly, these new meanings were hotly contested – was August 24 a day of Treason or a day of Deliverance? – and the authors of calendars and almanachs found ways to convey their ideological orientation, even in the short space afforded by these genres. The Almanach or calendar could, moreover, accommodate a certain degree of elaboration while still retaining its basic structure. This is the case with Thomas Galiot's 1599 *Inventaire de l'histoire journalière*, which offers short historical annotations for every single day of the calendar year.[17] Galiot's journal includes an account of the *dies Alliensis* as the very first entry for July 16 (154v), and describes the assassination attempt on the protestant Admiral Coligny on the 22nd of August, 1572 (180v). The St Bartholomew's Day massacre, identified as such, occupies the large majority of the entry for August 24 (just two other events are mentioned briefly). Galiot's overtly pro-Catholic entry overlays the massacre with the by then well-known story of a barren hawthorn bush that reportedly flowered miraculously that same day, as observed by no less than the king and by "infinite eyewitnesses":

> La journee dite St Barthélemy, en l'an 1572, en laquelle fut fait un pitoyable massacre sur ceux de la religion prétendue réformée, et au même jour au cimetière St Innocent une aubépine dénuée de feuillage commença soudain à pousser et à produire, si bien qu'à vu d'oeil on la voyait fleurir. Le Roi Charles IX la fut voir, la chose lui étant rapportée par une infinité de témoins oculaires (181v)[18]

---

16 *Guidon et practique spirituelle du soldat chrestien, reveu et augmenté pour l'armée de Sa Majesté catholique au Pays-Bas, par le R. P. Thomas Sailly, . . . avec un calendrier historial* (Anvers, 1590), n.p.

17 Galiot 1599.

18 Pierre de l'Estoile explains the story in his *Mémoires-Journaux*: "Le lendemain de la Saint-Barthélemy, environ midi, le bruit se répandit qu'au cimetière Saint-Innocent, une aubépine sèche et sans feuille aurait refleuri. Le peuple y accouru de toutes parts en si grande foule qu'il fallut y poser des gardes alentour; on commença à sonner et carillonner les cloches de joie. Le peuple mutin croyant que Dieu, par ce signe, approuvait le massacre, recommença de plus belle." Pierre de l'Estoile 1896, Tome XII, 378–379.

Despite Galion's obvious Catholic partisanship, there follows a list of some of the most prominent victims of the massacre, ending in a mention of the massacres that occurred in other cities in the days that followed: "plusieurs personnes de l'un et de l'autre sexe furent tuées durant la violence de ce massacre, qui depuis eut son cours à Toulouse, Rouen, et en plusieurs autres villes de la France" (181v). In short, despite Arnaud Sorbin's confidence in the Catholic calendar's capacity to frame History, St. Bartholomew's Day appears to have become a day that would live in infamy.

Reinscriptions of the name of Saint Bartholomew onto references to the massacre(s) on calendars, almanachs, and works like Galion's day-by-day history helped to ensure the phrase "la Saint-Barthélemy" would come to refer with increasing frequency not to the saint, nor to the saint's day, but instead to the violence – whether seen as treasonous or sacred – of the French wars of religion. A remarkable example of this inexorable displacement of the saint by the sixteenth-century event, which also refers very explicitly to the Roman example of Ovid's *Fasti*, occurs in a 1643 Latin work, the *Fastorum Rothomagensium* or *"Fastes rouennais,"* a versified calendar of saints' days that by and large rehearses the hagiography of Catholic tradition as it goes through the months and the seasons, commemorating the saints as it goes along. A glaring exception to the hagiographical tenor of the work is the passage on Saint Bartholomew:

> Bartholomae, tuae venerunt gaudia lucis:
> Calvini soboli lux ea flenda venit
> Haeretico nostri maduerunt sanguine vici;
> Invisum voluit Rex abolere genus[19]

In a striking departure from the rest of the poem, the author mentions nothing at all about the life and death of the saint at whose day his verses have arrived. Instead, he addresses Bartholomew directly in order to praise him for his association with the day upon which French villagers' hands were stained with the "heretic blood" of "Calvin's progeny."

---

19 Griselli 1643, 266.

From the Calendar to the Dictionary: Saint Bartholomew's Day as Lexeme

The calendrical consolidation of the status of August 24, or Saint Bartholomew's Day, as an event according to which historical time shall be measured, is further evident in the Catholic Himbert de Billy's 1587 *Almanach*, which introduces another form of shorthand for the history of Fall 1572: *les matines parisiennes*. The work opens with a list of between fifty and sixty memorable events, beginning with the creation of the world, along with the distance, in years, that separates them from 1587. A small subset of the entries on the list measure the temporal distance from one memorable event to another. This is the case with what Billy calls "les matines parisiennes," which, his almanach informs us, occurred 301 years after the "vespres siciliennes des François" (n.p.).[20]

As another form of commemorative shorthand that overlaid a pre-existing Catholic temporal framework with secular history, the term "matines parisiennes" occurs in a number of historical works published in sixteenth- and seventeenth-century France.[21] Unlike the *Réveille-matin's* baldly political "Journée de la Trahison," this sacred-secular hybrid seems to have caught on, even making it into Randle Cotgrave's famous 1611 *Dictionarie of the French and English Tongues*. After translating the French "Matins" as "Matins, morning prayer," Cotgrave lists a number of proverbial expressions that use the term. The very first among these is none other then "Matines parisiennes: the Massacre of Paris, which began about midnight."[22]

Cotgrave's dictionary brings us to the intersection of the dictionary with the work that the calendar has performed on the memory of Saint Bartholomew's Day. One might be surprised to learn that there are no fewer than thirty-eight mentions of the Saint Bartholomew's Day massacre in Émile Littré's late nineteenth-century *Dictionnaire de la langue française*. While some of these mentions occur exactly where one would expect to find them – under MASSACRE, for example, or ÉGORGEUR – many of them are inserted into entries for words that have a decidedly more

---

20 Himbert de Billy 1587. The term "sicilian vespers" refers to an uprising of the Sicilian people against the Capetian King of Sicily, Charles of Anjou, in 1282, during which members of Charles's French army were killed, and after which Charles never regained control of the island. It is beyond the scope of the present essay to probe further the links that were perceived in Billy's France between this event and the massacres of August 24, 1572 and after.

21 A few notable titles include the *Discours merveilleux sur la vie . . . .de Catherine de Médicis*; Innocent Gentillet's *Discours sur les moyens de bien gouverner*; and Henri Lancelot-Voisin de la Popelinière's *Histoire de France*. The term even earns a place in the index to François Le Maire's 1648, *Histoire et Antiquitez de la ville et Duché d'Orléans*, Tome I, n.p.

22 Cotgrave 1611, n.p.

general or even incidental connection to the event, such as HIER; LIÈVRE; LAPS; ODI-EUX; or VEINE (and this is not an exhaustive list). By associating the Saint Bartholomew's Day massacre with a wide range of terms, these mentions transmit something that is not merely another version of what is transmitted by the various works that deal directly with the event. Like their calendrical counterparts, the dictionary entries embed the term into the fabric of much larger discourses – indeed, into the fabric of language itself, intimating a wide range of commemorative residues and resonances. We could simply attribute these associations to Littré himself, on one end of a spectrum, but they are also linked to broader traditions of transmission, outside of overt works of history or memory, on the other end.[23]

Rather than try to propose a comprehensive analysis of all of the occurences of *Saint Barthélemy* in Littré's dictionary, let us stick with the key terms we have been discussing, namely, "Saint Bartholomew," and the concept of the "day." Littré's entry for "Barthélemy, Saint" is in its entirety given over to the 1572 event. Of course, as the fiercely republican son of an atheist father and a protestant mother, Littré emphasizes the secular associations with all of the saints that appear in his dictionary. The larger point, however, is that the 1572 massacre is apparently the only secular referent for St Bartholomew; in contrast to, say, Saint Michel, no military orders, liberal arts medals, or pears were ever named after him (all things mentioned in Littré's entry for Saint Michel). More striking in the context of my investigation here is the massacre's appearance in Littré's entry for "journée". The term "Journée," Littré explains, is used precisely for days that are associated with a particularly significant historical event. Put another way, we could say that a "journée," at least in this sense, is a "jour" that has earned a place on the historical calendar. By way of further explanation, Littré cites Voltaire: "La journée de la Saint Barthélemy fut ce qu'il y jamais eu de plus horrible; la manière juridique dont la cour voulut soutenir et justifier ces massacres fut ce qu'on a vu jamais de plus lâche."[24] Not merely an inheritor or exploiter of the tradition of calendrical commemoration, Littré here acts as a perpetuator of that very tradition, adding yet another link in the chain that yoked the massacres of Fall 1572 to a day, and that allowed a term as fundamental and ubiquitous as "journée" to serve as a mnemonic touchstone for the memory of the violence of the wars of religion.

---

23 Littré writes that he assembled a team that he directed to find examples from "les plus célèbres [textes] depuis le douzième . . . jusqu'au seizième siècle" en donnant la préférence "aux exemples intéressants ou par leur élégance, ou par l'anecdote, ou par l'histoire." Littre 1897, 6. This is a fascinating essay that describes the assistance Littré received from his wife and daughter; the vicissitudes of the Franco-Prussian War and of the Commune; and Littré's eventual illness and decline.

24 Littré 1874, Tome III, 205. The citation is to Voltaire's *Histoire du Parlement de Paris*.

April 13, 2016

When the city of Paris finally decided to dedicate a small plaque as a public memorial to the Saint Bartholomew's Day massacres in 2016, two lines from the verses of Agrippa d'Aubigné cited above were chosen to adorn it: "Jour qui avec horreur parmi les jours se compte/Qui se marque de rouge et rougit de sa honte" (Fig. 2). Although the plaque stipulates that it is a question of "le 24 août et les jours suivants," the choice of Aubigné's verses bring us once more to the *jour*, the single day.

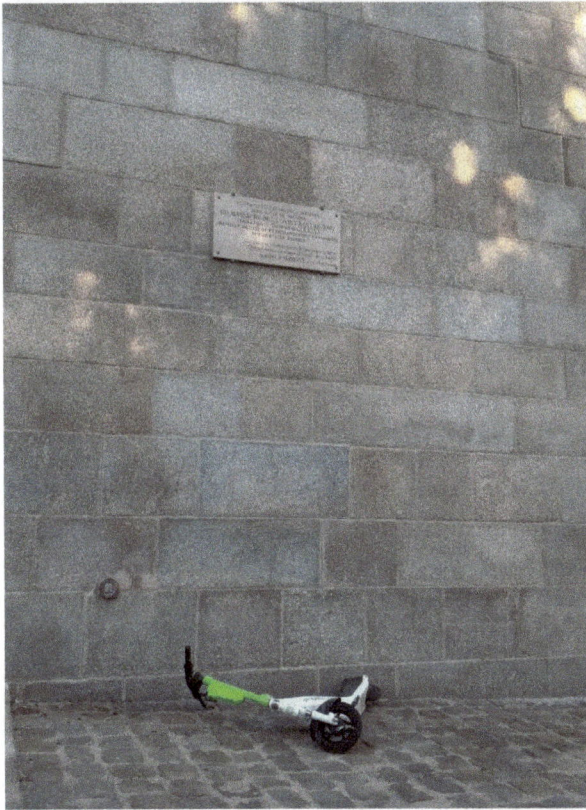

Fig. 2: Plaque dedicated in 2016 to the memory of the victims of the Saint Bartholomew's Day massacres, located near the Square du Vert Galant, Paris, Photo: Andrea Frisch.

The Roman rhetoric of the *dies ater*, emblematized by the *dies Alliensis* and reanimated in "la journée Saint Barthélemy," facilitates the concentration of a complex web of historical circumstances into a potent ideologeme that the calendar efficiently preserves, publicizes, and circulates. And like the *dies Alliensis*, "la journée Saint Barthélemy" returns each year in a slightly different guise. But the *mairie* of Paris did not choose August 24 as the date for the plaque's public unveiling ceremony. Exploiting the palimpsestic layering of meanings that the calendar affords, it chose the date of April 13 for this singular event. April 13 is not, of course, the fateful day mentioned on the plaque; it is that of Henri IV's entry into Nantes to ratify the famous 'edict of tolerance' in 1598. The choice of this date, rather than that of August 24, suggests a very specific orientation for the gesture of commemoration: rather than memorializing the victims of the massacres, the ceremonial unveiling of the plaque memorializes what French public culture promotes as the most consequential rejection of religious fanaticism in modern history: the Edict of Nantes. Whereas in Aubigné's poem, as I suggested earlier, the *topos* of a "jour marqué" serves to designate a singularly tragic and therefore eminently memorable event, the Parisian plaque has more in common with the rhetoric of the royal edicts of pacification. The quote chosen from Aubigné's poem serves to evade the question of human agency on that fateful day "et les jours suivants"; we are led to believe that the horror, the blood, and the shame that the poet describes are attributes of the *jour* itself, rather than of the French actors who sanctioned the massacre or of those who took part in it.

François Hotman's painstaking reconstruction of the policies that led to these "assassinations" has here definitively ceded supremacy to the simplified rhetoric of the fateful day. This day, long past, carries the entire burden of the massacres, which are thereby completely divorced from the beliefs, the institutions, and the practices of the human beings that made them possible, and that could potentially link them to life in the present. The passive voice of the official declaration that precedes the quote only confirms this reading: – just as "mistakes were made," "plusieurs milliers de protestants furent assassinés." We are not very far here from the "ce qui fut fait" of the sixteenth-century royal edicts. Engraved in stone under the Pont-Neuf, August 24, in its infinite adaptability, now stands neither as a sign of divine deliverance nor as the evidence of treason, but is rather framed as the epitome of the kind of very bad day that *other people's* religious fanaticism inevitably produces.

Bibliography

D'Aubigné, Agrippa. *Les tragiques* (1616). Ed. Jean-Raymond Fanlo. Paris: Champion, 2006.

Benedict, Philip. "Divided Memories? Historical Calendars, Commemorative Processions, and the Recollection of the Wars of Religion during the Ancien Régime." *French History* 22 (2008): 381–405.

de Billy, Himbert. *Almanach pour l'an 1587*. Paris: Benoist Rigaud, 1587.

Christin, Olivier. "Mémoire inscrite, oubli prescrit. La fin des troubles de religion en France." *Vergeben und Vergessen? Pardonner et oublier?: Vergangenheitsdiskurse nach Besatzung, Bürgerkrieg und Revolution. Les discours sur le passé après l'occupation, la guerre civile et la révolution.* Eds. Reiner Marcowitz and Werner Paravicini. Berlin: Walter de Gruyter, 2014. 73–92.

Cooley, Alison. "Commemorating the War Dead of the Roman World," *Proceedings of the British Academy* 160 (2012): 63–88.

Cotgrave, Randle. *A Dictionarie of the French and English Tongues*. London: Adam Islip, 1611.

Cousin, Gilbert. Calendarium in *Opera multifarii argumenti*, Basel: 1562.

Crespin, Jean. *Ephemeris historica*. Geneva: 1551.

Engammare, Max. "Mise en page des calendriers réformés (mi-XVIᵉ – fin-XVIIᵉ siècle)" in Charon, Annie, et al. Eds. *La mise en page du livre religieux (XIIIᵉ-XXᵉ siècle)*. Paris: Publications de l'École nationale des chartes, 2004. 27–60.

Engerbeaud, Mathieu. "Le 'jour de l'Allia' (*dies Alliensis*) : recherches sur l'anniversaire d'une défaite dans les calendriers romains." *Mélanges de l'École française de Rome – Antiquité* 130–131 (2018): 251–266.

de l'Estoile, Pierre. *Mémoires-Journaux de Pierre de L'Estoile*. Eds. Brunet et al. Tome XII. Paris: Lemerre, 1896.

Frisch, Andrea. *Forgetting Differences. Tragedy, Historiography, and the French Wars of Religion*. Edinburgh: Edinburgh University Press, 2015.

Galiot, Thomas. *Inventaire de l'histoire journalière*. Paris: Jacques Rezé, 1599.

Grafton, Anthony and Swerdlow, Noel. "Calendar Dates and Ominous Days in Ancient Historiography." *Journal of the Warburg and Courtauld Institutes* 51 (1988): 14–42.

Griselli, Herculis. *Fastorum Rothomagensium*. Lutetiae: Gervasium Alliot, 1643.

Le Maire, François. *Histoire et Antiquitez de la ville et Duché d'Orléans*. Orléans: Maria Paris, 1648.

Littré, Émile. *Dictionnaire de la langue française*. Seconde édition. Paris: Hachette, 1874.

Littré, Émile. *Comment j'ai fait mon "Dictionnaire de la langue française."* Nouvelle édition, précédée d'un avant-propos. Paris: 1897.

Luce, T. J. "Design and Structure in Livy: 5.32–55." *Transactions and Proceedings of the American Philological Association* 102 (1971): 265–302.

Philadelphe, Eusèbe. *Le Reveille-matin des François, et de leurs voisins*. Eds. Jean-Raymond Fanlo, Marino Lambiase, and Paul-Alexis Mellet. Paris: Classiques Garnier, 2016.

Rosenberger, Veit. "The Gallic Disaster." *The Classical World* 96 4 (2003): 365–373.

Sorbin, Arnaud. *Le Vray Resveille-matin des Calvinistes, et Publicains François : où est amplement discouru de l'auctorité des Princes*. Paris: 1576.

Guidon et practicque spirituelle du soldat chrestien, reveu et augmenté pour l'armée de Sa Majesté catholicque au Pays-Bas, par le R. P. Thomas Sailly, . . . avec un calendrier historial. Anvers: 1590.

Michael P. Steinberg
The Cry of Laocoön. Myths and Countermyths of the Founding of Cities

1

In May 1981, François Mitterrand was elected President of France and lost no time conceiving of a remake of the monumental architecture of Paris on a scale rivaling that of the Second Empire and the era of Napoleon III and Baron Haussmann.[1] His informally named *grands projets* included a new opera house, the Opéra Populaire de la Bastille, the so-called opera of the people, an answer to the Second Empire's Palais Garnier. The new house was inaugurated finally on July 13, 1989, the eve of the anniversary of the storming of the Bastille, the *fête nationale*, and in 1989 the bicentennial of the French Revolution. The celebration was enormous and included over sixty heads of state, all seated in the auditorium according to President Mitterrand's personal tastes and rankings. There were some surprises. No love of any kind had ever been lost between Mitterrand and British Prime Minister Margaret Thatcher through their shared decade of service, a predicament only exacerbated by Thatcher's remark on this occasion that much too much fuss was being made about the commemoration specifically and about the French Revolution more generally. After all, the French had not invented democracy in 1789; the Brits had beat them to it by close to six centuries with the Magna Carta, signed at Runnymede in 1215. As her reward, the British Prime Minister was seated high in the upper rafters of the new auditorium.

At more or less the same time, a recent PhD holder from the University of Chicago was revising a dissertation into book form. Its first chapter, "The Ideology of the Baroque," included a survey of nineteenth-century opera houses and opera festivals conceived as temples of national and sometimes imperial culture and power. In France and elsewhere, the decade of Mitterrand's presidency had spawned repertoires of neo-baroque architecture, theory (Gilles Deleuze's *Le Pli* and the canonization of Walter Benjamin serve as two examples), and style. Bur-

---

1 My thanks to Michèle Lowrie and Barbara Vinken for the invitation to offer the first version of this essay at the June 2022 conference *Paris: a New Rome*, as well as to fellow participants for their comments. The assignment gave me the chance to revisit some key work and concerns of Aby Warburg (as cited below) and to recontextualize some of the material from my recent book Steinberg 2022.

https://doi.org/10.1515/9783111334776-011

ied in a footnote of "The Ideology of the Baroque," was the observation that Paris, in 1989, was at it again. The footnote read:

> It will be interesting to see in the next few years whether an attempt is made to revive a sense of a national operatic genre, perhaps through a focus on Berlioz and Meyerbeer, in conjunction with the new Bastille Opera. The initial signals are mixed: the choice of architect was made in the same way as that for the Palais Garnier in 1860 – by open contest. But the winner was an Uruguayan: Carlos Ott. The socialist government's January 1989 dismissal of Daniel Barenboim as director of the Bastille Opera suggests that some kind of national program is desired; Barenboim's plans would have emphasized Mozart and Wagner.[2]

Historians occasionally get away with spasms of prophecy. As it in fact turned out, when the Opéra Bastille mounted its first fully staged opera, in May 1990, it presented Hector (I repeat, Hector) Berlioz's immense masterpiece *Les Troyens*, set to his own translation of Vergil. A parable about the founding of Rome thus served as a parable of the refounding of Paris. The immense opera's composition dates between 1856 and 1858. Its second part, *Les Troyens à Carthage*, was premiered at the Théatre Lyrique in Paris in 1863; the first of the opera's two acts, *La prise de Troie*, was performed first in Karlsruhe in 1890, more than two decades after Berlioz's death.

Berlioz introduces the hero Aeneas in Act 1, Scene 2. Following a self-imposed cut to his own text and music, he has Aeneas make a rushed and agitated initial entrance, recounting to Priam's court the horrible death of the priest Laocoön, strangled along with his two sons by two serpents emerging from the sea, punishment by the Greek gods for his attempt to expose the ruse of the wooden horse now parked inside Troy's gates.

ÉNÉE
accourant du peuple et des soldats
ô roi! la la foule s'enfuit et roule
Comme un torrent; on ne peut l'arrêter!
Un prodige inouï vient de l'épouvanter:
Laocoon, voyant quelque trame perfide
Dans l'ouvrage des Grecs, a d'un bras intrépide
Lancé son javelot sur ce bois, excitant
Le peuple indécis et flottant
A le brûler. Alors, gonflés de rage,
Deux serpents monstrueux s'avancent vers la plage,
S'élancent sur le prêtre, en leurs terribles nœuds
L'enlacent, le brûlant de leur haleine ardente,

---

2 Steinberg, *The Meaning of the Salzburg Festival: Austria as Theater and Ideology* (Cornell, 1990), 9n–10n.

> Et le couvrant d'une bave sanglante,
> Le dévorent à nos yeux.

This agitated and clipped account sutures several passages from Aeneas's account in Vergil's Book 2:

> Then Laocoön, a huge mob in his wake,
> Runs down in a hurry from the city heights . . . .
> With all his force, he flung a giant spear
> At the jointed curving belly of the beast . . . .
> Suddenly, twin snakes from Tenedos –
> I shudder at the retelling – headed for the shore,
> Their giant coils cutting through calm waters . . . .
> They made a beeline for Laocoön. First
> They twisted round his two sons' tiny bodies,
> Feeding on their helpless flesh with fangs.
> Then they snared the father as he ran to help
> Bringing his spear. They bound him with huge loops . . . .
> As he tried to break their knots with both his hands,
> his headbands slimed with venom and black gore,
> his awful shrieks rose to the sky – like the bellows
> of a wounded bull when he's escaped the alter
> and dislodged the ax half-buried in his neck.[3]

Berlioz's scene continues with a long choral ensemble, recording and repeating the reactions of Vergil's Aeneas's audience.

Berlioz's introduction of Aeneas in real time, so to speak, prior to the sack of Troy, and not as a storyteller to the court of Dido, as in Vergil, posits him as a witness and affective twin to Laocoön, whose demise he reports. As Aeneas's story continues – in Vergil, but not Berlioz – he will, on the one hand, tarry peacefully between the generation of his father and that of his son, able to carry his father to Sicily and honor him there after his death. On the other hand, his story will continue as one of an exile and a refugee, responsible for several important deaths, most notably of course that of Dido, and henceforth responsible as well for the sworn enmity between Carthage and Rome. Berlioz's story matches the city of Hector, Priam, and Aeneas, for whom the future, to say nothing about the prospect of founding of a city or a civilization, is shadowed by the memory of defeat and exile. Berlioz's answer to Napoleon III may echo Vergil's to Augustus. In musical reception history, Berlioz himself has come to figure as an answer, a contra-foundational antagonist, to Richard Wagner. Jacques Barzun made such a move shortly after World War II as his magnum opus *Berlioz and the Romantic*

---

3 Vergil, *The Aeneid.* Trans. Shadi Bartsch 2021, 2:40–41, 50–51, 203–08, 212–16, 221–224.

Century dislodged Wagner as the paradigmatic voice of the nineteenth century, shifting, so to speak, the accent of modernity from one side of Baudelaire's iconic equation ("the absolute and the immutable") to the other ("the fleeting, the transitory, the contingent").[4] Berlioz's music, especially his operas and most especially *Les Troyens*, rivals Wagner's in duration but differs fundamentally in its comparatively counter-teleological pulse and temporality.

The agitation of Aeneas's entrance and account are offset somewhat by the formal, grand-operatic genre and style that deliver them to Berlioz's (rather than Aeneas's) audience. To listen to the scene I recommend the 1969 Phillips audio recording of record, conducted by Colin Davis and with Jon Vickers as Aeneas. The timbre of Vickers's voice along with the style of his intonation and delivery offer a signature combination of beauty and pain that make his Aeneas (together with his Tristan and Peter Grimes) unmatched sonic, musical, and dramatic portrayals. Nevertheless, if Vickers's sound sympathizes in any way, along with his text, with Laocoön's pathos, it cannot compensate for the fact that Laocoön's cry is never heard, in other words, never represented through auditory art. G.E. Lessing's treatise on the Laocoön group as an argument for the superiority of narration over image for its superior combination of verisimilitude and representability (about which more below) does not and cannot engage the presence or materiality of sound. In post-Lacanian operatic criticism, the *cry* accrues significance as the Other of song, voice, and music. It exists beyond art – where Lessing had no interest in going – in the same way that *jouissance* (as the loss of self) exists beyond pleasure (the satisfaction of expectations). The cry therefore approaches the status of the Lacanian Real, beyond the symbolic order and therefore beyond mediation and representation. But a cry uttered onstage as part of a dramatic plot, no matter the sound, retains the dimension, the middle ground, of mediation and representation. It becomes literally obscene – *hors scène* – to match or to imagine any sound to the cries of the *Laocoön* sculptural group or to Vergil's narration.[5]

The notion of Aeneas, who sings, as the twin of Laocoön, whose cry is unrepresentable, may therefore be problematic if not false; the question I want to ask here may itself be expressed with a similar exaggeration: namely, what happens when we think of the Laocoön figure and trope as foundational, historically and politically– or, perhaps rather counter-foundational? *Les Troyens à Carthage* ends contrapuntally with the suicide of Dido and her prophetic intonation of the name of Hannibal as Carthage's future avenger against Rome. (Berlioz/Dido's

---

4 Barzun 1950. The reference is to Baudelaire's essay "Le peintre de la vie moderne" of 1859.
5 See Poizat 1992. The very construction of the Bastille Opera during a period of economic crisis, Poizat adds, points to the "jouissance machine" of opera itself (11).

Hannibal prefigures in symbolic function the Hannibal of Sigmund Freud for the latter's imaginary conquest of Rome as the overdetermined seat of both empire and Church.) In the opera's final tableau, the chorus of abandoned Carthaginians curse the descendants of Aeneas against a downstage vision of the Trojans entering Rome to an accompanying musical recapitulation of the latter's earlier triumphal march – a mere ironic quotation in the context of the perspective from Carthage in flames. The signal here is in fact musically, dramatically, and historically inconclusive and redolent of defeat, indicating an ongoing temporality that is melancholic and transitory rather than foundational. Berlioz, channeling both Hector and Laocoön, is not a founder – did not present himself as one, and has not been so lionized by musical historiography. Its indisputable selection as the work most suitable for the opening of the Opéra Bastille notwithstanding, *Les Troyens* is not a national opera, let alone an imperial one, but rather, conceivably, a counter-national opera. With its final point of view belonging to Dido, it stands as an anti-imperial one as well.

2

Laocoön's iconic future is perhaps even richer than Aeneas's.

The young Hector Berlioz would have seen the Laocoön group in Rome during his two years there (with interruptions) between 1830 and 1832. He might also have known, previously or subsequently, of Hubert Robert's painting *La découverte du Laocoon* (1773), which wound up in the collection of Maurice de Rothschild in Switzerland before being sold via the dealers Rosenberg and Stiebel to the Virginia Museum of the Arts in Richmond, its current home (Fig. 1).

Robert's painting is set in the Louvre but recounts the renowned unearthing of the sculptural group from Rome's Esquiline Hill in the presence of the young Michelangelo, dispatched to the site by his patron, Pope Julius II. The work was identified in part from its description by Pliny the Elder as "preferable to any other production of the art of painting or of statuary."

Laocoön and the threatening figure of the serpent carried profound and overdetermined meaning through the career of Aby Warburg (1866–1929), the pioneering cultural historian of the image. Laocoön followed Warburg from his early study of G. E. Lessing's 1766 treatise *Laocoön: An Essay on the Limits of Painting and Poetry* as a Gymnasium student to the youthful ethnography of his trip to the Hopi mesas of the American southwest in 1895–96 to his eventual recapitulation of that journey in his 1923 lecture "Images from the Region of the

Fig. 1: Hubert Robert, La découverte du Laocoon. *The Finding of the Laocoon*. Virginia Museum of Fine Arts. Public domain.

Pueblo Indians of North America" and beyond. Here, Warburg centered his ethnography on the Hopi ritual dance with poisonous snakes, a ceremony that he had in fact not witnessed. Thirty years after his two-part sojourn in the American southwest, he delivered the lecture as a patient in Ludwig Binswanger's sanatorium in a wager to gain his own discharge, following a stay of four years. The lecture's themes of culture, violence, and healing shadow uncannily Warburg's own psychic predicament. From the 1923 lecture:

> This idea of the serpent as a destroying force from the
> underworld has found its most powerful and tragic symbol in the myth and in the sculpted
> group of Laocoön . . . .
> The vengeance of the gods, wrought on their priest and
> on his two sons by means of a strangler serpent, becomes
> in this renowned sculpture of antiquity the manifest in-
> carnation of extreme human suffering. The soothsaying
> priest who wanted to come to the aid of his people by
> warning them of the wiles of the Greeks falls victim to the
> revenge of the partial gods. Thus the death of the father
> and his sons becomes a symbol of ancient suffering: death

at the hands of vengeful demons, without justice and
without hope of redemption. That is the hopeless, tragic
pessimism of antiquity . . . .

The serpent as the demon in the pessimistic worldview of antiquity has a counterpart in a
serpent-deity in
which we can at last recognize the humane, transfigured
beauty of the classical age . Asclepius, the ancient god of
healing, carries a serpent coiling around his healing staff
as a symbol. His features are the features carried by the world savior in the plastic art of
antiquity.
And this most exalted and serene god of departed souls
has his roots in the subterranean realm, where the serpent
makes its home. It is in the form of a serpent that he is
accorded his earliest devotion. It is he himself who winds
around his staff: namely, the departed soul of the deceased, which survives and reappears in the form of the
serpent. For the snake is not only, as Cushing's Indians
would say, the fatal bite in readiness or fulfillment, destroying without mercy; the snake
also reveals by its own
ability to cast off its slough, slipping, as it were, out of its
own mortal remains, how a body can leave its skin and
yet continue to live.[6]

In 1907 Warburg wrote to James Mooney of the Smithsonian Institution that his
time with the Hopis had proven key to his evolving understanding of the Italian
and northern European Renaissance as the moment of symbolization, in other
words as a moment of distance-taking via representation from the divine, and
hence also and inseparably from the demonic. Months before his death in 1929,
Warburg made a final trip to Rome, a story recounted in his inimitable voice by
my teacher Arnaldo Momigliano:

Gertrud Bing, the Director of the Warburg Institute, used
to tell with great gusto a story that apparently has not
found its way into the biography of Aby Warburg by Ernst
Gombrich. Bing happened to be in Rome with Warburg,
the founder and patron saint of the Warburg Institute, on
that day, February 11, 1929, on which Mussolini and the
Pope proclaimed the reconciliation between Italy and the
Catholic Church and signed a concordat, the first bilateral
agreement to be reached between post-Risorgimento Italy

---

6 Warburg 1996, 39–42.

and the Church of Rome. There were in Rome tremendous
popular demonstrations, whether orchestrated from above
or from below. Mussolini became overnight the "man of
providence," and in such an inconvenient position he remained for many years. Circulation in the streets of Rome
was not very easy on that day, and it so happened that
Warburg disappeared from the sight of his companions.
They anxiously waited for him back in the Hotel Eden, but
there was no sign of him for dinner. Bing and the others
even telephoned the police. But Warburg reappeared in the
hotel before midnight, and when he was reproached he so-
berly replied something like this in his picturesque German: "You know that throughout my life I have been inter-
ested in the revival of paganism and pagan festivals. Today I had the chance of my life to be
present at the re-paganization of Rome, and you complain that I remained to watch it."[7]

The triumph of fascism as a pagan comedy, via Warburg and Momigliano, gives way
to multiple tragedies. Perhaps none is more evil than the Gestapo's roundup of Rome's
Jews of October 16, 1943. The some 1,200 people herded for deportation included Ludwig Pollak, citizen of Rome since 1893, director of the Barracco Museum of Comparative Ancient Sculpture, and in 1906, four centuries precisely after the unearthing of
the Laocoön group, the discoverer of its principal figure's authentic right arm.

Hans von Trotha's recent novel *Pollak's Arm* (2021; English translation 2022) imagines an interview between Pollak and an emissary from the Vatican on October 17,
1943, as the latter attempts unsuccessfully to rescue the aged scholar and his family
from arrest and deportation. Von Trotta's portrait of Pollak also restages the iconography of the *Laocoön* group itself. In Ingrid Rowland's summary:

> Von Trotha's Pollak . . . believes that his discovery of Laocoön's bent arm has entirely
> changed the meaning of the statue. The outstretched arm, reaching upward through the
> chaos, expressed the priest's extremities of suffering as an epic struggle toward immortality.
> The bent arm, the real arm, has brought Laocoön and his agony crashing back down to
> earth, bound by the incurable pain of being human.[8]

Rowland continues with a quotation from Pollak as imagined by von Trotha:

> He's no hero, and neither nobility nor grandeur is on display. Simplicity, maybe. And a
> bloodcurdling scream ringing in the silence . . . .
>   The extended arm is monumental, sublime, and wrong. The arm that will never reach
> out again. My arm – the arm of a doomed man – is the real arm (Fig. 2), (Fig. 3).

---

7 Images, 108–109. Momigliano 1986, 181; reprinted Momigliano 1987a, 297; also in Momigliano
1987b, 92.
8 NYRB 7 April 2022, 25–26.

Fig. 2: *Laocoön* with arm from 1523. Originally taken from Richard Brillant, *My Laocoön*, published in May 2000 at University of California Press. C. 1850 photograph of Laocoon sculpture showing pre 20th century restoration. Public domain.

"Pollak's memories," Rowland continues, "are indissolubly linked to the glorious, weighty heritage of Judaism, and hence to anti-Semitism, the serpent that has confined him in its coils since his birth, a monster unleashed by an angry God for some unfathomable reason – or perhaps the same reason that drove Minerva to throw snakes at Laocoön . . . ."

For Aby Warburg, the serpent's coils carried the threats to the ego of both antisemitism and religion itself: "The poisonous reptile symbolizes the inner and outer demoniac forces that humanity must overcome."[9] As with Sigmund Freud, Warburg's sensitivity to antisemitism was matched by an intellectual intransigence that disallowed the exemption of Judaism from the critique of religion. In a letter of 25 November 1889, he wrote to his mother from the University of Strassburg of his depression at the antisemitic barbs to which he was subjected; several times a day, as he heard voices in the street behind him saying, in Alsatian dialect, "Desch ischt e Jud" (That is a Jew). The participation in ritual performance frightened him, an

---

9 *Images*, 53.

Fig. 3: *Laocoön* with Pollak's arm from 1906. *Laocoön and his sons*, also known as the Laocoon Group. Marble, copy after an Hellenistic original from ca. 200 BC. Found in the Baths of Trajan, 1506. Vatican Museums. Photo by Livio Andronico, 2014. Public domain.

attitude that prevented him, the eldest of four sons, from attending his father's funeral in 1910 – in other words the generational struggle of fathers and sons in addition to the inter-cultural one. He wrote to his brother Max:

> The whole celebration acquires, in a natural and subjectively absolutely justified manner, the character of a demonstration for the faithful Jews. I do not wish to disturb this. I am after all in the eyes of others an unreliable customer, but in my own eyes a political opponent of clerical elementary schools such as the Talmud Torah School, and above all I am a 'Cherem' [banned] through my mixed marriage and as the father of non-denominational children whom I shall never lead to Judaism . . . . The Mourners' Kaddish is a matter for the eldest son: it signifies not only an external act, but at this public memorial service demonstrates acceptance of the moral inheritance. I will not make

myself guilty of such public hypocrisy. No one is entitled to demand this of me.[10]

The Jewish troping of Laocoön has additional examples, including El Greco's placement of the group in front of the city of Toledo (1610–1614) in the throes of the Inquisition (Fig. 4).

Fig. 4: El Greco, *Laocoön*, National Gallery of Art. Public domain.

It adheres as one of the auras of Lessing's treatise. Indeed Lessing's central metaphors of *Nebeneinander* and *Nacheinander* [the sequential and the simultaneous: i.e. the poetic against the visual, Vergil's *Aeneid* vs. the sculpture] carry themselves a certain Jewish shadow in light of Lessing's sustained (and frankly incomprehensible) attention to the status and integrity of Germany's Jews. In the German canon, Lessing seems to me equal only to Nietzsche in his dismissal and intolerance of antisemitism. The slaughter of innocents is regularly depicted both

---

10 Steinberg 1988, 452.

literally and allegorically as the murder of children. Hence the survival of the Laocoön trope with its simultaneous murder of multiple generations – the core of genocide – into the Jewish twentieth century. The assault on the fathers impacts the sons. The generation of the *fin de siècle* – Freud's and Warburg's – added to the predicament of multi-generational pathos the additional dimension of Oedipal resentment against the fathers who could not protect them.

3

Fig. 5: Michelangelo, *Moses.* Photo: Jörg Bittner Unna. Public domain.

Michelangelo's memory of the unearthing of the Laocoön group followed him to the creation, some thirty years later, of his Moses statue, also associated with his patron Julius II and destined for the latter's tomb. Like the *Laocoön* group, Michelangelo's *Moses* operates between ongoing story and momentary image, as well as between rage and recalcitrance. Kenneth Gross suggests, moreover, that the *Moses* "contains some quite obvious visual echoes of the central figure in the *Laocoön* group, revises and repossesses that sculpture most fully insofar as it takes *within* itself the supernatural serpent that enwraps the Trojan priest and his sons, relocating the energy of that demonic reptile within the beard, drapery, and serpentine pose of the isolated figure of the patriarch. It is a revision that furthermore manages to transform an image of entrapment into one of mastery (Fig. 5)."[11]

Sigmund Freud recalled his repeated encounters with "the Moses of Michelangelo" in a memorable passage of his 1914 essay of that name:

> How often I have mounted the steep steps from the unlovely Corso Cavour to the lonely piazza where the deserted church stands, and have essayed to support the angry scorn of the hero's glance! Sometimes I have crept cautiously out of the half-gloom of the interior as though I myself belonged to the mob upon who his eye is turned – the mob which can hold fast no conviction, which has neither faith nor patience, and which rejoices when it has regained its illusory idols.[12]

There is a coy charisma to this memoir of an interior theatricality, a performance for the audience of oneself, now shared with the reader. Freud recalls a methodical staging of his own experience, his emergence from the bustle of everyday life into the countenance of "the hero's gaze." He then imagines himself unworthy of his spectator's privilege, placing himself in the doomed position of the mob and the idol worshippers. The passage becomes a kind of ritualistic self-test, an exercise that will summon the strength to pursue the forthcoming analysis as a man of science. Freud and Moses have a unique and private relationship, and Freud owns it.

"Der Moses des Michelangelo" offers a counter-biblical reading of the Moses statue, in which Freud replaces the raging Moses with an icon – complex, to be sure – of Renaissance *sophrosyne*, or temperance. Through a painstaking reconstruction of the sitting Moses's bodily position, Freud establishes that Moses cannot be seen as if about to spring up in anger, about to hurl the two tablets clutched under his right arm into the crowd of idol worshipers gathered below him. This is indeed the biblical account of Moses, rising now in holy anger ("*heiliger Zorn*"), but repeating the same rage that had led him earlier in life to kill the Egyptian slavemaster who had abused a Hebrew slave. Contrary to this standard view, Freud argues, Michelangelo's Moses must be seen as having overcome his righteous rage and therefore having reassumed a seated position. His powerful, muscular body now becomes the "physical expression of the highest psychic

---

11 Gross 1992, 192.
12 Freud 1955, XIII, 213.

achievement possible for a human being," namely the suppression (*Niederringen*) of passion in favor of an entrusted purpose – namely the preservation of the Decalogue written into the tablets. Thus sublimation produces not only culture but politics and law as well.

No version of Freud's solitary delight or experience of personal discovery, intimacy, or ownership has been available to visitors approaching the aggressive, almost embarrassing placement of the statue inside the Lincoln Memorial in Washington, D.C. No solitary discovery or intimate experience is permissible against the visual rhetoric of the seated statue, measuring nineteen feet high and weighing two hundred tons, encased within its equally massive, elevated neoclassical pavilion. The theatricality overwhelms. But not quite. The statue is seated. Its downward gaze seems melancholic and preoccupied, but at the same time protective. The statue does not appear to notice its comparatively dwarfed human viewers, but it seems to recognize us, to take us into account (Fig. 6).

Fig. 6: Daniel Chester French, *Lincoln.* Photograph of the Abraham Lincoln statue by Attilio Piccirilli for Daniel Chester French, 1920, in the Lincoln Memorial. Public domain.

Abraham Lincoln's marble eyes have gazed across space and time over the National Mall and Memorial Parks of Washington, D.C. since 1922. The memorial's planning and funding had moved through Congress from early in the Lincoln centennial year of 1909. The rallying theme– national unity, not emancipation or racial justice – recapitulated Lincoln's own political priority. The same year, during the week of Lincoln's February birthdate, civil rights pioneers issued their famous "Lincoln Birthday Call" for a meeting to organize what became the National Association for the Advancement of Colored People (NAACP). As Scott Sandage shows, this double history tracked the early years of the memorial, until the momentum and iconography of the civil rights movement came to control its significance. Behind the statue, the following lines are engraved: "In This Temple as in the Hearts of the People for Whom He Saved the Union the Memory of Abraham Lincoln Is Enshrined Forever." Their author, art critic Royal Cortissoz, explained them to Henry Bacon, architect of the neo-classical pavilion: "The memorial must make a common ground for the meeting of the north and the south. By emphasizing his saving the union you appeal to both sections. By saying nothing about slavery you avoid the rubbing of old sores."[13] The memorial's May 1922 dedication saw its public segregated according to Jim Crow practices, with distant and uncomfortable seating supplied to Black spectators.[14]

Though standard accounts maintain a strange silence on the matter, Daniel Chester French's Lincoln colossus sustains an inevitable iconographic dialogue with Michelangelo's Moses. Inevitable because the trope of Lincoln as Moses is obvious: both men are emancipators, freers of slaves, political leaders, martyrs to their own careers. The iconographic comparison begins with the seated positions of both figures. Correct or not, Freud's account of Moses's conflicted emotions and contorted body, caught between action and resignation, the *vita activa* and *vita contemplativa*, speaks powerfully to the idea of the leader as negotiator of knowledge and authority. Freud understood that authority remains a function of both knowledge (science) and power. He finds his clues to the statue's ambivalence in the positions of the hands and feet. The rear, left foot remains poised to lift the figure in anger, while the right foot remains or has returned to the position of seated contemplation. The hands are curled in tension, the left fingers clutching strands of beard; the right hand balancing a tablet. The gaze looks to the distant left, trying to find the optics of "the noise of the people," *der Lärm des Volkes*. Lincoln's booted feet are also asymmetrical: the right foot oversteps the pedestal. The right hand (except for the index finger) occupies the armrest in some middle ground between comfort and tension, while the four fingers of the left hand are clutched tightly together. The gaze, however, is direct, encompassing the viewer in its arc of attention, compassion, and protection, while simultaneously overseeing the long vista of government ahead of it. The armrests are

13 Sandage 1993, 135–67. Quotation from 141. Powers 2003, esp. 30–48.
14 See Sandage and Holzer 2019, 13–18. Holzer cursorily mentions the young French's reactions to works of Michelangelo. The question of the Lincoln statue's iconographic dialogue with Michelangelo's Moses goes bizarrely unasked.

adorned with the fasces: the enduring symbol of Roman republican solidarity, fused by Jacques-Louis David and others with the iconography of 1789, and overtaken in 1922 – the year of the Lincoln Memorial – by Mussolini's fascism.

Like Michelangelo's Moses, French's Lincoln possesses an extraordinary degree of human verisimilitude. But the intention and resulting experience of his presence and gaze are simpler; they are benevolent. There are two ways to make the case for the vivification of Daniel Chester French's statue of Lincoln, in other words for the *experience* of the statue as a living, benevolent presence. The first would locate that experience on the occasion of its dedication in May 1922. But that placement seems to me to lack the requisite folkloric power, the power that would distinguish this commemorative statue from countless other instances of "official" art. The second option, which I prefer, claims that the seated Lincoln's life as a living national icon *and agent* debuted on Easter Sunday 1939, when Marian Anderson sang a concert at the Memorial, with Lincoln's gaze streaming from behind her and approximately seventy-five thousand listeners poised in front of her. Martin Luther King, Jr. entered the same iconographic space when he delivered his "I Have A Dream" oration in August 1963, marking explicitly the centennial year of the Emancipation Proclamation.

The political ownership of a statue's gaze brings into relief the very nature of the sustained human and emotional cathexis to an inanimate block of stone. The fantasy of its animation relates to its aesthetic and psychic importance and must work against the artifice of its representational verisimilitude. In seeking "a way of gaining purchase on our phantasmatic intimacy with the sculpted image," Kenneth Gross writes, the way forward is unlikely to be found in the "illusory feeling of an expressive human character or selfhood residing in a statue, something that depends on particular artifices and conventions of mimetic representation – for example, the ways in which a stone figure invites us to read its features, its complexly coded gestures, and thus to posit a set of emotions or an intentionality behind those gestures." Rather, "the statue in its paradoxical ontology (its opacity, otherness, fixity, also its anonymity and substitutability) resembles those entities that fill, indeed constitute, the hypothetical domain of the unconscious mind . . . . products or relics of an archaic process of internalization, yan 'introjection' of images, persons, gestures, and relations derived from our early experience of the external world."[15] In question, then, is possible parallel between, on the one side, the residue of Lincoln's dubious politics of race alongside the winning alternative narrative of emancipation and, on the other, the residual presence of the un-

---

15 Sandage and Holzer 2019, 32–33.

canny, death-in-life of the statue alongside the benevolence and inspiration of its gaze.

Laocoön's cry is silent. Moses, Freud would have it, turns away from the "noise of the people." This statue's silence is diegetic; the figure is himself silent in his decision to sit down, to impose Sophrosyne on himself. How much inner turmoil does this self-imposition generate? Do we see reconciliation, or rather defeat? Is the physical tension of the limbs a prefiguration of release? Or are the limbs redolent inner ambivalence and conflict, like those of Jacques-Louis David's Brutus, aware that the bodies of his sons, executed for treason on his own orders, are being carried behind him, attempts a stoic posture but is betrayed by the lower half of his body (Fig. 7)?

Fig. 7: Jacques-Louis David, *The Lictors Bring to Brutus the Bodies of His Sons.* 1789. Louvre Museum. Public domain.

French's Lincoln exudes a melancholy silence that seems beyond speech, as if the statue has lost confidence in the words inscribed around him. This Lincoln is never given voice. That denied voice is claimed in both sonic materiality and political potential by Marian Anderson.

4

The occasion is well known. Assistant secretary of the interior Oscar L. Chapman granted permission to use the Lincoln Memorial for the open-air concert, after the Daughters of the American Revolution (DAR) had refused to book Marian Anderson into Constitution Hall because of her race. The request came from an unnamed civil rights leader, and not from Eleanor Roosevelt, as legend would have it, who in fact did not attend the concert. (She did publicly resign her membership in the DAR.) Scott Sandage describes the event as a "tactical epiphany" and cites activist and educator Mary McLeod Bethune's comment the following day: "We are on the right track. Through the Marian Anderson protest concert we made our triumphant entry into the democratic spirit of American life." Between 1939 and 1963, Sandage writes, "Blacks strategically appropriated Lincoln's memory and monument as political weapons, in the process layering and changing the public meanings of the hero and his shrine." He asserts justifiably that "[i]n one bold stroke, the Easter concert swept away the shrine's official dedication to the "savior of the union" and made it a stronghold of racial justice."[16]

The ambiguity of the Memorial as a contested space follows the contested legacy of Lincoln himself. It continued to serve the agenda of racial justice, for example in the NAACP organized event in May 1957 on the third anniversary of the Supreme Court's Brown v. Board of Education decision, a precursor of the August 1963 March on Washington for Jobs and Freedom. Martin Luther King, Jr. crafted the rhetorical culmination of the March on Washington, first riffing on the Gettysburg Address– "Five score years ago, a great American, in whose symbolic shadow we stand today, signed the Emancipation Proclamation," and reciting the words to "My Country 'Tis of Thee . . .," with which Marian Anderson had opened her concert in April 1939.[17]

Various photographs of Anderson, the blurred statue hovering behind her, suggest their own political iconography. The principal category here is voice. Anderson is singing and the statue appears to recede into the background while listening to her. Active listening is active learning – even for statues. This statue – unlike Mozart's Commendatore, its most famous operatic predecessor – will remain, literally, silent. Anderson, therefore, gives it voice, literally here, as well as metaphorically. The literality, actuality, of this event in its gift of voice to the silent statue can hardly be underemphasized. So I add this gift of voice to the general claim that racial justice claimed the right to Lincoln's gaze and ownership of

---

16 Sandage, "A Marble House Divided," 135, 136, 145, 146–47.
17 Sandage, "A Marble House Divided,", 157.

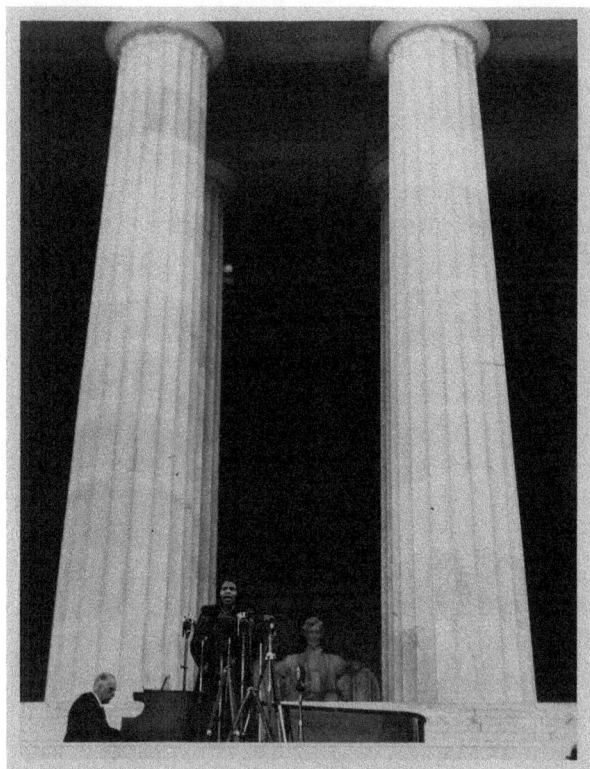

Fig. 8: Kosti Vehanen, *Marian Anderson*, Marian Anderson Collection of Photographs (Ms. Coll. 198, 7.3.2), Kislak Center for Special Collections, Rare Books and Manuscripts, University of Pennsylvania.

it. The stone gaze that peers over Marian Anderson's shoulder sheds its white gaze, to invoke Toni Morrison's key formulation.[18] As to the legacy of the man Lincoln, the same claim took hold of the preservation/emancipation pendulum and moved it to the side of emancipation as a persistent goal. Moreover, racial emancipation disqualified the notion of national preservation, as it disqualifies the notion and force of the original national constitution. Appropriation of the stone gaze insists on a politics of reconstitution. It embraces a certain kind of melancholy, which I would define as the refusal of ignorance, and the critique of historically transcendent foundations. Marian Anderson recast French's Lincoln as a testament to a counter-founding (Fig. 8).

---

18 Morrison cit. Grant 2015.

5

Foundings tend to cite, indeed seek, the status of myth. But as operations of history, they potentially have the wisdom to understand the difference.

In his important early work as both a literary and political critic, Edward Said posited "the notion of *beginning* as opposed to *origin*, the latter divine, mythical and privileged, the former secular, humanly produced, and ceaselessly reexamined."[19] An origin carries within itself a claim of essence, marking the development of an originary phenomenon through its life with an identity and a telos, a goal of truly becoming itself. This may seem like a tautology, and indeed it is. As distinct from a *beginning*, an *origin* also carries a certain non-evidentiary aura. Beginnings, in Said's important inflection of the term, carry a certain intentionality, whether in the context of the opening of a novel, the initiation of a work of art of any genre, the production of new knowledge, or in the context of a social or political action. This sense of potentiality is what Hannah Arendt calls *natality*: "the new beginning inherent in birth can make itself felt in the world only because the newcomer possesses the capacity of beginning something new, that is, of acting."[20] Myths of origin are thus multiply different from histories of beginnings. In modern history and specifically in the history of modern nations, these two cosmologies coexist and battle each other constantly. A sacred or sacralizing cosmology cohabits easily with myths of origin, as the latter point to a universe beyond the human – to gods and demons, to God alone, to God and the Devil, and so forth. In a disenchanted world, however, the reduction or origins to beginnings can prove emotionally unsatisfying. Historians who like laws, that is who replace God with Nature or Reason, the power of supernatural origins with that of natural origins, can opt for a strong replacement, such as determinism, or a weaker one, such as causality. Students of history are usually instructed to understand major historical events in terms of multiple causes: major and minor, long-term and short-term. Historians who choose, rather, to pay heed to contingency, human agency, and unpredictability can downgrade causality to sequence: from antisemitism to imperialism to totalitarianism, in Hannah Arendt's genealogy. Such is the deeper logic implicit in Leopold von Ranke's comment that history is "What happened." It does not follow, however, that the principle – or rather the fiction – of causality must be obeyed in

---

19 Said [1985] 1975, xii–xiii.
20 Arendt [1959] 1998, 9. The idea of natality emerges already in her 1929 dissertation *Love and Saint Augustine*, where natality is "embedded in the power of love (*caritas*) that, following Augustine, replicates creation in each new birth . . . ." See Scott and Stark 1996, 181.

the retrospective analysis of historians. A political principle is different from an analytical one.[21]

Two years after "The Moses of Michelangelo," Freud theorized these opposing affective directionalities in his key essay "Mourning and Melancholia." He opposed the process of mourning, a reintegration of the self following a traumatic loss, to melancholia, which he understood as an ongoing and pathological disintegration of the self in a similar context. Melancholy amounts to a pathology, whereas mourning is a performance, over time, of mental health. The year 1916 – midway through the Great War and its horrors – points to a clear political context and aura in Freud's binary, though his argument limits itself to personal loss. The nature and very category of recovery, in the aftermath of such experience, becomes complex, as does Freud's classification of melancholy as a pathology.

As a pathology, melancholy can be characterized as a refusal of loss, as opposed to the process of mourning, understood in turn as the gradual acceptance of loss in favor of the reintegration of the self. There are many kinds of losses, and what happens if we think of one experience or posture of melancholy as the refusal of the loss of innocence – in other words as the refusal of innocence itself? If we understand the state of innocence as equivalent to the state of ignorance, then I would like to risk an understanding of melancholy as the *refusal of ignorance*. The enduring political as well as ethical and aesthetic viability of the marble Lincoln's gaze involves its recognition of flawed foundations and unfinished business.

In this counter-foundational spirit I offer concluding words to the voice of Ludwig Pollak, as imagined by Hans von Trotha:

> I have spent a great deal of time thinking about Laocoön. Destiny saw to that. I have, however, also spent a great deal of time contemplating the notions of founding cities and destroying them. When Paris was slated to become the new Rome after Napoleon's victory over Italy, what, Pollak asked, did Napoleon have brought in from Rome and paraded through the streets of Paris?
>
> It was lost in Paris, by the way, the right arm they'd made for Laocoön in 1523, out of terra cotta.[22]

---

21 Ezrahi's example is the deadlocked 2000 U.S. presidential election, where the fiction of causality collapsed and was replaced by the alternative fiction of "finality" as decided by the Supreme Court. Ezrahi 2012, 168–70.

22 Trans. E. Lauffer (New York: New Vessel Press, 2022), 92.

Bibliography

Arendt, Hannah. *The Human Condition*. Chicago: University of Chicago Press, 1998.

Barzun, Jacques. *Berlioz and the Romantic Century*. Boston: Little Brown, 1950.

Ezrahi, Yaron. *Imagined Democracies: Necessary Fictions*. Cambridge: Cambridge University Press, 2012.

Freud, Sigmund. "The Moses of Michelangelo." *The Standard Edition of the Complete Psychological Works of Sigmund Freud*. Trans. James Strachey. London: Hogarth Press, 1955.

Gross, Kenneth. *The Dream of the Moving Statue*. Ithaca, NY: Cornell University Press, 1992.

Holzer, Harold. *Monument Man: The Life and Art of Daniel Chester French*. New York: Princeton Architectural Press, 2019.

Meyer, Anne Marie. "Aby Warburg in His Early Correspondence." *American Scholar* 57 (1988): 445–452.

Morrison, Toni. "Our lives have no meaning, no depth without the white gaze. And I have spent my entire writing life trying to make sure that the white gaze was not the dominant one in any of my books." Cited in Stan Grant, "Black writers courageously staring down the white gaze – this is why we all must read them." *The Guardian*, 15 December 2015.

Poizat, Michel. *The Angel's Cry: Beyond the Pleasure Principle in Opera*. Trans. Arthur Denner. Ithaca, NY: Cornell University Press, 1992.

Momigliano, Arnaldo. "How Roman Emperors Became Gods." *American Scholar* 55 (1986); reprinted in the *Ottavo Contributo alla Storia degli Studi Classici e del Mondo Antico*. Rome: Edizioni di Storia e Letteratura, 1987a; also in *On Pagans, Jews, and Cbristians*. Middletown, Conneticut: Wesleyan University Press, 1987b.

Powers, Richard. *The Time of Our Singing*. New York: Vintage Books, 2003.

Said, Edward W. "Preface." (1985) *Beginnings: Intention and Method*. New York: Columbia University Press, 1975.

Sandage, Scott A. "A Marble House Divided: The Lincoln Memorial, The Civil Rights Movement, and the Politics of Memory, 1939–1963." *Journal of American History* 80:1 (1993): 135–67.

Scott, James V., and Joanne C. Stark. "Rediscovering Hannah Arendt." *Love and Saint Augustine*. Chicago: University of Chicago Press, 1996.

Smith, John. "The Afterlife of Moses: Exile, Democracy, Renewal." Stanford, CA: Stanford University Press, 2022.

Steinberg, Michael P. *The Meaning of the Salzburg Festival: Austria as Theater and Ideology*. Ithaca, NY: Cornell University Press, 1990.

Steinberg, Michael P. "Warburg's Kreuzlingen Lecture." Warburg, Aby. *Images*. 1996.

Steinberg, Michael P. *The Afterlife of Moses: Exile, Democracy, Renewal*. Stanford: Stanford University Press, 2022.

Vergil. *The Aeneid*. Trans. Shadi Bartsch. New York: Random House, 2021.

Warburg, Aby. *Images from the Region of the Pueblo Indians of North America*. Trans. M. P. Steinberg. Ithaca, NY: Cornell University Press, 1996.

Michèle Lowrie
Epilogue: Before Rome

La France insoumise, the name of Jean-Luc Melanchon's populist left-wing party, channels triumphalism at odds with its lack of electoral success. It nevertheless reflects a strand in French popular culture, available to all sides of the political spectrum, that asserts a nativist fantasy of France, free and untouched. France unbeholden to the European Union is figured as Gaul before the Roman conquest.

The *Astérix* comics by René Goscinny and Albert Uderzo have promoted a clarifying dichotomy. The Romans are imperialist invaders and colonists who seek to dominate an idealized France instantiated in a largely peaceful village community. Their greatest disharmony comes from the harsh and tuneless twanging of the hopelessly self-deluded bard, Assurancetourix. The Romans are inept and foolish, foils for the clever and brave native Gauls. Obélix can be relied on to expostulate, "Toc toc toc, ils sont foux, ces Romains!" – a meme to be appropriated against the craziness of the powerful in any structure. The Romans stand for everything awful about dehumanizing modernity. They are stand-ins for Americans as well as the Third Reich.[1] Technological progress may deliver a modern water system via aqueducts, but it has a downside in the destruction of landscape (*La Serpe d'Or* 10; *Le Domain des Dieux* 5). The Romans in *Astérix* figure power as illegitimate, modernity as invasion. They are outsiders in contrast to a pure and native Gaul in resistance. The nativism in *Astérix* arises less from xenophobia than from the resistance to domination that animated both the Revolution and Napoleon's Empire.[2]

But such clarifying dichotomies are fragile. The difference between Gaul and Rome is at least partially undermined. Assourancetourix's name inscribes insurance, a particularly modern institution redolent of liberalism, within the Gallic village. It is pilloried as requiring the insured to take on all the risks, obviating the benefits of having insurance to begin with. The French, of course, also had an empire, but all the ways the French resemble the Romans are denounced.[3] On the Roman side, Julius Caesar is a perennially frustrated and grumpy autocrat. The one last unconquered village in Gaul is a thorn in his side. But he is at least par-

---

1 Clark 2004, 2.
2 Nicholas Sarkozy attempted to harness Astérix to bolster a fantasy of pure Gallic ancestry for his right-wing agenda, but was rebuffed by Uderzo: https://www.radiofrance.fr/franceculture/pod casts/le-mot-de-la-semaine/apres-nos-ancetres-les-gaulois-breve-histoire-politique-d-asterix-3460236. Accessed Date: June 13, 2023.
3 Clark 2004, 6–7.

https://doi.org/10.1515/9783111334776-012

tially redeemed by the typically Gallic humor he displays against his fellow Romans, among whom the senators are the most bone-headedly uncultured (e.g., in *Astérix et le bouclier Arverne*, Caesar puns sardonically on the senators' lack of memory of the Gallic wars, offering "no comment" in an allusion to his own *commentarii*: "sans commentaires," 8). Caesar is author as well as autocrat. In several layers of topsy-turvy reversal, the Romans turn out to be less literate than the Gauls, but Caesar's wit rivals theirs. Satire, in its generosity, targets fools all around.

If it is tempting to shrug off the figuration of Paris as a new Rome in recent times as trivially comedic, a mere lingering anachronism from the intense engagement with the trope from before Charlemagne to the Second World War, we must confront the fact that this discourse still circulates, in highbrow and street culture alike. The question of Rome's and which Rome remains vital. In June, 2019, Barbara Vinken and I found ourselves face to face with a *Gilets jaunes* march, protesting the expense of transportation, the perennially Roman topic of roads. Emmanuel Macron had raised fuel taxes to nudge France toward more sustainable energy consumption to fight climate change. Backlash came from the working classes, who could not afford to foot the bill and felt that the new president's alignment with Europe came at the expense of the French nation. The banner of the protest (Fig. 1) figures the European Union as a modern Roman Empire. As Rémy Brague says in *Europe: La voie romaine*[4] – where *voie* (road) puns on *voix* (voice) – Europe has coherence as the place where people have at some point cared about Latin.

In the photograph, multiple puns depend on Latin's continued legibility. The banner's main motto inscribes *Vinci autoroutes* into Julius Caesar's famous declaration of victory over Pharnaces II of Pontus at the Battle of Zela (46 BCE), *veni, vidi, vici,* "I came, I saw, I conquered" (Suetonius, *Divus Iulius* 37). The banner substitutes *vinci*, the name of the French organization governing road infrastructure, for *vici*. *Vinci* were particularly excoriated for exploitative tolling when the *Gilets jaunes* were staging road blockages in protest. What looks like an elementary grammar mistake, substituting the verb for binding and fettering for conquering, turns out to be a pun on the name of the organization. But for those who know Latin, fettering still resonates. A further pun turns on Macron's name, Manu for Emmanuel. The motto looks like it is signed with his nickname within a heart, figuring the declaration as an ironic f-you letter from Macron, a Caesar-wannabe who declares a victory he cannot even spell correctly. But that is not all – *manu* in Latin means not just "by hand," but "by force." The motto figures the president

4 Brague 1992.

Fig. 1: *Gilets jaunes* protest, June, 2019. Photo: Michèle Lowrie.

of the Fifth Republic as a conquering, imperialist outsider, an overconfident fool who does not know he has met his match in the native Gallic little guy. The European Union is now the new Rome and France has gone nativist. Of course, the story is never that simple. Rightwing mega-funding was fueling the *Gilets jaunes*, undermining their appealing grassroots worker narrative. Nevertheless, the banner reappropriates the traditional figuration of Paris as a new Rome to say no, *we* are not a new Rome, but you, Macron, are a new Caesar, no true Gallic republican, but an imperial, exploitative outsider who tramples on France as if it were Persia.

As often in this discourse, gender ideology is a defining battlefield: masculinist republicans tar imperialists as effeminate. Marine le Pen accused Macron of being under the boots of Angela Merkel. The classic trope of decadence emasculates Macron by putting the woman on top – a dominatrix to boot. His signature on the banner, in a little heart, figures him as a teen-age girl, undoing the force of *manu*. Ironically, it is a strong woman who makes the declaration, one about whom the media exercised itself in debating, furiously, whether or not she is fascist. It took a court decision that Melanchon was not committing libel in calling her such to settle the case.[5] The Roman symbol of force endures.

The banner of the *Gilets jaunes* instantiates a conundrum for ideological struggle around which figurations of Paris as a new Rome turn. The trope of Rome's return is never comfortable. It comes at moments of violence, of political upheaval. It questions whether renewal is possible and under what terms. The identification comes in antithetical guises, each of which carries positive and negative valences. But Rome can never be fully overcome. France would throw off Caesar, would find itself – now truly itself – free from imperialist Roman domination, now read as the E.U., to be finally her own true self. But in making this declaration, France, however nativist, still speaks Latin.

Bibliography

Clark, Andrew. "Imperialism in Astérix." *Belphegor: Popular Literature and Media Culture* 4.1 (2004): https://dalspace.library.dal.ca/bitstream/handle/10222/47692/04_01_Clark_Asterx_en_cont.pdf.
Brague, Rémi. *Europe: La Voie romaine*. Paris: Gallimard, 1992.

---

5 https://www.lemonde.fr/politique/article/2017/02/28/marine-le-pen-definitivement-deboutee-contre-jean-luc-melenchon-qui-l-avait-qualifiee-de-fasciste_5087106_823448.html.

List of Contributors

Tristan Alonge, HDR (Sorbonne Nouvelle), Ph.D. (Sorbonne Université), Associate professor (MCF) in French literature at Université de La Réunion (France). Selected Works: *Racine et Euripide. La révolution trahie* (2017), *Racine, Special issue of the revue Europe* (2020, ed. with Alain Génetiot), *Les origines grecques de la tragédie française: une occasion manquée* (2021).

Susanna Elm, DPhil oxon., Fellow, The British Academy, Sidney H. Ehrman Chair and Distinguished Professor of History and Ancient Greek and Roman Studies, Department of History, University of California, Berkeley. Selected publications: *Sons of Hellenism, Fathers of the Church: Emperor Julian, Gregory of Nazianzus, and the Vision of Rome* (2012; winner of the 2013 Goodwin Award); *Dressing the Empire: Queering Christian Imperial Rule* (2024).

Andrea Frisch, Ph.D. (Berkeley), Professor of French and Comparative Literature at University of Maryland (USA). Selected Works: *The Invention of the Eyewitness. Witnessing and Testimony in Early Modern France* (2004); *Forgetting Differences: Tragedy, Historiography, and the French Wars of Religion* (2015).

Philip Hardie, M.A. (Oxford), M.Phil. (London), Ph. D. (Cambridge), Fellow, Trinity College, Cambridge, and Emeritus Honorary Professor of Latin Literature, University of Cambridge. Selected Works: *Virgil's Aeneid: Cosmos and Imperium* (1986); *The Epic Successors of Virgil* (1993); *Ovid's Poetics of Illusion* (2002); *Lucretian Receptions. History, The Sublime, Knowledge* (2009); *Rumour and Renown. Representations of Fama in Western Literature* (2012); *The Last Trojan Hero. A Cultural History of Virgil's Aeneid* (2014); *Classicism and Christianity in Late Antique Latin Poetry* (2019); *Celestial Aspirations: Classical Impulses in British Poetry and Art* (2022).

Anselm Haverkamp is Emeritus Professor of English in NYU New York, and Professor of Philosophy at LMU Munich. Selected work for the present purpose: *Typik und Politik im Annolied* (1979); *Theorie der Metapher* (1983); *Shakespearean Genealogies of Power* (2011); *Productive Digression: Theorizing Practice* (2017); *Latenz: Zur Genese des Ästhetischen als historischer Kategorie* (2021).

Stephan Leopold, Dr. phil. habil. (Munich, Germany), Distinguished Professor for French and Spanish Literature at Johannes Gutenberg Universität Mainz (Germany). Selected Works: *Die Erotik der Petrarkisten: Poetik, Körperlichkeit und Subjektivität in romanischer Lyrik Früher Neuzeit* (2009); *Liebe im Ancien Régime: Eros und polis von Corneille bis Sade* (2014)*; Zusammenbruch und Erinnerung: Prousts Recherche (2022).*

Michèle Lowrie, Ph.D. (Harvard), Andrew W. Mellon Distinguished Service Professor in Classics and the College at the University of Chicago. Selected works: *Horace's Narrative Odes* (1997); *Writing, Performance, and Authority in Augustan Rome* (2009); *Exemplarity and Singularity: Thinking through Particulars in Philosophy, Literature, and Law* (2015), co-edited with Susanne Lüdemann; *Civil War and the Collapse of the Social Bond: The Roman Tradition at the Heart of the Modern*, co-authored with Barbara Vinken (2022).

Larry F. Norman, Ph.D. (Columbia University), is the Frank L. Sulzberger Distinguished Service Professor of Romance Languages and Literatures and Theater and Performance Studies at the

https://doi.org/10.1515/9783111334776-013

University of Chicago (USA). Selected Works: *The Shock of the Ancient: Literature and History in Early Modern France* (2011); *The Public Mirror: Molière and the Social Commerce of Depiction* (1999).

Michael P. Steinberg, Barnaby Conrad and Mary Critchfield Keeney Professor of History, German Studies, and Music, Brown University. Selected works: *The Afterlife of Moses: Exile, Democracy, Renewal* (Stanford, 2022); *The Trouble with Wagner* (Chicago, 2018); *Listening to Reason: Culture, Subjectivity, and 19th-century Music* (Princeton, 2004); *Austria as Theater and Ideology: The Meaning of the Salzburg Festival* (Cornell, 2000), translated as *Ursprung und Ideologie der Salzburger Festspiele* (Anton Pustet Verlag, 2000).

Christine Tauber, Dr. phil. habil. (Bonn / Konstanz). Member of the research department and chief editor of „Kunstchronik" at the Central Research Institute for the History of Art (Zentralinstitut für Kunstgeschichte). Professor at the Institute of Art History at the Ludwig-Maximilians-University Munich (Germany). Selected Works: *Bilderstürme der Französischen Revolution* (2009); *Manierismus und Herrschaftspraxis* (2009); *Armand-Guy Kersaint, Abhandlung über die öffentlichen Baudenkmäler 1791/92* (2010); *Politikstile und die Sichtbarkeit des Politischen in der Frühen Neuzeit* (Ed. with Dietrich Erben, 2016).

Barbara Vinken, Dr. phil. habil. (Konstanz / Jena), Ph.D. (Yale), Professor for French and Comparative Literature at Ludwig-Maximilians-Universität Munich (Germany). Selected Works: *Renaissance Rome: Du Bellay und Petrarca* (2001); *Flaubert: Durchkreuzte Moderne* (2009)/ *Flaubert Postsecular (*2015*); Bel Ami (2020); Civil War and the Collapse of the Social Bond: The Roman Tradition at the Heart of the Modern,* co-authored with Michèle Lowrie (2022); *Diva* (2023).

Figure Credits

Anselm Haverkamp

Fig. 1 Mit freundlicher Genehmigung von Stefan Krabath, NIhK Wilhelmshaven —— **35**
Fig. 2 Österreichische Nationalbibliothek Vienna —— **36**
Fig. 3 Bayerische Staatsbibliothek München, P.o.germ. 1036, urn:nbn:de:bvb: 12-bsb10115840-6, page 17 —— **39**
Fig. 4 © Domkapitel Aachen, Foto: Klaus Bednorz (Augustusseite) —— **43**
Fig. 5 © Domkapitel Aachen, Foto: Klaus Bednorz (Augustusseite) —— **44**
Fig. 6 © Domkapitel Aachen, Foto: Klaus Bednorz (Augustusseite) (detail) —— **44**

Philip Hardie

Fig. 1 © RMN-Grand Palais (musée du Louvre) / Christian Jean / Hervé Lewandowski —— **96**
Fig. 2 © RMN-Grand Palais (musée du Louvre) / René-Gabriel Ojeda / Thierry Le Mage —— **98**
Fig. 3 © RMN-Grand Palais (musée du Louvre) / Hervé Lewandowski —— **99**
Fig. 4 © RMN-Grand Palais (musée du Louvre) / Thierry Le Mage —— **100**
Fig. 5 © RMN-Grand Palais (musée du Louvre) / René-Gabriel Ojeda / Thierry Le Mage —— **101**
Fig. 6 © RMN-Grand Palais (musée du Louvre) / Jean Schormans —— **102**
Fig. 7 Paris, France / Bridgeman Images —— **104**
Fig. 8 © RMN-Grand Palais (musée du Louvre) / Christian Jean / Hervé Lewandowski —— **105**
Fig. 9 © RMN-Grand Palais (musée du Louvre) / Christian Jean / Hervé Lewandowski —— **106**
Fig. 10 © RMN-Grand Palais (musée du Louvre) / René-Gabriel Ojeda / Thierry Le Mage —— **111**

Christine Tauber

Fig. 1 https://upload.wikimedia.org/wikipedia/commons/1/19/Fête_de_l'Etre_suprême_2.jpg. Public domain —— **113**
Fig. 2 Stein 2022, cat.no. 55, 194 —— **114**
Fig. 3 https://gallica.bnf.fr/ark:/12148/btv1b69476006/f1jpg —— **115**
Fig. 4 https://upload.wikimedia.org/wikipedia/commons/6/6d/Le_Serment_du_Jeu_de_paume.jpg. Public domain —— **117**
Fig. 5 Stein 2022, 25 —— **118**
Fig. 6 Stein 2022, cat.no. 56, 197 —— **119**

https://doi.org/10.1515/9783111334776-014

Fig. 7   https://commons.wikimedia.org/wiki/File:Jacques-Louis_David,_Le_Serment_des_ Horaces.jpg. Public domain —— **121**

Fig. 8   https://en.wikipedia.org/wiki/The_Lictors_Bring_to_Brutus_the_Bodies_of_His_ Sons#/media/File:David_Brutus.jpg. Public domain —— **122**

Fig. 9   https://upload.wikimedia.org/wikipedia/commons/f/fe/Jacques-Louis_David_-_ Brutus_-_WGA6108.jpg. Public domain —— **125**

Fig. 10   https://images.metmuseum.org/CRDImages/ep/original/DP-13139-001.jpg. Public domain —— **127**

Fig. 11   https://upload.wikimedia.org/wikipedia/commons/2/2b/Leónidas_en_las_Termópi las,_por_Jacques-Louis_David.jpg. Public domain —— **131**

Fig. 12   Wildenstein 1973, Frontispice —— **135**

Andrea Frisch

Fig. 1   Gilberti Cognati Nozereni Opera Mvltifarii Argvmenti 2 [. . .], München, Bayerische Staatsbibliothek, Sign. 2 Opp. 21-1/3, bsb10148156, S. 254 —— **186**

Fig. 2   Photo: Andrea Frisch —— **197**

Michael Steinberg

Fig. 1   https://fr.m.wikipedia.org/wiki/Fichier:Hubert_Robert_-_1773_-_Finding_of_the_ Laocoon.jpg. Public domain —— **206**

Fig. 2   https://en.wikipedia.org/wiki/Laoco%C3%B6n_and_His_Sons#/media/File:Laocoon photo.jpg. Public domain —— **209**

Fig. 3   https://upload.wikimedia.org/wikipedia/commons/b/bd/Laocoon_and_His_Sons. jpg —— **210**

Fig. 4   https://en.wikipedia.org/wiki/File:El_Greco_(Domenikos_Theotokopoulos)_-_Laoco %C3%B6n_-_Google_Art_Project.jpg. Public domain —— **211**

Fig. 5   https://upload.wikimedia.org/wikipedia/commons/0/0f/%27Moses%27_by_Michel angelo_JBU140.jpg. Public domain —— **212**

Fig. 6   https://en.wikipedia.org/wiki/Daniel_Chester_French#/media/File:Lincoln_statue, _Lincoln_Memorial.jpg. Public domain —— **214**

Fig. 7   https://en.wikipedia.org/wiki/The_Lictors_Bring_to_Brutus_the_Bodies_of_His_ Sons#/media/File:David_Brutus.jpg. Public domain —— **217**

Fig. 8   Marian Anderson Collection of Photographs (Ms. Coll. 198, 7.3.2), Kislak Center for Special Collections, Rare Books and Manuscripts, University of Pennsylvania —— **219**

Michèle Lowrie

Fig. 1   Photo: Michèle Lowrie —— **225**

www.ingramcontent.com/pod-product-compliance
Lightning Source LLC
Chambersburg PA
CBHW070930150426
42814CB00025B/183